The Empath's Journey

What working with my dreams, moving to a different
country and learning about Carl Jung taught me
about being an empath.

By Ritu Kaushal

To my dear husband Rohit, for all your love, support and kindness.

This book wouldn't have been possible without you. You are the man behind the woman.

Table of Contents

Chapter 1

Diving into the Emotional World

After I moved from India to the United States six years back, in 2012, I journeyed up and down my emotional currents, feeling caught up in the swirls of life changing all around me. I had never thought that I would ever live outside India, someone like me who often clung to the familiar so fiercely, someone who hated making big changes. But through chance or synchronicity, here I had landed, and here I was, trying to cast myself into the shape of a completely new life.

I had already been on my own personal journey for a few years before I met my husband Rohit, got married, and made this move. Now, in this new country, in the middle of what sometimes felt like overwhelming change, it felt as if something else was making the process of adjusting even harder. It was something essential about me, something I had *been* forever. Once again, it felt like I was noticing and feeling too much, as if hundreds of waves of raw energy were pounding me down. This was an exciting move, so full of possibilities. But then, there were also these other times, when everything felt too much and more than I could ever handle.

What the hell was wrong with me? Why couldn't I just get on with it like other people? They didn't seem to have these extreme reactions and intense feelings that I always seemed to be having. All my life, I had been called "*too sensitive.*" Now, it felt like my sensitivity was acting like a roadblock, all over again.

1

At different times in my life, I had had different relationships with these words. Sometimes, they had been thrown at me like an accusation. They had implied weakness, something out of control. Then, I had railed against them. *Too sensitive.* No, I would not be *too sensitive.* I had felt cut by the charge of these words, cut by the shame of not being as tough as others. Why was I the one who always took things to heart, felt them deeply, got affected by everything? Why wasn't I like those people who could remain detached and above it all?

At different times in my life, I had tried to change myself, to get rid of this "weakness." There had been times when I had completely numbed out. I had clamped my intense feelings shut. Then, I had looked calm and collected from the outside, but inside, those stormy feelings had just created a whirlpool. There had also been those other times when I had isolated myself. I had felt as if other people's feelings were coming rushing out at me, as if I was porous and permeable, as if I could catch people's feelings like you would catch a cold. Then, being on my own had felt like the only solution.

There had also been those times when I had moved towards people. But more often than not, I "attracted" people who needed me to listen or to take care of them. Somehow or the other, I just got entangled, and then, there would come a time when I would swing to the opposite side, choosing to be completely on my own. That felt safer. At least that was something I could control.

But through all of this, there had run a common thread. Through all these different stages of my life, as a child, as a teenager and as an adult, I had always tried to mould myself into something different, something more

2

acceptable than who I was.

Now, in this exciting phase of my life, in this new-to-me country, this part of me, this sense of being "*too sensitive*," "*too soft*" and the frustration that went with it, came up once again. Here I was, in my early 30s, feeling, for the umpteenth time, that what was easy for other people was terribly hard for me. I had often felt like this, as if I was always two steps behind everyone.

When I looked around now, it felt as if adjusting to this new rhythm of life, so different from life in India, was easy for others while I was drowning in this too-much-change. In my dreams, lakes and rivers often overran their boundaries. Sometimes, I was overtaken by masses of overflowing water, and all I could do was flail around. I just couldn't seem to get to a stable and secure place, to dry land. This didn't feel fair.

Why was this always so hard for me? Why was I always this intense? It was as if my peaks were high but momentary, and then, I was plunged into a deep, dark valley.

While I was feeling like this, both the exciting newness of life opening up with someone who was wonderful as well as feeling held back by this constant churning in my emotional life, I was also building pieces of my new life. As a spouse on a dependent visa who couldn't work, soon after the move, I had started volunteering as an ESL (English as a Second Language) teacher for adult students as part of a reading program at the local library. Here was a little window into my new life in the Silicon Valley.

Every week, I met Jennifer, my Korean student, in a small ground-floor room in the library. Jennifer, a sweet woman with a child in middle school, seemed settled in her skin even though she didn't speak fluent English. America had been her home for a long time. After our weekly lessons, we sometimes talked about the differences we found between Silicon Valley and New Delhi and Seoul.

I told her about all the little differences that I had come across that seemed to point to some big difference. At an American birthday get-together, everyone chipped in to pay for the person whose birthday it was. This was the opposite of what we did with our Indian friends, where the person whose birthday it was "treated" the others. Jennifer told me how mortified she had been when her son told his teacher that they were from North Korea, instead of South Korea. It had been a long while since they had gone back home. I thought then of how life might be like ten, fifteen, twenty years from now. Already, home felt like a place far away. Already, life was morphing and changing in unexpected ways.

This sense of looking back, of letting go was, of course, just part of the process. Life had also become new again. There were numerous little adventures to be had as Rohit and I made our life together. We travelled, saw more art exhibitions than he probably liked, and created our home together. We went to one store after another before we found a dining table we could both agree on. He liked classic. I liked distressed. I wanted to do up our home almost like a Pinterest board, a place for inspiration. I didn't want it to look too finished, but instead, look alive and changing. Rohit, of course, preferred a more put-together look.

Over the years, we found our middle ground. The furniture was all brown or black, just as he liked while I put up colorful frames and covered almost all the walls with things I had painted, giant puzzles he had made, and gifts we had been given. Think of this house as a springboard, Rohit had said and that's what it became for me, a place from which I explored, a place in which I created. It also became a promise, an empty canvas for creating a new definition of home, away from the home I had grown up in.

Standing near Coyote Creek, not actually a creek but a river, named in the late 1700s, the house bore witness to our journey together. It heard us negotiating our life as a couple, with me insisting that Rohit not call the food I cooked "Indian food." It was just *khaana*, the Hindi word for food. We didn't have to put Indian before it like we would for Chinese or Italian food. It was food, just food. But for Rohit who had grown up in different countries all around the world, it was actually "Indian food," a little removed from his experience. He talked sweetly and I felt, a little frustratingly, about how I would be just like him in a few years. I would not have any one place to which I belonged.

But no, I thought, it was different for me. India had been the only place I had ever lived in. Of course, it would remain a place I belonged to. But then, what exactly did that mean? Would America be my home too or would I just remain an outsider here, never quite belonging?

In the next few years, I would dip in and out of these different feelings. I would cycle through homesickness, feeling like a piece that didn't fit anywhere. At times, I would feel like an unfinished person, belonging neither here nor there. But in time, as the years added up, I would see that a home is what you create with your hands when you join together the past and the future, when you express pieces of your soul and when you work at

5

something and that effort deepens your connection with it. India, with its red *palash* trees, with its gorgeous red-orange suns, its languid *nehars* and canals is home. America, with its cathedrals of redwoods, with its moons so close you-can-touch them, its never-ending blue sky is home as well.

Our little house has seen me changing, from dislocated to coming together, from an emotional morass to finding structure. All those years ago, in mid-2012, it had seen my first step. One of Rohit's friend's wives had sweetly welcomed me on my first day in the States by pouring mustard oil outside the front door. Then, like generations of Indian brides entering their new homes, I had pushed the little pot of rice she had kept on the ground into the house with my right foot. I was bringing my own luck, my own destiny inside it. Outside, across the road, the American flag had waved in front of the post office. Farther in the background, I could see the rolling hills that encapsulated the Valley and gave it its name. *Home.*

Quite soon afterwards, sheltered in my new space, I had taken another step in the construction of my new life. For many years, even before I met Rohit, I had been moving closer and closer to reclaiming my lost self, my artistic soul. Seven years of working in the corporate world in India had underlined who I really was, first a creative person desperately lost, and then, one tentatively finding her way back. In Delhi, I had done my first writing workshop and had then started freelancing while working full-time.

With this move to the States, the door to my true self nudged open even further. Soon after the move, I found my first writing workshop and soon, signed up for another, and then another. Taking the train from the

6

South Bay an hour up north to San Francisco, in these classes, I met kindred spirits who wanted the same things that I did, who were also figuring out how to make things happen.

Here, I met different kinds of writers. There were those who created the most beautiful imaginary worlds. They submerged themselves so deeply that the lines between fantasy and reality disappeared. These were the ones who could create exquisite beauty. These were also the ones who could drown in illusion. Then, there was the other kind of writer. These were the people who looked at the world with a critical eye. They sized up everything, including people. They had a decided cutting-edge to their voice. One such person's writing reminded me of Roald Dahl's biting, sarcastic wit and the laser-like precision with which he sometimes looked into the human heart and its follies.

In his stories for adults, Dahl has talked about frightening things, people caught by accident in the conveyor belt in factory farms just like the pigs who had hung there; a wife bullied by her husband all her life who locks him in the house and leaves him to die; a man with a great work of art tattooed on his back, abducted and stripped of his very skin. Like Dahl, these writers wiped the veneer off quickly and talked about things that others weren't talking about. In them, there was less of that empathy that makes some writers great. There was a different genius, sharp and probing. It weighed us up and often found us lacking.

I wasn't anything like these writers. Both beauty and illusion seemed to call out equally to me. But meeting all these different people, some like and some unlike me, showed me that the elusive thing that writers often search so hard for, their "voice," wasn't something that you just made up. It was something that you were. It came from inside the markings of your soul and if you could just set it free, you could possibly have things to say. You could possibly reach out and connect.

It was also somewhere during this time, during the initial few years after the move, when I was doing my writing workshops, when I was working with Jennifer, and when Rohit and I were creating our life together that I read Dr. Elaine Aron's book *The Highly Sensitive Person*. My sister in India was reading it and I picked up the book on her recommendation. I think I had come across it in India as well but the "highly sensitive" title had put me off. These were the very words I had tried so hard to escape from almost all my life. These weren't words I felt comfortable being, comfortable associating with myself.

But now, in the middle of this transition to a new life, feeling as if I was again lagging behind, these words seemed relevant to me. Once again, they called out to me.

Experiences with Sensitivity

Even as a child, this being "too sensitive" had often left me feeling as if the world was too much for me. It was too big, too large, too hurtful. One of my earliest memories is of walking to a neighborhood Delhi market with my *naani* (my maternal grandmother) for some errands she had to do. My family stayed in a small government DDA flat, and in the evenings, we often wound our way through the neighborhood parks to go to the market.

It was the kind of market that sits next to blocks upon blocks of low apartment buildings that you find in that part of the world. It had a grocery shop, a tailor, a stationery shop plus a *halwai* (sweet seller). If you walked further down from the concrete marketplace, in the evenings, you would find an entire road taken over by vegetable and fruit-sellers with their hand-pulled carts.

Often, as a child and definitely when my *naani* was visiting, there was some kind of treat involved in these evening outings. We would finish our chores and then buy some syrupy-golden *jalebis* from the *halwai*. Afterwards, we would thread our way through a jumble of people to get to the vegetable market. It was a place I dreaded as a little child. On busy evenings, there was the din of people haggling. Sometimes, there was pushing and shoving, jostling for space. But to get to it, we had to first walk in front of a row of beggars sitting on the pavement - old men and women huddled under their blankets in that smoky, foggy Delhi winter.

Sometimes, we stopped to give them some change. Sometimes, we just passed them by.

I remember coming home after many of these outings and hiding to cry. There was so much suffering in the world, so much pain and just by going out, by being near these people, I had absorbed it. It was as if their pain had seeped inside me, colored me through. I couldn't control it. Even as a child of six or seven, I knew it was weak to cry like this. So, when we reached home, I would escape to another room to cry by myself.

I had to get over it, I would tell myself, shaking with sobs. I might be shamed for going on like this, and I didn't want to feel hurt by that, on top of the pain I was already feeling. In the beginning, I hadn't quite been able to do this. Trying to scold myself into *not crying* didn't work. But over time, I would become a little better at numbing myself, turning away from that pain, escaping up into my mind. This was one of my early experiences of my sensitivity.

It was a double-edged sword, this ability to feel other people's feelings. Even then, I had known this was the best part of me, this ability to feel compassion. But it also made me vulnerable. Feelings were like wispy monsters out to get me, such uncontrollable things, and just as the market had gradually become a place to avoid as a child, avoiding people and situations would become a pattern that criss-crossed the length of my life.

As I had grown up, some of my sensitivity, this part of me that I most hurt with, this part of me that I most valued, deadened somewhat. I had already numbed some of it purposely, and some of it numbed by itself. It just wasn't possible to make it from day-to-day feeling so acutely in a country where you encountered poor, starving people every day, almost around every corner.

In the decades since those childhood days, I had developed an ambivalent relationship with my feelings. By the time I got to America, I knew that my feelings cut both ways. I had spent the last few years learning to listen to my feelings instead of being in a constant battle with them. I knew my feelings were the sensors I extended out into the world. They nudged me this way or that. They also gave me important messages about my own reaction to the world. Whenever I hadn't listened to the messages inside my feelings, I had crossed into dangerous territory. But my feelings were also those problematic things they had always been. They made me feel like something whose shell had been removed, whose flesh had been exposed.

So, when I first read *The Highly Sensitive Person*, it felt as if I already knew what it was saying. I knew all of this. After all, this had been my life. At first, I just quickly leafed through the book. But later on, as I came to terms with the fact that this transition to the States, something that other people thought *should* only take a year or two would probably take longer for me that I thought about the book again and reread it. During one of our early conversations about the book, my sister had told me to start with the possibility that it might take me *double* the amount of time to adjust to the move than it normally took other people.

Double the time? Intellectually, I knew she had a point. But emotionally, I felt a growing resistance. It *did* feel like being so sensitive only held you back. If change was going to always be this hard for me, wouldn't I always be at a disadvantage? Again, I felt that old feeling of not-good-enough, of not being tough enough to cope quite as well as others.

But when I picked up *The Highly Sensitive Person* again and read it more slowly, this time, I thought consciously about what Dr. Aron was saying. If *Sensory Processing Sensitivity (SPS)* was rooted in biological differences, then everything in my life, everything I had experienced meant something different than how I had framed it before. It hadn't been a matter of just willing myself to be "tougher" or "stronger." There was something basic in my makeup that was different from other people. I couldn't change it at will, just as I couldn't change the color of my eyes. Until now, I had only looked at myself through the lens of other people's perception. I had thought I was *"too sensitive"* because others told me so. I had thought I was "weak" because that's the label that is stamped on you if you can't push through things.

11

But if I really thought about it, I could see that in my life, I had been both weak as well as strong, both *"too sensitive"* and completely numbed out. Maybe, as Dr. Aron was saying, SPS was a neutral trait. In itself, it wasn't either good or bad. It just was. It wasn't an exact comparison but I started thinking of it sort of like being left-handed in a right-handed world. There had been a time when left-handedness was thought to be "wrong," and children had been punished for it.

But it wasn't wrong. It was just different.

If this was true for being a Highly Sensitive Person (HSP) as well, then this meant that maybe, my struggles were at least partly because of how I related to the SPS trait. Often, I was forcibly trying to change myself and become something different. Maybe, this trying to fit myself into a box, this was the actual problem and not the fact that I was *"too sensitive."*

Even as I was starting to think like this, it sometimes felt as if feeling and noticing this much *was* often a problem. It didn't really seem to help. After the honeymoon period of the move was over, there came a time when it felt like all the hundred big and small changes, all the new information that was rushing towards me, was only overwhelming me. I wanted to hide under a blanket and escape what I was feeling.

While I was experiencing this push and pull with my emotions, I also reached a point in my writing journey where doing any more writing workshops only felt like a stalling tactic. I needed to put my work out there in the world. So, I decided to stop doing any more workshops and instead start a blog. But what exactly would I write about?

It was somewhere during this time that I happened upon Peter Messerschmidt's *HSP Notes* blog, one of the oldest HSP-centric blogs on the internet. In one of his posts, he had talked passionately about the fact that while at least 15-20% of the general population was Highly Sensitive, sensitive people were conspicuous by their absence in the online world. We were invisible, hidden in the nooks and crannies of the internet. If we couldn't claim our space, Peter said, who could blame others for disregarding us?

This question became the catalyst I needed. Because my sensitivity had become such a big factor in my new life, it also felt like the most natural thing to talk about. I would write about being an HSP and the gifts and challenges that came with it. So, I started a blog hoping to offer something useful from the tumultuous experience I was having.

Maybe, my explorations could help not just me, but also other people. At first, I only had questions. Was sensitivity really such a gift? The online world seemed to be slowly bursting with HSP-related articles and memes. But were these memes affirming the sensitive spirit right? My sensitivity didn't *always* seem like such a great thing. It often felt like I was noticing and feeling too much and drowning in too-much-information.

During the honeymoon period of the move, right at the beginning, I hadn't felt like this. In fact, I had even wondered a little superiorly about all those poor souls who found moving to a new county so hard. Look at me, I thought. I was doing so well. I had lived in a big city like Delhi, so I wasn't wide-eyed about anything. When people asked me, the only noticeable difference I talked about was the difference in the traffic between Delhi and the Bay Area, which was, of course, much less and much better here.

But this sense of adjusting amazingly well, so much better than others, hadn't lasted very long. In just a few months, after Rohit had gone to work, I often spent my time at home watching YouTube videos about cultural differences. Sometimes, I walked to the nearby library in the blazing sun to check out books because I still didn't have my driver's license. I had aced the written test and flunked the actual one. It would take me a couple of tries to actually get that much-needed license to feel independent in this suburban life.

After the initial excitement of visiting museums and galleries and trying the different food options in multi-cultural Silicon Valley got over, the real differences between India and America started peeking out their heads. Sometimes, for weeks, here in the States, no one ever rang the bell to our house. My memories of India were tinged with an ache, even for the kinds of things that had irritated me there, such as how you couldn't pass a day at home without multiple people interrupting, from the washerman come to collect clothes for ironing to someone selling special Kolkata *sarees* door-to-door to some third person who had come asking for donations. Here, in the deafening silence of America, the chaos of India felt like a rhythmic heartbeat.

Soon, the subtle differences between India and America started to add up. Sometimes, I would wonder if I was reading too much into it and whether I was even noticing anything real. For example, when I had first moved, I had noticed that the rhythms of conversations I had with Americans and Indians were different. It was something intrinsically different in the structure of the back and forth. I still couldn't pinpoint exactly what it was but there seemed to be many slight differences.

In the beginning, Americans, at least some of them, seemed to be lacking in subtlety to me. They had a tendency to explain things in the most tedious manner. Even if you asked something simple, like directions to a nearby store, they would give you long-winded, step-by-step instructions instead of telling you something like: *Go straight, then watch out for the Starbucks. The shop will be nearby.*

Sometimes, this worked out really well, like the first time I took the train to San Francisco to attend my first writing workshop. The place was supposed to be within walking distance of the train station, just a few blocks away. When I asked a girl about the address, noticing my nervousness, she gave me precise directions and in around 15 minutes, I had gotten where I needed to be. Afterwards, I felt a little more confident about exploring things on my own.

But most of the time, it felt as if I was being given precise, detailed explanations even when I didn't need them. Sometimes, I even felt like I was being talked down to. Surely, no one needed such small things explained to them in this manner, like they were some stupid child who didn't understand. I felt I was being disrespected.

When I hesitantly tried to talk about these kinds of observations with other people, they often gave me blank looks. They didn't seem to have noticed any such differences. What was I talking about? This reaction made me doubt whether I was even feeling something valid. Was I sensing a real difference, or was I imagining things?

Trying to explain and not being understood also seemed to underline my feeling of being different and weird. Again, it felt like something was wrong with me, as if I was just noticing superfluous stuff that no one else cared about. Again, I felt alone, not mirrored back, almost as if my discomfort didn't really mean anything, as if what I sensed was rendered null and void because someone else couldn't see what I was seeing.

But as time passed, I started thinking more about what being an HSP really meant. Tentatively, unsure of myself at first, I started learning more about culture and cultural differences. If I *did* notice subtleties, and if this multitude of subtleties was overwhelming me, then maybe learning about what they meant could help me.

So, in time I started looking for explanations for all the differences I was sensing.

Sensing Subtle Differences and Validating My Own Experience

Some answers came when I read the work of cross-cultural expert, Erin Meyer. Meyer was a professor at INSEAD, the world-renowned business school, and an expert on cross-cultural communication and how it impacted transactions in the business world. One of the topics she talked about was the difference between *low-context* and *high-context* cultures. High-context cultures were cultures with a long-shared history. Countries like India, China and Japan have very high-context cultures. These are places with relationship-oriented societies in which networks of connections are passed on from one generation to the other.

In these kinds of places, the focus is on preserving harmony in relationships. A lot of *reading between the lines* happens in these cultures. Lots of things are not said out loud. They are simply understood. Let's say, a hypothetical aunt of mine becomes miffed about something I have done. She will probably not tell me this directly. Part of the reason is that open confrontation could bring up other issues that might hurt our relationship. She might also think it's impolite to bring up this topic. But still, underneath it all, she is angry.

Although she doesn't communicate her anger in so many words, as someone listening to her, I read between the lines and realize that something I have done has caused a reaction. Now, it's up to me to figure out my faux pas. In this situation, there is the additional layer of her being older than me, and so a certain amount of respect is automatically hers in this relationship. That's just how I have been raised. That's how my conditioning is, for both good and bad.

So, explicit communication is *not* necessarily considered a good thing in my culture, and as Erin Meyer tells us, in high-context cultures in general. There are behaviors that will be considered rude, like calling out someone directly *even if* you know they're lying because the concept of saving face is so highly valued.

Of course, no one passes on these rules of culture to us in so many words. We just pick them up from the air, so to speak. We learn them from the way people around us dance in conversations, from sensing unspoken rules and expectations, from internalizing the way of being that is all around us and that creates us.

When I read about how India was a high-context culture, while America was, in fact, considered *the lowest-context* culture in the world, a lot of my challenges with communicating with Americans or Indian-Americans became clear. Now, I knew that all that step-by-step instruction that had felt like overkill, at best, and talking down to me, at worst, was because of this cultural difference. Unlike India, where the onus of communication is as much on the listener as the one doing the talking, in America, good communication was the exact opposite.

It was the person doing the talking who was responsible for getting their message across. They had to talk directly, specifically and almost spell out things in a way that often ended up feeling to me, as a person from a high-context culture, as being talked down to. Someone like me would think, all of this didn't need to be explained. Maybe, this was why Americans had felt so *obvious* and lacking in subtlety to me. It had felt like they tried to hammer their point home.

But now, I realized the opposite was also true. To someone meeting Indians or people from other high-context cultures for the first time, it can also seem like we are hiding and hinting at things. To them, we can come across as not transparent enough.

The cultural research pointed to the different historical backdrops that had given rise to these differences. America, like other low-context cultures such as Canada and Australia, is a place where people from all around the world have come and made their homes. It has many immigrant groups, each with its own language, its own culture, its own stories. Because of this lesser shared context, good communication is whatever gets your point across. Good communication is clear and precise. Even if you have to repeat the same thing twice, that's fine. It's the person doing the talking who is responsible for "good" communication, for getting their message across.

This noticing of a subtle difference and the ensuing dissonance was just one example of what being in America had often felt like for me. It had felt like being in a world where the rules I had learnt had been turned upside down. What was normal here was often the opposite of what was normal in India. In the beginning, I had the same kinds of experiences that other immigrants often have, experiences that left me feeling like I was out in the cold, unsure of how to orient myself.

Going to an Indian-American family's house, for example, would be a completely different experience from a social outing in India. There would be none of the warmth of India, where the lady of the house usually keeps on asking you to have one more *roti* or try something she had cooked specially for the occasion. No one here would understand that if you said *No* the first time, you were just being polite. No one here would try to press on and offer you things again. If you tried that here, you might go hungry. It felt like a cold world to live in, and I wasn't sure if this was about being individualistic or something else entirely.

The underlying bits of it seemed unclear. It wasn't just one thing, like saying clear Yeses or Nos, the result of being a culture that valued explicitness. It was almost as if these small interactions pointed to the many other things that were going on underneath. They were almost a confluence of how the entire society was structured. In one book on culture I borrowed from the library, there was a picture I still remember hazily. It showed how people in different cultures view themselves in relationship to their environment.

The example it gave was between Japanese and American culture. For Japanese culture, the photograph showed a

Japanese person sitting on a chair with the details of the room clearly visible. For Americans, the picture was zoomed in to the person themselves. When the Japanese talked about themselves, they also described their relationship to their environment. But Americans didn't talk about their own self in relation to something else. They were zoomed in to their very self.

Was this good? Was this bad? Did this mean Americans were self-absorbed like I sometimes thought? Did this mean that the way we see the world is so determined by our culture that we can't really ever see what life looks like for someone very different from us?

As someone coming from a more collectivist culture, it wasn't that my allegiance was clearly with the collective. I came from a rational-minded family. I had lived in big cities like Delhi and Mumbai (Bombay). I had also suffered enough of the downsides that come from the collective to know that being more collective wasn't all good. In the American and Japanese example, I could sense that India was somewhere close to Japan although not quite as collectivist.

For years, my creative self had been buried under the typical Indian refrain of "*log kya kahenge*" or "*What will people say?*" What other people said and what other people thought about you meant a lot. At least, it meant a lot in the part of India I came from and for me, in my own conditioning. It was that age-old comeback that resounded in my head when I thought of doing anything that was other than nice, anything other than what was accepted, other than what everyone else was doing.

My kind of writing, which I am only now starting to learn about, is the kind of writing that sometimes touches on personal things. Sharing the hidden, the ugly, the hurtful - the frayed ends and the dried twine, the combustible and the crying parts of the psyche - is something that America made possible for me. Being in the States was a big factor in my discovering my way back to my own voice. *"Log kya kahenge"* versus *"What do I think?"* There is a healthy part to not caring about what others think, in being self-focused not in a self-absorbed way but in a self-affirming way, when you really zoom in to yourself and stand up for what's true for you.

At one point here in the States, I took photography classes at a local community college. They consisted of 17-year-olds, a few retired people come back to pursue their interests and spouses like me, mostly women, who had followed their other-halves into a new life in a new country. On dependent visas, we women probably already felt a little constricted. But we also seemed to have something else in common. Whether Indian or Chinese or Korean, many of us seemed more malleable than the 17-18-year-olds. We didn't seem to question as much or as rigorously, unlike the American kids or the second-generation kids born here. Many of us were probably not as aware of our "rights." We were all very nice though.

This was an interesting education for me, even more than developing film in the darkroom for the first time or creating a presentation on the Indian photographer Raghu Rai. The cultural differences were palpable. The teenagers debated, were more able to stand on their own and felt more like grown-ups than all the women in their 20s and 30s.

Of course, in the early days of the move before all these experiences had come, when everything was not quite clear, before I had put everything into a context, I had only felt lost and displaced. Sometimes, I had tried to *act* direct and clear, in the way I imagined Americans were. But that actually came across as rude. It didn't *feel* right. Forget culture, I am not even the kind of person who is direct or blunt. I try to take care of others' feelings. I try to say things carefully, unless, of course, I am really angry.

Some of this carefulness is unhealthy. But there's also a part of it that's just me. I am also not directive in the sense that things are just one way or the other for me. The gray, the shades of light and dark, the history of people and of things are all changeable, variable factors. When I had tried to *act* American, I was trying to match some foggy image in my head.

But assimilating was not about trying to copy Americans, like those Indian-American families who came across as a little off when they tried to be American by not offering things a second time, even though many of them knew of our different norms. Assimilating was being me and then connecting with America in my own way, connecting to those parts that I genuinely understood and admired and loved. I could grow from adopting these parts of America - from its spirit of questioning to its openness to difference and valuing of hard work.

In the first few years of the move though, the feeling of being displaced, even though the move had been a conscious decision and even though I had a lot of amazing support from Rohit, was strong. I felt uprooted, as if no one could understand me here and also as if no one could understand me in India. How could I explain all these hundred little details that seemed to be washing me ashore? Sometimes, I was so ungrounded that it would take someone else pointing it out to see these differences. It took me forever, for example, to figure out that the light switches in our home looked and worked the opposite way in which switches worked in India. What was "*Off*" there was "*On*" here and vice versa.

In the middle of all this newness, familiarity urgently tugged at my sleeve. There felt a real danger of losing touch with my roots. Neither Rohit nor I were particularly religious but things like not getting to celebrate festivals like Diwali on the same day as in India pricked at me.

People here celebrated Indian festivals on the weekends when they were free. In this space of letting go of the old and building the new, this felt like a big loss. It loomed large for me and I tried to pull together the threads of the familiar. In one of my first Diwalis, I made a stencil out of cardboard, cutting it into the *ambi*, a simplified pattern based on a mango and used it to make a circular *rangoli* like the ones I used to make in India during Diwali. *Rangolis* are patterns made both outside and inside homes on festivals. In some parts of India, they are even made daily. Drawn on the floor, they can be made with either fresh flowers or rice flour or with the colored powders that are popular in bigger cities.

That Diwali, I had taken my makeshift *rangoli* stencil outside and spent two to three hours, shivering a little in the November cold, as I filled in pink and green colors in my little mango shapes arranged in a circle. On one hand, it had felt so sad, being all alone on this day. But there had also been that feeling of newness and excitement about doing something in our home together.

Later on, when someone would ask me about the meaning behind *rangoli*, I would try to find out. It was one of those things I did in India without really thinking about it. But any reasons for it seemed to be lost in the mists of time. The closest explanation I found talked of how making it with rice flour was both a daily creative ritual as well as a way to offer food to the natural world. To me, it felt like one of those things without a goal. It was about the sense of beauty and meaning you got from making something.

Maybe, making a daily *rangoli* joined you a little bit. Then, afterwards, you left it there as an offering, and a little bird might come and peck at it. The next day, it would be the same steps, the same stitching together, the same give-away.

During another Diwali, some years down the road, when I was feeling down and sad, I made another big *rangoli*. This time, I had gotten stencils from India - tiny swans and flowers - and I made this one on the edges of the path in front of our home. When I had started, my heart felt hurt and empty. But by the time I had finished making it, my heart had been filled again, either with the colors I was using or with just being in the present moment. I thought then about how so many of the things I had discounted about India were those feminine things that are the bridge between this moment and that.

Even here in the States, when I was asked about the significance of these kinds of rituals, I often tried to find logical explanations for them instead of talking about my own feeling. I didn't think the first person who started doing something creative like making a *rangoli* or creating jewellery and adorning themselves knew exactly why they were doing it. I was just like them.

Learning about creating was about giving myself permission to make things without knowing exactly *what* I was making. All I knew was that just like those people, when I, in my modern home in modern America made my little creation, I felt renewed by it. Maybe, this is simply something embedded deep within our beings, this impulse to create things that pull the thread of the sacred into the mundane world.

Managing Overwhelm - Creating a Framework for Diffuse Feelings

When I initially started these explorations into learning about culture, they were a way to connect with myself, with my past as well as my present. They were an attempt to find inner tools at an overwhelming time. But as the years passed, I could start seeing what my overall process had been like.

At first, once the honeymoon period of the move was over, I had felt inundated by the rush of changes I had to deal with. I had felt like I couldn't cope with them, as if I couldn't make sense of them. But *other* people didn't seem to get exactly *why* I felt so overwhelmed in the first place. So, I had even doubted whether I was actually noticing any real differences or whether I was imagining them. So for a time, I had just kept on feeling overwhelmed. I had tried to cope by *not seeing* and doubted whatever I did pick up on.

But then, at some point, my natural interest in people and learning about this new culture had slowly started giving me a context. Instead of having just unformed feelings and sensations, I now had a framework inside which I could put all these feelings and sensations.

I *was* catching on to real subtleties and differences. My

noticings might have been irrelevant for other people. But they weren't irrelevant for me. If I wanted to work with my sensitivity instead of against it, I had to honor the wisps of information it brought me. I had to take my noticings seriously even if no one else took them seriously. I had to put them inside a context. It was only when I gave myself permission to find out more about what I was sensing and then started contextualizing it that I started to feel much more in control and much less overstimulated.

It was a bit like when I used to do photography in Chandni Chowk in Old Delhi. Without my camera, I was overwhelmed by the sensory overload - the cart-pullers pulling humongous bags of spices from *Khari Baoli*, Asia's largest spice market, streams of humanity pouring from all directions on cycle-rickshaws and scooters, families shopping around for the right wedding card design. Without that camera, the whole world seemed to be rushing at me.

But when I was behind the camera, it was as if the camera imposed a framework on the world around me, as if everything was condensed and filtered through, as if everything had a purpose. Then, I was in control. Working with my sensitivity meant finding a similar kind of framework to catch all the subtleties that seemed to pour in from all different directions.

I had to make a net to catch what I sensed, which would then make it easier to examine it.

Here, in the States, I had created this framework by consciously learning about cultural differences. This understanding then gave me rules and guides that told me the *meaning* behind the things I was noticing. They were no longer undifferentiated bits of information, all glommed together. I had put at least some of them in their assigned buckets. Just as cleaning the clutter in my kitchen or finishing up the dishes gave me a feeling of lightness, parsing this too-much-information and clearing its clutter helped me feel more in control.

Of course, this was not always a cut and dried process. Culture is an intersection of many things. But even a few dropped clues felt like a way to look inside this new culture. One concept I had come across that felt quite helpful was formulated by Kurt Lewin, the pioneering German-American psychologist who is considered the founder of modern social psychology. Lewin's theory talked about how whole cultures could be identified as *Peaches* or *Coconuts*.

Peaches are people who are soft on the outside, the ones who are friendly and familiar right from the beginning. But if you mistake this friendliness for real intimacy, you will soon encounter the hard pit that protects their innermost life. On the other hand, *Coconuts* are people who have tougher exteriors, but once you get past that hard shell, once you get past that reserve and make it to their inner circle, then the softer aspect of the person is revealed. Americans, taken together as a culture, are considered *Peaches* while cultures like the French and the German are considered *Coconut* cultures.

I knew this was a broad-strokes generalization. I could think of Americans I knew who could easily fit into the opposite stereotype. Some of the *Peaches* versus *Coconuts* idea seemed to also be connected with personality, how introverted or extroverted you were and how that might come across to others. But on a broader level, I did feel that there was some truth to this idea.

It felt like a clue for why my interactions felt different with some Americans and some Indians. Americans did seem to live up to their reputation of being friendly to strangers. Even in daily interactions, even if I just went to get a haircut at *Supercuts*, the hairdresser would tell me about their weekend plans or about their family. This was innocuous and I was, in fact, interested in people and getting to know about them. But what bothered me were some other, more personal interactions than these.

With a few people, at least to my introverted self, divulging of personal details felt like an offer of friendship or increased closeness. But after a time, I would realize that there was a part of the person I just couldn't access. It did feel like the pit of the peach, as if I had come to a locked gate, as if I had mistaken friendliness for friendship.

For some time, I wasn't sure if I had these kinds of experiences because India was a *Coconut* culture. When I had first come upon this theory, I had tried to find out but I couldn't find any references online. At any rate, I concluded that whether India was a *Coconut* culture or not, I was definitely a *Coconut* in many ways. I seemed to match many of those descriptions of people from *Coconut* cultures, like the French. I was reserved. I didn't like to ask people personal questions and was a bit wary of sharing personal information. Although I could be friendly, my inner world was definitely completely out of bounds to other people in the beginning.

Also, coming from a country with multitudes of people, I had some ingrained *Coconut-like* habits. I didn't go out of my way to greet people who were just passing by, for example. Some of this was about being an introvert. Some was simply habit and the norm that I grew up with.

This was probably the reason for many small crossed communications that left me feeling like I had done something wrong. I had made a social mis-step I couldn't quite decipher. But there was no mistaking the other person's reaction in these cases. I registered that completely.

One time, flying by myself to Washington D.C, I sat beside an American guy who I said *"Hi"* to. But I hadn't really been in a mood to talk, so later on, I had just kept quiet. I hadn't initiated any small talk, and the man had talked with the woman sitting on his other side. Reaching D.C., when I had said *"Bye"* to him, he had given me *the look*. Obviously, I had done something wrong. He had thought I was rude while I had thought that I had been polite and had done what was necessary. *Why were Americans so extroverted?,* I had thought then.

But looking back on these kinds of interactions, I realized there was also that layer of the cultural norm to them. If I had talked for a few minutes and then actually excused myself in some way, maybe saying I had a headache and wanted to be quiet, that interaction would have gone down better. I had probably left this person feeling that he had made an effort to be friendly while I had possibly come across as snobbish.

Did this mean I always had to talk? In time, I decided that wasn't so. I just needed to be a little more mindful. I didn't need to be super-revealing when I didn't want to be, when that was not who I was. But often, a few lines were enough. As an HSP, I was extremely tuned in to the other person's reaction. Maybe, someone else in my place wouldn't have cared if they made this cultural faux pas. But I did. I noticed the other person's feelings. I felt like I had made a mistake. I registered that I had given a wrong impression of myself.

Understanding that many of these differences in expectations were cultural and not personal, I could slightly angle my conversations depending on who I was interacting with here in multicultural, diverse Bay Area. Now, even when I am walking inside my gated community and encounter some unknown neighbor, I am okay either way.

I often expect to say *"Hi?"* to the Americans except for the decidedly introverted ones. If someone passes me by and doesn't even look at me, I think of both culture as well as personality differences. As an introvert and a reserved person, that's my natural tendency as well. But when I come across someone with different norms, as an HSP who registers other people's reactions, I often change my response slightly.

Responding slightly differently like this doesn't feel fake to me. It feels wholly authentic. It takes care of the reality of the situation. It also helps me take care of myself and avoid feeling like I have made an emotional misstep. Being here in Silicon Valley with people from different nationalities and cultural norms means I get to practice this. More often than not, I can almost predict the nationality of the person depending on how open or closed they are to small talk and how they reply to me when we've just met.

I have also stopped trying to *act* extroverted, which just left me feeling fake. I just have to be me, smile and just notice who is around me. Of course, I hardly do this perfectly. But just knowing the context helps a lot. It makes me feel more comfortable and less like I did in the beginning, when I felt I was making mistakes all the time.

How I hated making those mistakes!

Learning about culture has also showed me just how Indian I am. In India, I didn't think there was something especially Indian about me. But there is. Like other people from Asian cultures, open disagreement often leaves me feeling attacked. This is interesting because India, as such, falls on the "emotionally expressive" side of the international spectrum. But as is the case with people from other countries that are *both emotionally expressive and also avoid confrontation*, open confrontation has often felt like disrespect to me. It's not that there are no areas in which I can't be direct. But in many things, I am very much Indian. More than ever, living bang in the middle of this melting pot of different cultures, I see both the inherent possibilities that exist in the meeting of these differences as well as the real challenges this brings up.

Culture makes us. But it's ever-changing. It's not something as simple as the place we've originally come from. When I listen to people talking with surprise about the increasing number of marriages between second-generation Indians and Chinese, I think of how two people like these have more in common culturally with each other than they would have with someone from their "own" original culture who had grown up in India or China. They are both American, second-generation immigrants. I also think of how much commonality there can be underneath our outer differences.

But what I most think of now is how sensing the subtle has brought me to this deeper understanding. If I hadn't tried to learn about these differences, I would have concluded that Americans were fake when it's their culture, with its amazing openness to diversity and differences that makes up social norms that can be interpreted in different ways, as open and friendly or as superficial and fake. It was also because I almost felt other people's reactions in my body whenever I made a mistake that I actually had an impetus to learn about what was all around me.

Being in America has not just given me a window into a different way of thinking, as valid as what I grew up with, but a window into my sensitivity. When I consider my feelings and the things that I sense as important, only then I can do something to stop being overwhelmed. Only then can I start moving in the direction of what I am noticing, delve deeper into it and really understand it for myself.

This journey has taken me deeper into my inner world, the real world within this world where all things happen.

Expressing Emotions Kinesthetically - Coloring Books, Jung and Mandalas

It was also because I needed to depend on my own self in this new country that I started exploring something else that took me even deeper inside myself. As I settled more into my skin, as I worked with Jennifer, and as Rohit and I fell into a more familiar groove, I opened the door to something that would give me a further insight into the nature of my own mind.

My mind (like the minds of many other HSPs, I suspect) often hooks on to a thought and then chomps on it endlessly. It's like a dog with a bone, gnashing on the same old things. This over-thinking, this rumination, has long been a part of my adaptation. But it was here in the States that I accidentally happened upon a practice that gave me an inroad into understanding and dealing with this part of myself.

Like many other good things in my life, it began with following a curiosity.

Adult coloring books had just started becoming popular, and my sister had gotten one. It was also around this time that I started diving deeper into Carl Jung's work. Carl Jung, the great Swiss psychiatrist, was born in 1875 and is the man who formulated many psychological concepts that are now part of our collective vocabulary - Introvert, Extravert, Shadow, and the Complex. Because I both wanted to do something my sister was doing in India and because I had read about Jung's experiments with art therapy and his work with *mandalas* (a Sanskrit word for sacred circular designs drawn in Hinduism and Buddhism), I picked out a book on coloring *mandalas* by Jim Gogarty.

As I colored in my *mandala* book, I also started learning more about Jung and Jungian Depth Psychology. As one of the great psychologists in modern history, Carl Jung was once considered heir apparent to Sigmund Freud. But after a long association, Jung's ideas had taken a sharp turn away from Freud's, and there had come a rift between the two great men.

Both were interested in plumbing the innermost depths of the human psyche (both Freudians and Jungians use the term Depth Psychology because they both delve deep into the unconscious) but both thought that there were different things inside the unconscious. Freud maintained that it only contained our repressed desires and feelings. Jung thought that it also contained the proverbial "gold" in our psyche, our greatest gifts. I was fascinated by

Jung's conception of the unconscious.

As I dived deeper into his work, it was also fascinating to learn about the origins of his theory of Psychological Types. Jung's theory is, in fact, the foundation for the extremely popular MBTI (Myers-Briggs Type Indicator), constructed by Katharine Cook Briggs and her daughter Isabel Briggs Myers, which gives us 16 personality types. According to MBTI, I am an INFP personality type, a very rare personality type in the MBTI universe.

INFPs (Introverted, Intuitive, Feeling and Perceiving) are highly tuned in to the inner world of their feelings, for both good and bad. Increasingly, as I went up and down the currents of my emotions, I realized the truth in that popular meme that depicts INFPs' feelings in the shape of an iceberg. Only the tip of my feelings was visible to other people, while my inward orientation hid the rest of the iceberg.

Because I processed my feelings internally and only shared them with a select few people, often people who didn't know me well didn't realize the depths of my emotions. This is also why although I am generally laid back, I can also dig my heels in at times. This can come as a surprise to others, and it's usually when some value I hold dear has been violated.

Because I had found MBTI so helpful and prescient in my own life, it was fascinating to read about its foundation, Jung's theory of Psychological Types. Jung had, in fact, formulated it after his bitter break with Freud. Neither one of them had been able to convince the other about his own conception of the unconscious. They just couldn't see eye to eye. It was almost as if they were seeing completely different things. Later on, when

Jung thought deeply about this impasse, he realized that innately, both of them were oriented differently to the world. They picked up on different aspects of the world and interacted with it differently. This kernel of a thought became the starting point for Jung's theory of Psychological Types, which says that people experience the world using four main psychological functions - *sensation*, *intuition*, *feeling* and *thinking* - and that *one* of these four functions is dominant for a person.

As someone who meets the world first through feelings and then through intuition, I had found this understanding helpful in my own life. I knew how difficult it was for me to communicate with someone with a very different dominant orientation. As someone who gave more importance to shades of feelings and intuitive details, concrete, day-to-day details sometimes slipped me by. So, I had always been fascinated by these differences in how we look at the world. As I read more and more, Jung's insights felt enthralling and utterly captivating, as if they were pulling me deeper inside a mystery.

Once I started learning about Jung, I also started exploring my dreamworld, what Depth Psychology thinks of as the bridge to the unconscious. I started writing down my dreams every morning to try to find clues for what was happening in my inner world. The move to the States seemed to have opened the portal to my dreams. But before I began this inner journey, I would first learn about Jung through another path.

As a true pioneer, Jung was also one of the first people in Europe to include art therapy in his therapeutic process. He had come upon art as a tool for healing during a dark time in his own life. Because he was familiar with Indian philosophical writing, he had started a personal ritual of doing a small circular drawing each and every day. Over time, he had started noticing how these drawings changed as his feelings changed.

Later on, he also started incorporating this idea of drawing *mandala*-like circular designs in his therapeutic process. As different people worked with him, as they made their own circular drawings, and as client and therapist, they together interpreted the meaning of these drawings, an utterly fascinating thing started to become clear to Jung.

He found that just like him, his patients were not only soothed and calmed after they created these images, but there was also a great deal of similarity between the images they created at different points of the therapeutic process. So, as an example, clients who had recently started therapy would create circular designs that resembled each other's drawings. At later stages of healing, when they created new drawings, they would again just "happen" to create drawings very similar to others at a similar point in their inner work.

This was true even though these people who came to Jung for therapy had no prior knowledge of *mandalas* or any symbolism associated with them. They just did the drawings because it was part of the process, because it was a tool that Jung had found personally useful and handed to them to use. But now, it seemed like they were dipping into some ancient, universal aspect of themselves and pulling out similar images to represent the psychological change happening inside them.

As their inner world became more ordered, their drawings shapeshifted and changed into similar patterns.

When I read about this, it felt fascinating to me, just like it had fascinated Jung when he had noticed this pattern. As people's inner lives became more ordered, the images they drew changed and different people, who knew nothing about each other, drew similar images at similar points in their journeys. There was a common thread of humanity, a common reservoir of images that everyone seemed to have dipped into.

To Jung, it became clear that the circular drawing, the *mandala*, was the template for the mind, a resolution of the chaos within. It was almost as if creating the circular form compensated for the confusion and disarray inside the person. In his work, he also started seeing that the urge to create these circular patterns came up spontaneously for people during intense periods of growth and change. It seemed as if drawing these images or creating them in some other way helped people integrate the changes that were happening in and around them. It helped them come back to their center.

To me, it seemed like my *rangolis*, with their often circular, traditional patterns were an everyday expression of that same impulse to get back to center that Jung and his patients had found in drawing *mandalas*. I was vaguely aware of *mandalas* in Hinduism and Buddhism. These circular designs were sometimes said to represent the universe. They were often used as tools for meditation.

While the word *mandala* had been adopted by Jung because of his own first encounter with these images, these circular patterns are found across religions, across cultures. Only the word is foreign sounding. But circular images themselves can be found everywhere. When I think of *mandalas*, I think of the beautiful stained-glass rose windows in Notre Dame in Paris. I think of Grace

Cathedral in San Francisco with its replica of the Chartres labyrinth, which you can use for a walking meditation. Just as Jung's patients had found with their *mandalas*, the circular labyrinth is linked to mystical traditions that help you get centred. When I think of these archetypal patterns, I think of both sand mandalas in Tibetan Buddhism as well as Native American sand paintings.

Tibetan Buddhism tradition is especially poetic. It involves first creating and then destroying these ephemeral paintings made with colored sand. To me, this feels like a representation of the essence of the creative process. You create something outwardly. You give it all your attention. The process connects you to your very soul. Then, that thing is let go of. It's not the "having created" that joins you, it's when you are inside the moment, inside the process, inside the labyrinth, inside your center.

To me, the *mandala*, the labyrinth, the stained-glass windows, they speak not of any one religion but of the motifs and patterns that underlie all religion. Why is it that across different religions, in different contemplative practices, the same kinds of images are used as a centering device? There are probably many anthropological and historical reasons behind it, but I think one big reason is that these images *work*.

It doesn't matter what formal religion you believe in, when you dip into the pool of these archetypal, universal images, they seem to have inside them, something mysterious, something that connects you to the very core of your larger self. To me, the Instagram pictures I see of flowers laid out in circles or the artiste displaying her paintings of circles studded with semi-precious stones in a San Francisco park, are all people dipping into that same universal pool of images, expressing the same archetypal patterns.

Maybe, this is why making my *rangolis* had felt so centering. It was meditation but a different kind of meditation. It brought me right into the present moment. But it wasn't about trying to get my mind empty. Instead, it was about connecting and filling up with my very essence. It was a feeling of fullness, not emptiness.

This promise of greater order in my inner life in the rush of change felt like something precious to hold onto. After coloring umpteen *mandala*-like patterns in Gogarty's coloring book, I soon found another quite fascinating little coloring book. It was Susanne Fincher's *The Mini Mandala Coloring Book,* based on American Art Therapist Joan Kellogg's work.

Joan Kellogg had developed her ideas about *mandalas* and personal growth in the 1970s. She called her theory *"Archetypal Stages of the Great Round of Mandala"* (or simply the "Great Round.") She had identified circular designs associated with twelve stages in a complete cycle of growth related to the ebbs and flows of human experience. These stages are visited again and again, at different times in our life. Every time we come back to a particular stage, it helps us gain deeper understanding and realize more of our potential.

When I started coloring the circular patterns in this book, it was fascinating to see how I naturally gravitated to the kind of drawing that corresponded to the stage I was myself in. I would flip through the book quickly and instead of moving linearly, pick out a pattern that called to me. In periods when I was feeling as if things were coming apart at the seams, I would naturally pick out the designs associated with the *Fragmentation* stage of Kellogg's "Great Round" of psychological growth.

The explanation given on the page opposite to the drawing would almost exactly match what I was feeling. When I felt fragmented, when parts of my old identity were withering away but my new identity hadn't yet come to fruition, the text described something that was exactly true for me, like the feeling of my bones being picked clean or my dreams being full of alien creatures or ones in which I was lost in the parking lot.

In the beginning of the move, I had especially felt this way. It seemed like my identity was breaking down. Suddenly, I was "brown," a word I chafed at. I wasn't Asian even though India was in Asia. It felt like I had to describe myself to people again and again and give explanations not just for myself, but for my culture. I felt like an in-between person who didn't belong in the Indian diaspora.

There were already many things I had left behind, like the way I related to God. I didn't want to celebrate festivals or do things that connected me to India in the accepted, traditional way. So, it felt like I neither belonged to the Indian community nor was I American. I really was becoming some third thing, especially once I committed to an artistic path, a thing that most people didn't quite get.

Later on, as I settled down, there would come a time when I felt more at home. My roots seemed to go a little deeper into my everyday life. Then, I intuitively picked out the patterns from the *Squaring the Circle* stage. The descriptions talked about how I was in the stage where figuring out my place in the scheme of things was creating the foundation of a firmer identity. The combining of circles and squares denoted how the female and male energies in my own self were now more balanced.

Again and again, over a few years, as I went through the different cycles in my life, I intuitively picked out patterns in this coloring book that corresponded exactly to where I was. Sometimes, I felt attracted to "*Void*" patterns such as the image of a circle in which an old woman, who I thought of as the healer, encircled a still-being born woman. At different points, I went through different stages of my own process and felt delighted when I saw them being reflected in the images I was picking, like *Crystallization*, when creative projects coalesced together and even when I was going through the *Gates of Death*, walking down the steps into the basement of my unconscious and letting many things dissolve.

Over the years, I went through many copies of *The Mini Mandala Coloring Book*. Its patterns laid out the ebbs and flows of my journey. There were times when I was called to the circles with spiralling lines inside them. This was usually when I was feeling excited about something new. When I liked the patterns with the several concentric circles around a center point, it *did* feel like I was gathering my personal power, just as the book said.

This precious little book was an opening into the symbolic world, a world of images, a world of possibilities. But even more than the *a-ha* moments and the delight at seeing my own changes mirrored back in its patterns, I felt the shifts in feelings that happened inside my body when I moved my hand over the page.

Always, without fail, after I had stopped coloring, I felt a visceral feeling of being nourished, literally in my heart, at the very center of my being. Always, without fail, I felt less scattered and more cohesive afterwards. Going through book after book, I found some much-needed encouragement.

It was okay to be fragmented, to feel like you were in the void, to build stronger boundaries while soft, new vines were taking root inside you. These were all essential parts of changing.

Working through this book also brought me closer to the value of colors. I had always loved colors. Here, in the States, I had wondered why lack of color was a fashion statement. Did it have to do with not being feeling oriented? Was it that color was seen as a distraction? Whatever the reason, it felt like a loss, the disappearance of an entire spectrum of color after moving from India to the States. So, coloring seemed like a way to bring myself some of that.

When I had first started coloring, I had let myself pick out colors intuitively, based on my attraction to them instead of doing what I used to do once upon a time as a child - debating endlessly about the perfect choice, feeling like I could never ever make the right choice. But this time, I had been tuning into my intuition and just as a little practice, I let myself go with what "felt" right instead of trying to match colors. Playing like this, it felt like I was picking out colors that called to me energetically and coloring within the lines of my heart as well.

A year or so before I started coloring, at a time when I was struggling with feelings of homesickness and feeling little tremors in my identity, I had sat myself down on the floor of my room and drawn my body and how it felt energetically. This exercise of "drawing the body" comes from somatic therapist Anodea Judith's work. It tells you to draw the "felt" experience of your body.

Does your body feel big, or does it feel small? Does it feel densely packed, or does it feel diffuse? Are your shoulders tight as a screw while your middle is flopping around? How can you visually represent the different parts of your body?

At that time, I had drawn a head much bigger than my body. It was completely out of proportion. That hadn't come as a surprise. I always felt like my attention was way up in my head, instead of down in my body. What was surprising was the fact that I had drawn an extremely tight and small heart. I was always giving and feeling responsible for others. I was always finding one stranger after another, even in this new-to-me country who often, finding someone listening to them, vented to me. It was as if the very attention that made me a good listener seemed to pull away the mask and cause people to tell me all these things.

When I was giving so much of my attention away, why then had I drawn such a small, clenched heart?

Until now, although I routinely got drained by all this listening, it had never even occurred to me that my heart could be closed. Didn't giving like this mean that my heart was open? But obviously some part of me didn't think so. No, my heart was clenched tight into a fist. It was there on the paper for me to see.

Why did I think that was?

As time passed and I thought about this question, I would start seeing that the heart lives on a balance of giving and receiving. When I gave when I was already overdrawn, I was not opening my heart but snapping it shut. It was as if my heart clenched to protect itself, to guard its happiness and joy.

At that time though, I didn't understand why my heart felt like this even though there was so much good in my life now, even though Rohit was a wonderful source of support for me as I figured out my new life. I didn't yet realize how I was almost leaking energy. With these *mandalas* and through using color, for the time being, at least, I had found a practical way to nourish my heart.

I didn't always use this tool. Sometimes, I was just caught up in rescuing people and neglecting the ones who actually gave to me. But whenever I did, whenever I remembered, this was an easy way home to myself. This expressing with art, sometimes in coloring books and then later on with painting, also brought me closer to understanding how my emotions worked. Moving my hands while coloring or playing with clay was physical. It was expressing kinesthetically. It was like all these blobs of feelings could be put onto a page. I could pour out the blackness of my feelings and almost physically move them out of my body.

What was even more amazing was that right from the first day that I had picked up my first coloring book, my mind quieted down almost instantly, predictable like clock-work, as soon as I started coloring. Just a minute before, it would be turning back on itself, locked into the same old thoughts, looping again and again. But as soon as I started moving my hand, that rush of inner destructive chatter stopped. It just stopped.

It did not slow down. It did not become less. It went away.

Nothing like this had ever happened to me even when I had tried meditating. It was almost as if the raw, crackling energy inside me that had no channel before, that was dancing in destruction, now had a way to flow out. It could take shape, instead of creating a ruckus inside me. It was as if that dog with a bone, obsessively thinking about the same thing again and again, had been given something else to chew on.

This experience led me to become even more curious about color. In the past, at different times in my life, I had been drawn to specific colors. There was a time in my corporate life, a time when I felt stuck, when I was very attracted to yellow and wore it a lot. Yellow, of course, is associated with the solar plexus chakra in Yoga philosophy, and the solar plexus is the seat of power in the body. I was instinctively pulled towards the color that I most needed to make a change. There had been other times in my life when I had naturally gravitated towards red, a color associated with grounding and to purple, a color that helps us think clearly.

Today, research is telling us more about the healing effects of color, and color therapy is becoming more mainstream. Color is vibration and energy, and it seems like we instinctively know what energy we most need at a particular time.

Bit by bit, organically, as I started doing watercolors and acrylics and drawing more, I also started diving deeper into the meanings of colors. Soon, I had discovered intuitive healer Inna Segal's work. She had a deck called *The Secret Language of Color Cards,* which was a collection of cards with individual colors on them and a booklet talking about the healing properties of different colors and ways to visualize with them. I worked with these cards intuitively. I would pick out a color that called out to me and then read about it.

Always, without fail, I had picked out the exact thing I needed.

As a sensitive person, I had gone through life feeling like what was inside me was all wrong, as if my out-of-control feelings had to be disciplined, as if they were always turning against me. Over the years, I had lost a lot of faith in my ability to choose what was right for me. But with picking out these colors, first with coloring and now with these cards, it felt like there was a part of me that knew exactly what I needed.

There were times when I spontaneously picked out the lemon card when I needed to think of my writing in creative, innovative ways. Lemon, as it turned out, is a color that helps us think innovatively. At times when I was working on building better boundaries and grounding myself, I naturally picked out brown and auburn and breathed them in.

I also saw how other people used colors, even without knowing anything of its properties, almost instinctively picking out exactly what they needed. I knew someone with breathing problems who wore peach instinctively, a color good for breathing problems. Rohit loves eating watermelons, so much so that I feel like any watermelons we get are his. Watermelon is a color that resonates with the inner child, that encourages playfulness after a day of hard, intellectual work. Like him, I found that watermelon resonated with my inner child. It has also been a color that helps me honor the feelings of this little child inside. Whenever I have visualized breathing in watermelon, it's as if I am in closer contact with my hidden feelings. If the

46

little child inside is feeling hurt or sad, for example, watermelon helps not just soothe it but also helps me express her feelings.

For someone who has often worn the shroud of *Be Strong*, whether things are going good or bad or terrible, who has often stamped down on her feelings, even though they are so big and large, these ways to let my feelings flow, these ways to be in touch with them, have felt valuable.

Over the last few years, after I discovered the magic of colors, I have used them to support myself at different times. In the beginning, it was with the help of tools like Inna Segal's color cards. Later on, I used colors simply by paying attention to colors in my environment and visualizing myself as being full of them. Always, without fail, I have felt my emotions shift and change as I used a specific color. Often, I have felt myself get instinctively pulled into the constellation of colors I need.

Now, with all these years of exploring behind me, I know that I can draw in energy from all sorts of things, from the sight of the purple-flowered vine that grows near my house or the green on my dentist's wall when I go in for a cleaning. It's good to know that the kind of energy I need is available, anytime, anywhere. It's good to know that the sensitivity that often makes my life challenging also opens me up to receive the whole wide world around me.

Chapter 2

Going down into the Well of My Dreams

I have always been fascinated with the image of the explorer - the one who goes down into a cave and finds beautiful stalagmites nestling in the earth, the one who dives deep into the ocean and finds colors shimmering and shifting and life enacting its multifaceted dance. These are the people who dare to go inside the deep, dark fold. These are the people who risk getting lost in the void.

But then, at some point, in a moment made possible by their own daring, a membrane cracks, and the darkness crumbles under their fingers. It opens up to reveal a world spinning with colors and teeming with life, pulsing with an ecstasy that has left its imprints everywhere.

Some of these explorers go out into the external world. But some walk down into the underground caves of their own selves to find what lives there.

For all of us, a time like this comes, in that space when the tide turns, when the current of our own soul beckons. It nudges us to lift the curtains. It pulls us closer to that something more.

At the beginning of the move to the States, I felt this time of little coming-alives in my inner world. I had always had vivid dreams. But now, it felt as if my dreamworld had tilted even closer, as if my dreams were alight with meaning. In the first few years after the move, as I

48

adjusted to my new life, as I rode up its hills and down its valleys, the images in my dreamworld also shape-shifted along with me.

During the periods of intense change, there were often images of water in my dreams. Lakes and rivers often overran their boundaries. Sometimes, I found myself drowning. The symbolism seemed apparent. In my day-to-day life, my emotions were often overflowing and threatening to take over me. But apart from what seemed like obvious metaphors, there were also harder to understand images in my dreams.

More than a year after my actual wedding ceremony and the subsequent move, I still had dreams of one wedding after another. Sometimes, I was the star of the show and getting ready for my own wedding. Sometimes, it was other people's weddings that I was a part of. Often, I was trying on new outfits. Sometimes, there was dancing and celebration involved and an accompanying feeling of joy.

When the door to my dreamworld had first opened, I hadn't paid too close of an attention to it. But as time passed, it felt as if my dreams were so richly-colored, so alive, they almost seemed to have a voice of their own. Soon, I couldn't help feeling that they meant *something*. Something seemed to be both showing me my face in the mirror and also revealing things I hadn't consciously thought of before. If I just let myself pay attention, this *something* was speaking back to me.

Was I the only person who felt curious about her dreamworld?

I had always had this curiosity. I was one of those people who looked up dream interpretations online. I was also one of those people who believed in signs and portents. Dreams had always tugged at me. Even as a teenager, I had thought of dreams as signs from somewhere deep inside me. But then, at a pivotal point in my life, things had happened that had caused me to become sceptical and disillusioned, that had made me wary of taking my dreams too seriously.

This had happened when I was fifteen or sixteen. It was then that a dream had come that I had taken both literally and seriously. It came at the cusp of a major change. Soon, I would be stepping out of the protected space of my all-girls' Convent school into Junior College in what was then called Bombay. Already, in the last few years, my friends had become more interested in boys. Some of them even had boyfriends. Life was changing all around me. It felt as if I was stepping off the edge into the unknown. It felt as if the outside world was coming rushing towards me.

But the thing was, I wasn't ready. I couldn't quite put it into words, but something was rising inside me. It felt uncontrollable, something I was frightened by. This not having control any longer, this coming to a point where I was going to be out in the open, this felt like a huge risk, a risk I couldn't afford to take.

The world was not to be trusted.

This sense of the world being dangerous had its roots in my childhood when something traumatic had shaken up my life. This feeling had been my companion for a long time, but I had thought I had left it behind. But as I later realized, at this moment of stepping into the larger world, this belief was activated again. Its underlying charge and feeling hadn't been snuffed out. It had lived in the shadows, waiting for a weak moment, waiting to capture me.

It was while I was feeling this shakiness that I had, what would later turn out to be, a fateful dream. It went like this. It was late at night. I was being followed in the dark, deserted Bombay streets by someone coming for me, someone who I knew had a knife in their hands.

In my dream, I ran faster and faster with my heart pounding in my chest. But no one was around, not at this time of the night. I was utterly alone, almost jumping out of my skin, petrified. Frantically, I tried to find a place to hide. As the minutes counted down, I could hear the man's footsteps going *thud-thud*, getting closer and closer. With every minute, he was gaining on me. At last, I could feel him right behind me. Now, there was nowhere to escape, nowhere to hide. Frightened out of my wits, I finally turned to look at him.

This is where the dream had ended, truncated like many other dreams, or maybe, that was all I remembered when I woke up. I could still feel that sense of impending doom. The dream felt like a warning of things to come. Something bad could happen once again. I had to protect myself, guard myself. I couldn't get injured. It was too painful, too vulnerable. What was I going to do?

Although I tried to push down the residue of this feeling from the dream, it slowly spread its tentacles inside me. It latched on to my fear. It found a place in a gaping hole. It grew.

Now, with more than two decades between me and that dream, I know that this dream simply showed me a fear that I already carried inside. It wasn't telling me that something terrible was going to happen. Instead, it was drawing, in fleshed-out pictures, what was happening in my emotional life. It was showing me my place in my psychological terrain. But for those of us who have experienced trauma, whether it is abandonment, abuse or something else, it changes everything. Our worlds become a shaky, unstable place, prone to shifting at a moment's notice. We start feeling that *anything* can happen because once upon a time, something terrible *did* happen.

At sixteen, I wasn't conscious of this. The dream hung over my head like a knife that could strike at any time. Something seized me, paralyzed me. Somewhat unconsciously, somewhat willfully but driven with acute fear, I started responding to the feeling of foreboding looming inside. One of my close friends had been getting interested in boys. I made up a little drama that served as an excuse to pull away from her. Some other things had been making this friendship difficult, but this feeling became the catalyst for cutting off from her entirely.

Another close friend had already moved to a different city a while back. This ended up leaving me all alone, isolated from people at a crucial time when I needed them the most. But there was also a weird sense of having stemmed and delayed an ocean of change, of having controlled it. Alone, I could be lonely. But also, alone, no one could get to me.

That decision to skirt away in my teens coupled with my shyness created a cascading effect. I stalled at an important developmental stage. For years afterwards, I would find it difficult to relate to men. The world around me seemed to give me some more reasons for shoring up my beliefs. In a country swarming with patriarchy, all sorts of things *did* happen in the world around me, and I used them as justifications for keeping myself shut.

I had protected myself. I had walled myself in.

I did what a lot of people who believe in dreams tend to do. I took my dream as the literal truth instead of as a symbolic tale of my own struggles. It seeped into my life. My beliefs, in turn, colored it. I think that dream was trying to tell me something different. Something in me was turning against me.

Looking into that dream decades later was like looking into a pool of water. In it, I could see the reflection of my emotional life at that time. It was as if I had internalized the image of the aggressor, which was going on a rampage inside me. It fed on my fear and gained life and strength from the male-dominated culture that thrived outside.

Something poison-like had flowed into the uncontaminated parts of myself. Maybe, I was already weakened by my oversized fears. Maybe, I just gave in to the pictures in my dream, to the threat of violence inside it. Maybe, if I had known about dreams then, I could have prevented all of this from happening.

Jungian depth psychologists talk a lot about these "dark men" dreams that many women have. They tell us that women who have dreams like these have often suffered what the ancients called soul loss. Some psychological injury has left them reeling. Their instincts are not so sharp anymore. In the dreams of these women, who have effectively started turning against themselves, thieves and rapists lurk just around the corner. They are held hostage, threatened, made to keep quiet. What Jungians call the *animus*, the masculine principle inside women, has turned negative and is going on a killing spree. Their aggression has become twisted and turned against themselves.

While sometimes, dreams like these may be associated with the trauma of an actual assault, even women who haven't experienced assault often have these kinds of dreams. They indicate that we have internalized the discounting we might have experienced outside. They tell us that our reserves are dipping dangerously low. Maybe, we don't have enough that is nourishing and life-giving in our lives. Maybe, we don't have enough support to help us journey ahead. Over the years, whenever I have abandoned myself, whenever I have listened to injunctions from the outside and collapsed within, I have had dreams like these.

Now, I know that they tell me my negative beliefs are hacking away at my soul, that I need more support in my day-to-day life. Of course, as an almost-child of sixteen, I didn't know all this when my dream came. I had been longing for connection and longing to feel safe, so later on, it felt like the dream had purposely misled me.

For years afterwards, I felt faulty, as if I couldn't navigate through life on my own, as if I couldn't trust myself, as if my inner world had betrayed me. I also felt ashamed of being someone who believed in such irrational things as dreams. How stupid was that? How stupid was I?

I had listened to my dream, and look where it had gotten me. Maybe, this was the reason why people tended to discount the inner world. There was no map for it. You could get lost in it. It had places in which you could slip and fall. Shadows could come out and threaten you. Maybe, that's why it feels better for so many people to just deal with concrete reality. It feels better to just push the inner world away.

I wish that inward-looking child had someone telling her that she had nothing to be ashamed of, that her impulse to look inside her dreamworld was correct, even if her interpretations were not. I wish I could show her that her feeling of being wrong had been compounded by growing up in a rationalistic family. Moving up in the world, we had left behind the superstitious, portentous dreams and dreamers of old India. Moving up, we had gotten rid of all that nonsense.

It was because of this that I had often pushed away, without quite knowing why, anything that couldn't be proven beyond any shadow of a doubt. When it felt like my dream had also led me astray, I became ambivalent about my dreamworld. I turned away from it, even when my dreams came rushing into the daylight from under the cover of night.

But still, the inner world, even though I mostly don't understand it, has always felt like my real experience, my real life. Even when nothing momentous is happening outside, nothing to tell people about, my inner world is always changing, my emotions are going up and down and it feels like I am responding to everything. Everything good and bad, big and small, important or inconsequential gets inside my skin.

Whether it's a farce or a tragedy, an adventure or a downfall, it all happens inside. So, I have always been interested in dreams, right through those years when I wasn't interested in them. Even when I got disenchanted, I was still fascinated. Who was this cast of characters who came out to play at night? Who created them? What did it all mean?

Some part of me had always thought that dreams were like a safety valve. In them, all the things I'd pushed down could combust when they were finally given some space. Then, they wouldn't spill out and affect my everyday life.

But this is only part of the story of dreams. There is more to it. Dreams are the mirror that show us our face behind the facade. But they are also something else. An intelligent something often shows up in my dreams. It's almost as if it's seeing what I am doing and commenting on it, sometimes even suggesting ways of doing things in a better way.

Maybe it's because I have always been this close, for both good and bad, to my inner world that moving to the States flung open the door to my dreams once again. Once again, my dreams were swarming with rich stories. Once again, they were hinting at things behind the curtain.

I had been finding it hard to fit myself inside this foreign life. Maybe, if dreams really had something to say, if they were really intelligent, they could help me. Maybe, they could point the way out and guide me. Maybe, I could look inside myself and trust myself fully again.

Carl Jung, Jeremy Taylor and the Lost Language of Dreamwork

When I decided to learn about my dreams, I felt a surge of enthusiasm. But like anything else, the actual process was a little circuitous, a little uneven, a little choppy. The first book I picked up was a simple introduction to Carl

Jung's work. I had already come across Jung earlier in my life in India, in my 20s, when I had seen a mention of him in an article. My interest had been piqued even then.

But when I had tried to learn more, his work had felt obtuse and inaccessible. This had also felt like such an impractical exercise, such an irrational attraction. What was the point of following some trail into the wilderness? It was important to be sensible and normal. So, I had turned away from my heightened curiosity. I had ignored the nudgings from my soul. So, now, this felt like a second chance, getting to know someone whom I had missed meeting in the first place.

But that wonderful encounter was not to be. The book I had picked out, a slim introduction to Jung, managed to turn me off, in one big, fell swoop, from both Jung and his work. One of the things the author talked about, quite early on, was how, this supposedly great man was a philanderer who famously had a mistress. Later on, after I had actually learnt more about Jung, I would go to a lecture in which a Jungian analyst ignored this fact when someone in the audience asked him about this aspect of Jung's life.

At that time, when I read the book, this information felt damaging. I guess we all want our heroes and heroines to be faultless. But here, the author had talked about Jung not as a hero, but in a biting, sarcastic way, talking about all the things he felt were wrong with him. Obviously, he was not an admirer. I was so repulsed I didn't even finish the book. I dropped it and shrunk back.

For some time, the tone of this book left me feeling disillusioned, not just with Jung but with the entire topic of dreams itself. It was a stupid thing, anyways.

Dreams. Who cared about them?

But as time passed, my hopeful curiosity was still there and so was the feeling of wanting to learn more. Hadn't I learnt things from people I did not agree with and sometimes didn't even like? Wasn't it true that in a sense, there were no heroes when we come up close and look at someone? People's lives are marked and chequered, not a perfect, presentable line.

Didn't I want to know what following my curiosity would bring? Didn't I have enough regrets in my life about not following up on my own intuitions? I didn't have to agree with everything or everyone I came across. I could just take what resonated and let the rest go. There was something here, something pulling me, something I could learn about if I just let myself do it.

After months of this push and pull, I finally let myself do just this. I let myself follow a feeling. As chance would have it, I had noticed a Dreamwork section in a second-hand bookstore in the nearby city of Mountain View. After moving to the States, the Mountain View downtown had soon become one of my favorite places. It had not one, not two, but three great bookstores, a second-hand bookstore called *Bookbuyers*, a branch of *Books Inc*, the American West's oldest independent bookstore as well as *East West*, my favorite, full of metaphysical books and gifts, a pilgrimage stop for all seekers and book lovers who passed through Silicon Valley.

I had gone to *Bookbuyers*, the second-hand bookstore, a few times, but had always retreated, almost never buying anything, feeling overwhelmed by the giant floor-to-ceiling bookshelves. The books seemed to tumble out of them and felt haphazardly arranged, except for being organized into broad categories. This should have been heaven, but oddly, I mostly felt overstimulated by so many options and such little direction.

But in one of these visits, I had noticed the *Dreamwork* section. Like other second-hand bookstores, *Bookbuyers* had many interesting categories, from books on *Eastern Philosophies* to the *Occult* to this, their *Dreamwork* section. Once, I had even tentatively picked up some books but had then felt befuddled and put them down. These were heavy tomes on Freud and Jung, the two names most often associated with the modern study of dreams.

Most of them had felt inaccessible. They were big, dense volumes. I also didn't want to buy the other, more simplistic books, dream dictionaries with meanings laid out. Those felt like an internet search. So, even though I had looked curiously at this section many times, I had never ended up buying a book.

But one fateful day, I decided that I was done overthinking and doubting my interest. I was going to go in and pick anything that called to me. So, I entered the bookstore, blocked out all the other books that seemed to be falling towards me, and walked straight to the *Dreamwork* section. As I glanced over it, the title of one book jumped straight out at me. It was a book tantalizingly titled *Where People Fly and Water Runs Uphill* written by someone called Jeremy Taylor. It felt like the right size. It felt like the right fit. There had been a time in my life when I would have tried to second-guess even this, this buying of a book that talked about something I wasn't even sure I *should* take seriously. But that day, I let myself buy it.

It turned out to be exactly the book I needed.

Jeremy Taylor, I came to know later, had worked with dreams for over forty years. He had taught dreamwork to therapists, social workers and seminary students. He had used dreamwork as a tool for social change and facilitated dreamwork groups in various prisons including San Quentin. He thought of dreams in almost the exact opposite way as what we are taught by default in our "modern" lives.

We are usually told that dreams are insignificant, meaningless or simply a rehash of the events that happen in our waking life. But Taylor thought that dreams were not just significant, they were extremely important. They were the markers of being human. Across the world, if we were to fly from mountain to sea, from deserts to island paradises, even though the language or culture changed, we would find that people have many similar images in their dreams.

Many of us dream of flying, of going into underground caves and basements, of being found naked in public, of falling into nothingness. Our dreams show us our similarities, how similar our hopes and fears are. They are that unifying element that can help us penetrate our masks and peer inside our shared hopes and dreams.

The context that *Where People Fly and Water Runs Uphill* provided showed me how significant working with dreams really is. My curiosity was valid. It wasn't stupid. There had been countless people who had not just taken dreams seriously, but also explored them in depth. These included some of the most influential psychologists in modern history.

All of them had something important to say, although I resonated with some more than others. Freud was on to something when he said that all dreams have an element of forbidden desire. Dreams did seem to sometimes enact wishes I had repressed. That matched up to how I had thought of dreams as being a kind of safety valve for our psyches, releasing pent-up energy so it could collide and explode in our inner world before it set off some major explosion outside. So, Freud's "wish fulfillment" theory resonated with me on one level.

But it was Carl Jung who talked about dreams and the unconscious in a way that most attracted me. Unlike Freud, Jung thought dreams didn't only contain repressions, those feelings and desires we wanted to get rid of. The unconscious was not a mere rubbish heap, a dump. Our repressions were just part of what it contained. The unconscious also had inside it the "gold" in our psyche. It contained parts of us that if we could just access, if we could just integrate, could help us become whole.

Just as Taylor had said in *Where People Fly and Water Runs Uphill*, I also thought that the different viewpoints held by Jung, Freud and a host of other psychologists, all had something important to say about the nature of dreams and the unconscious. It was not an either/or but rather a combination of. I was going to learn more and think about what felt true. I could look at my own dreams, observe what was happening there, and then, make up my mind.

Reading *Where People Fly and Water Runs Uphill* was exciting. The book gave me a context that helped me begin. It got me started with writing down my dreams as soon as I got up. Even if I remembered a fragment, a little shard of a mirror, I jotted it down to see myself better, just as Taylor had suggested. It was amazing how sometimes, just writing something down by hand could connect things. It would cause a physical sensation, as if my body was putting disparate pieces together, re-membering disjointed parts.

There were also those other times when I would write down my dreams, and they would make no sense at all. The dream would lie fallow on the page for months. Then, after reading a book on dreamwork or one on ancient myths, I would have that longed-for "*a-ha*" moment that dream workers tell us is the only true test for whether a dream image has revealed something to you. No one else has the final word on your dream. All others can do is offer suggestions. It's this internal resonance, this eureka moment that's the only reliable indicator of whether you have uncovered something true for you.

Taylor's book led me on to other books on dreams, such as books by the humanistic psychologist Erich Fromm and books by Jung and Jungian depth psychologists like Joseph Henderson. Each one had its own insights. In more than one book, the author talked about how dreams were hard to understand not because they were hiding something unpleasant or covering up some untoward wish but just because dreams spoke in images and pictures. This was the language of symbols and metaphors, a language we had long forgotten, but which was, in fact, nature's language, the language in which it communicated.

In Erich Fromm's book *The Forgotten Language*, Fromm talked about dreams in a similar vein to what I had found in Taylor's work. In *The Forgotten Language*, I also happened upon a dream that deeply resonated with me. It was very much like a dream I had recently had. My dream had gone like this. It was again night-time in my dream, but in a place I didn't recognize. I was walking alone on the empty, desolate streets. The few buildings I saw were dilapidated and empty. No one was in sight, and it was completely quiet and barren. There was also no transportation nearby, no way to get out of this cold, bleak place, nothing that could whisk me away. I felt all alone, unutterably lost.

In his book, Fromm had described a dream almost exactly like mine. He had used it to explain how dreams communicate with us. Think about a time, he had told the reader, when you were in a dark, despondent mood. At such a time, if you had tried to describe your feelings to a friend, desperately looking for connection, you probably didn't quite find the right words. Try as you might, your friend just didn't understand the depths of your despair. That left you feeling frustrated, unable to find the warmth you were seeking. Then, the following night, you might have had a dream.

Fromm then went on to describe a dream almost exactly like mine. Dreams, he said, described in images what's so often hard to put into words. They were a forgotten language.

Just as in Fromm's example, my dream had showed in moving images exactly what I was feeling. After the honeymoon period of the move was over, I had often felt like I had bitten off more than I could chew. I hated the sameness of Silicon Valley, right down to its similar-looking houses. It was a place, it seemed to me, with very little past. It was always marching on ahead. There was none of the theatre of life in India, none of the crackling energy that seeped in with Delhi's inefficiency.

The efficiency that everyone seemed to love about America felt cold and mechanical to me. It felt like it came at a cost. This was ironic because in India, I had often felt overwhelmed, like a leaf being blown by forces bigger than me. This more ordered life had many benefits. But in the throes of my misery, I felt like something important had been taken away from me.

Someone told me I was homesick. *Homesick*. That word itself felt small. It did not begin to capture the way my heart felt collapsed on itself. It did not touch on how I missed not just the people, family and friends, but the very underpinnings of life in India, the way it unfolded, the way it was familiar inside my skin. Now, I was left gasping for something that I hadn't even realized was such a part of me.

It was when I was curdling with these feelings, when I was feeling lost and uprooted, hung upside down, that this dream had come. When I read Fromm's example, it spoke directly to me. My dream had cut right to the core of what I had been feeling on and off for months. It had stripped me right down to my basic emotions.

This is part of what dreams do. They show us our location on the map. As Fromm and other dream workers tell us, the picture offered by the dream often stands in for a feeling, a thought, or an experience. If we pause to look at it, we also take off the mask we normally put on. We can see all that is changing and shifting inside us.

As I kept learning more, I came upon more such examples, as more strings were plucked that made a sound, as more pebbles were thrown that created ripples in my consciousness. And the more I wrote down my dreams, increasingly, the more intelligent and meaningful they felt.

Colors and Symbols in Dreams and When Dreams Appear in a Dream Series

When I first started noticing my dreams, I hadn't been aware of any color in my dreamworld. But at some point, this had changed. The shift happened during a time when I was tuning in to the whispers of my feelings and letting my intuition guide me. The more I listened to and honored the information inside my feelings, the more colors seemed to spring up in my dreams.

One of the first colors to appear was red. In one dream, an old woman showed up, all dressed up in a red coat and red stockings and carrying a red handbag. Over the next few years, I would have many dreams with red in them, often showing up in clothes that I was wearing, like in the *sarees* I was trying on in my "wedding dreams." It felt like something dynamic coming through, something alive and new. In another dream, I was in the shower and a gooey, mango-like color ran through the water. In the morning, when I got up, I didn't just have the dream fragment in my hands but also the residue of the feeling in that dream. It had felt so good.

But there were also other dreams with not so good feelings. In some of them, it felt like things had gone wrong somehow. In one such dream, I was following my sister, and we were walking uphill to catch a train. I trudged behind her, willing myself to walk, looking wistfully at the purple amethyst crystals growing on the side of the road. I wished I could stop for a moment and really look at them. But my sister was walking quickly, afraid of missing the train. I followed compliantly behind, all the while looking longingly at those crystals.

As the dream had ended, the perspective had shifted, as it often does in dreams. My sister and I had reached the train. It was waiting patiently for us to board. In the end, it seemed that it would have waited for us after all. Over the next few months, I would turn this dream around, thinking about it. I would also have other similar dreams with amethyst crystals in them where I was always walking away.

In time, as I learned about dreamwork, I started piecing together my own understanding of this dream. In day-to-day life, I think of my sister as very task-focused. Amethyst crystals are something I love, both for their enchanting color and their beauty. In fact, amethyst is my birthstone and I have some amethyst jewellery. Obviously, I was walking away from something precious and beautiful, something I was longing for. My sister's image had stood in for that part of me that was very task-driven.

This part of me was marching ahead, oblivious of the beautiful crystals growing on the roadside. It was dragging forward that other wistful but compliant part, the one who had noticed the crystals growing on the roadside but who had given up this knowing all too easily.

In my day-to-day life, in those first few years in the States, I had been obsessive about keeping my house perfectly ordered. Part of this was healthy, a way to assert control over my environment, to not have one more thing that would overstimulate me. But there was a lot that was unhealthy about it too. As a new wife, I was caught up in the role of being "wifely," trying to create a picture-perfect house. It wasn't something Rohit told me to do. It was an internalized idea, some old conditioning that I was acting out.

Everything had to be just perfect. Everything had to look good. I hated it if one used glass was left behind on the table. I spent a lot of energy keeping things clean and organized. But this too-much keeping things in place was as unhealthy as too-much-mess. It wasn't me being me, the messy, creative person I was. It was me climbing into a box and then complaining I couldn't breathe. And I did this to myself.

The dream was telling me how I was acting. Caught up in the mundane, I was missing the beauty that was all around me. You will catch the train, the dream seemed to be saying. It will wait. But if you go on like this, trying to control everything, you will miss the beauties strewn in your path. During that time, one dream after another had come warning me of this. It was only later, as my relationship with my creativity deepened, as I settled into my skin a little more, that these dreams had finally disappeared. They had done their job. They were no longer needed.

This is why dreams are important. When we listen to our dreams, we change. When we respond to them, they change.

A long while afterwards, I would also learn that Jungian depth psychologists consider crystals as a symbol for the authentic self, our larger self that contains not just our ego but also our very essence. This is our real self, the one we are trying to become, the one we are trying to realize. In my acting out my conditioning of what my "wifely" role meant, I had been walking away from my own potential.

All these dreams with color in them also underlined another point that dream experts talk about. Dream workers say that when we consciously pay attention to feelings in our day-to-day life, the more aware we become of colors in our dream world. It doesn't matter whether you are a woman or a man. Our dreamworld doesn't reflect that common assumption some might make about women being the more "feeling" type. Instead, dreaming in color is about how much attention we pay to our emotions in our day-to-day life and how connected we are to our feeling life.

Over the years, my dreams have taught me a greater appreciation for colors. They have taught me how to relate to them. I have sometimes pulled colors out of my dreams and used them. If red appears in a dream, I think, maybe I need more red. After all, color is vibration. It's energy. So, I take a cue from my dreams and use color consciously. I wear it in my clothes. I pay attention to it when buying vegetables. I change up my towels or use colors I know I usually need. It works in the opposite way too. Okay, so I feel like picking up a yellow or orange pepper. What does that mean?

Almost always, the colors appearing in my dream indicate the kind of energy I need at that time. Maybe, I need yellow's power when I am feeling powerless or orange when I need to let my feelings flow, yellow being the color of the solar plexus or power *chakra* and orange being the color of the sacral *chakra*, which is associated with feelings, pleasure and sexuality.

In dreams and in life, color awakens me. Although I am

aware of these different color systems, like the Indian *chakra* system, what's most important is my own attraction. I know, for example, that red can mean different things for different people. But in my dreams, red has often felt like an archetypal color, a color coming up from a deeper layer in my psyche. It is a sign of positive life. It has also come up on occasion at times when something old, an illusion I had been holding onto, died. Then, I am often clothed in red. New seeds have been planted. New life is coming up, being consecrated.

Dream workers also talk about how red is often one of the first colors that we become conscious of. I wonder why that is. Maybe, it's because paying attention to our dreams happens after we have decided to come alive to our own self. Maybe, that's why archetypal red - the color of new life - shows up first. Again and again, in my dreams, I see something creative weaving patterns, weaving stories, filling in colors. In many "dream series," like the different dreams with amethysts in them, there seems to be something that is nudging me to see things differently and to notice what is escaping me in waking life.

Another "dream series" talking about something I was missing seeing came at a time when I was trying to give myself permission to take my writing more seriously. There had been a blank space after I had decided to stop doing any more writing workshops and started my blog. Although I had taken another concrete step forward, this also came with a gaping hole in my sense of belonging.

I missed the camaraderie of those workshops, filled with new strangers in every new class, but strangers who felt wholly familiar to me. These were people like me who were following a creative dream. In contrast, without the presence of this makeshift village, here, in the Valley, it felt hard to meet like-minded people. Most of the people I knew were engineers, creative in their own way, but interested in things I wasn't very interested in. I am sure they felt the same way about me.

Again, I was touching on an old wound. Always the one on the outside, looking in. Always the one who didn't belong.

It was during these months of a gap, months of teetering with my writing and then willing myself to walk forward that another series of dreams visited me. In one of them, a heavily pregnant woman was on the verge of giving birth. She was naked, surrounded by other women, in what looked like an ancient bath. These women were helping her as she tried to walk, writhing in pain, her hair flailing around. There was steam, sweat and a feeling of stepping into the unknown, into the mystery of birth.

In another similar dream, a heavily pregnant woman was cycling to the hospital on her own. She was trying to keep going, trying to pedal, but getting more and more exhausted, more and more spent until she finally slowed down to a crawl.

When these dreams came, I was so caught up in the mundanities of my life that their suggestion escaped me. All I registered was the dream was showing that I was giving birth to my creative self, which was true. I was. But where was that new *something* that dream workers say dreams always bring to us, that element I wasn't consciously aware of?

It was only later, when I had joined a writing group and these dreams had finally disappeared that I had connected the now quite obvious dots. The dreams had been suggesting the action I had finally taken. At first, while I had been feeling sorry for myself, I had also constantly questioned my need for a writing community. I had downplayed this need to belong and to be seen and discounted how important a nutrient it was for my growth. Finally, after months of not validating myself, I had done something about this. This is when my "pregnant women" dreams had disappeared.

My writing group met every week to write together. No critique or feedback was given. It was simply a place for like-minded people to get together and spend time writing. It had a short social period at the beginning. Then, there was the writing time. Afterwards, you could stay back and socialize or leave, as you chose. It was a place where all sorts of people showed up. There were people writing fiction and nonfiction, short stories and screenplays. There were also people completing their PhD thesis on literature-related topics. In short, it was a place to be around kindred spirits. I had finally taken my needs into account and reached for what I needed.

My dreams of pregnant women, sometimes being supported in birthing their creations, sometimes crumbling down exhausted, were images of the same creative process, but with completely different support structures. After this, how could I not believe that something creative, something expansive was making up these dream stories? Maybe, it was a deeper part of me. Maybe, it was a part that somehow belonged to the larger whole, that shared in the same collective pool. There wasn't any physical instrument I could lower into my dream well to measure how deep it went.

But there was no need to measure. In my dreams, I could

touch the edges of something, or maybe, it was not an edge, but a starting point for something ancient, something vast. This was something veiled in mystery but containing wondrous things that sometimes opened up to reveal themselves. The more I reached into my dreams, the more I pulled out these tantalizing images.

There was one other significant dream series that sealed my faith in dreamwork. I had the same dream repeatedly over many months, in one form or another. These dreams came, if I remember correctly, sometime in the second year after the move. One dream went like this. I am in an airport. I am trying to get somewhere. But I am completely surrounded by people, all of them shoving and pushing me in their hurry to get to their own flights. Some of them are moving me in a direction opposite to where I need to go. Caught in this swarming mass of humanity, it is hard for me to move. I am undefended. Even as I try to protect myself, there isn't much I can do against this burgeoning stream of people.

On the surface, it felt like the dream was saying that I was trying to move to a new psychological space in this new country but that I was constantly feeling left behind. Did it have something to do with my sense of being clogged up with feelings I didn't know how to let go of? Why was I missing the flight? This didn't feel right.

I tried to puzzle out the dream, but the meaning remained elusive. I already knew all of this. My old identity seemed to be falling to pieces. But I hadn't yet pieced together a new identity. It was as if I was on marshland. Nothing was secure. Everything was up for questioning. So, was this all the dream was saying? If the assertion made by dream workers that dreams bring something new from the unconscious was true, then there had to be something more. But I couldn't quite pin it down. I just noted down this dream and the other similar dreams that came with it, in quick succession.

Again, as had happened before, months later, this series of dreams suddenly stopped. I didn't quite realize when that happened. I wasn't paying as close an attention to my dreams then. It was only when I was reading a book later on that I thought back to these dreams. Once again, synchronistically, a dream almost exactly like mine had spilled into my lap. It was described in Jill Mellick's book *The Natural Artistry of Dreams*. In it, Mellick talked about a woman who complained to her that she just didn't have any meaningful dreams. Ever. Her life was drab and routine and so were her dreams. She travelled a lot for work, and guess what showed up in her dreams? Airports.

The dream that this woman had described to Mellick was very similar to mine. The suggestion that Mellick had offered to her gave me my *a-ha* moment. It was a tool that came from Gestalt psychology and was called *Being the Object in Your Dreams*. Think of an object or a place that actually appears in one of your dreams. When you think of yourself as this dream object, what kind of associations come to your mind? What do you think the object stands for? Could it be that the object or that place symbolizes a part of you?

Just as this woman with her dull, drab airport dream had identified psychologically with "being the airport," I too identified with being this kind of an overcrowded space. Like her, I was often a place people passed through to get to their own destinations. Just like she had associated the airport with her own role as the family peacekeeper and mediator, I resonated with similar associations that "being an airport" brought up for me. I was the place people came to vent.

The only difference between her and me was that I was almost like the "stranger bus station" instead of being the "family bus station." I almost seemed to "attract" people who needed help. Sometimes, strangers, finding someone listening to them, told me extremely personal stories. They offloaded their feelings, their concerns and their distress on to me. It was as if I was a place they could rest at before they passed on to get to somewhere else. But I, myself, couldn't get anywhere. I was being prevented from catching my own flight. I was being shoved here and there, pushed and pulled in a hundred different directions.

I often started these interactions genuinely wanting to listen. By nature, I am a listener. I was interested in people and interested in learning about them. But at that time, I was also a little desperate for connection, for friends of my own. I didn't want to believe any red flags I saw early on. I was also probably doing a lot of what psychologists call "rescuing," trying to help people when I needed to help myself first, when I already had a lot to adjust to in my own life. I also thought that I *had* to give. That's what "good" people did. Fueled by this mixed bag of feelings and intentions, these interactions often devolved into something unhealthy.

It was as if I was extending my energy in bits and pieces, first to one person and then another, till a whole chunk of it went missing. It left me feeling tired, frustrated, resentful. I didn't feel very "good" neither did I feel fulfilled by this giving, as if I had done something truly valuable for someone else. Instead, I felt ill used, as if I was a dump for people who came to me to get rid of whatever was bothering them. And for what? It seemed like no amount of my help *really* helped anyone. It didn't solve their problems. It didn't create anything meaningful. It just gave temporary relief.

All this rescuing also meant that I was irritable with Rohit, someone who gave me all of his energy and who surely deserved a lot more back. What was wrong with me? Why did I feel this compulsive need to give to anyone who asked but didn't give more to someone who was giving so much to me? Why was I always looking for connection in the wrong places? I was cutting pieces from my life and frittering them away. It was almost like I couldn't say no to anyone who asked.

This was how it it had gone on, on automatic, until I came to a dangerously low point.

A personal problem had cropped up. Rohit was there for me, but it was still a lot for me to handle. A small, infant part of me now started screaming loudly, clamoring, getting rageful whenever I didn't listen to my own needs. When someone I had given to did not return that in kind, when they did not listen to me or asked me how I was doing, although I still kept on nodding and listening, afterwards, it would feel like I had plummeted down an emotional abyss.

Energetically, it was as if a thousand hungry mouths inside, my anger at not being listened to, my wounded self, my valid need for being heard, were thrashing and moaning and wanting to lash out. I thought I had left some of my wounds behind years earlier, but here they were again. At one point, I even went to the doctor because my heart was pounding so hard, it felt like I was having a heart attack. It turned out these were, in fact, anxiety attacks. Something inside me was getting more and more agitated, bent over with the double whammy of the weight that I, myself, carried as well as the weight of taking on other people's problems.

During this chaotic time, I had a dream of a toddler. He looked like a human baby, but he didn't seem entirely human. He seemed to be composed only of one instinct. In the dream, he kept on wobbling up, walking and ramming straight into a wall. He would feel pain, get agitated, then wobble up again, getting caught up in something like a bedsheet, and make his way in the other direction, running straight into another wall. He was out of control. He just did this over and over again. It seemed like he couldn't help himself. In day-to-day life, my feelings veered in a similar fashion. I felt wobbly, out of control, ramming into one wall after another.

This rising sense of an urgent need to get a hold of my feelings led me to start setting more boundaries. It was slow, screeching work. My identity was so bound up in fixing and rescuing that it often felt like I was being "bad" when I set limits. But all my different experiences had nudged me towards asking some hard questions. In this new place, where I was attempting to build a new life from scratch, how could I accomplish that when again and again, I was falling on the wayside?

My energy wasn't unlimited. This wasn't sustainable. What exactly was I creating? I was giving my energy in bits and pieces that never seemed to amount to anything. Whatever I did give, even when it felt costly, never seemed to be enough to get the person to the other side. Once they had gotten things off their chest, it was back to the same old, same old. In the end, I wasn't helping anyone, neither them nor myself.

Why had I taken on this belief of "giving without any questions asked?" It didn't seem to work at all. Giving also didn't always lead to receiving. I had to admit, I did expect *something* back, even if it was just acknowledgement. Maybe, from now on, I should only give when I could really do it unconditionally, without expecting anything at all. Maybe, I should also stop creating more resentment by giving in situations or to people who didn't give back to me. Relationships needed a back and forth. Maybe, always giving wasn't such a great thing. Maybe, it opened you to people who thought that you were too "weak," instead of thinking you were being "nice" and giving to them. Maybe, I needed to stop being so "nice" and instead give authentically, give sustainably and give to the right people.

This was a hard process. It's something I am still learning, still failing at, still getting up and doing again. It calls to the heart of my beliefs - what being a "good" person means, what being a "good" woman means. It means looking at why I am giving in each and every situation. Is it out of the fear of not being enough, of not being liked? Then, this is not pure giving. It is tainted by my feelings. If I am people pleasing, then it is not clean giving but has another layer, which makes it murky and unclean.

Am I doing things at too great a cost to me? Am I giving at a time when I, myself, need my own help? Then, maybe I have to come to terms with the limits of what I can and cannot give. Am I giving to someone who is healthy and reciprocates or someone who either takes advantage of it or thinks that it is stupid for me to give like this? Why then am I giving to people like these? It seems up to me to become more discerning, to give up the child's magical thinking, to see that this is the real world where everyone plays by different rules, rules that come from their own beliefs. How am I going to navigate my way through this? This is a lot of thinking about giving, about what it is and what it isn't, about my own energy and my capacity, and about exactly why I have so defined myself by what I give away.

With time, practice, and trial and error, I have gotten a little better at knowing my limits and setting boundaries. When I started actively doing this, it was then that things began to shift. I was no longer as easily permeable, no longer as easily invaded. It no longer felt like my energy was being siphoned off by everyone else's concerns. Little by little, I was building up a more realistic assessment of myself, of others and of our relationships with each other. Little by little, I could become the one who could also give to herself, something I had no permission to do earlier in my life.

When I started listening to the little one raging inside, to her dire need, it was then that my airport dreams disappeared. No longer was I the place that people just passed through. I was protecting my space, giving myself more priority in my own life. I was no longer being pushed here and there.

As I continued to work with my dreams, it also felt like they were a direct testament to the Jungian view of the unconscious. Jung tells us that the unconscious functions independently, with autonomy. I could feel that in my dreams. They seemed to have a bird's-eye view of my life when I, myself, was drowning in details. They were like a hawk flying over my psyche, looking at me from far up above.

Still, sometimes, they did feel confusing, almost misleading. Was that because I had only scratched part of the surface of my dream symbols, both the personal as well as the archetypal ones? Was it because I had still only learnt some selective words of this new language? The rest of it lay unclaimed, waiting to be explored. Could it be that even though dreams were the language of nature, nature itself was indifferent to my fate? Or was it just that it felt indifferent because I had only now found the bridge back to my unconscious, relatively late in my life but maybe also early enough?

There are no simple answers to these questions. In the psyche, we are dealing with the light and the shade. There is no one simple answer as to how to interpret dreams. Are dream figures a representation of parts of my own self? Are dream figures telling me about interpersonal problems and the relationships I have with people in the outer world? Looking at my dreams, the answer seems to be yes for both these questions.

Depending on the dream and what's going on in my life, my dreams seem to be talking about many different things. There is a degree of ambiguity in dreamwork. I am also still learning about how to relate to my dream images. I have to look at them, not in a linear way, but in almost a circular fashion. There's a lot of overlay, a lot of layers in one dream, as if it's commenting on many different things, on many parts of my life, all at the same time, in one compacted time.

In my dreams, I have also seen the elaboration of another assertion that dreamworkers make. They say our dreams sometimes offer in pictures and images what is lacking in our everyday life. The unconscious is always making suggestions when our conscious attitude becomes too rigid and too one-sided. The Jungian view is that our psyche is always seeking this balance between the conscious and the unconscious. According to this perspective, sometimes, the unconscious will offer a startling image to shake us up.

Jungian depth psychologists give many examples of this from their own practice. For example, one example is of a woman who is cut off from her sexuality, whose conditioning about what it means to be "virtuous" discounts her sensuality. The only thing is, sometimes, this woman also dreams of being a prostitute. This shakes her up to her core. Her inner self seems to be betraying her. What's happening here? Obviously, this woman is not actually a prostitute. What the disturbing image is doing is calling attention to the one-sidedness of her conscious attitude. In her day-to-day life, the pendulum has swung one way.

In her dreams, it swings in the opposite direction. Maybe, what she needs to do is drop her rigid stance on morality. Maybe, she needs to give expression to some of the wantonness in her dreams. The dream is not suggesting that she is a prostitute or that she might become one. Its suggestion seems to be that it would be a good thing to bring a little bit from this opposing image into her day-to-day life. This could bring about a healthy change in her somewhat brittle attitude.

Again, the dream is speaking in story. It is offering up a stark contrast to a calcified image, to what has been consciously identified with. This point is something for all of us to remember. Dreams speak the truth, but not in a literal sense, but in essence. They are poetry, not prose. We have to unpack dream images and ask exactly why things have swung in the opposite way. What is missing in our lives? What are our horrific nightmares telling us about? To me, dreams feel like a magic portal, a way to find my center, a labyrinth in which I sometimes get lost but that also promises the adventure of moving closer and closer to something essential.

The Animus, the Wild Creatures and the Call to Home

As I have explored my dreams, one element that has often showed up in my dreamworld is what Jung calls the *animus*. In Jungian psychology, the psyche itself is androgynous. This means that every man has an aspect of the feminine inside him, in his psyche, and every woman has an aspect of the masculine.

In Jungian Depth Psychology, the masculine principle in a woman's psyche is called the *animus* and the feminine principle in a man's psyche is called the *anima*. Both the animus and the anima can have positive and negative facets. They are archetypes made up of many different layers. For one, they include our own experiences with members of the opposite sex.

Then, there is also a universal, mythic layer to these concepts. For example: Figures of the Wise Old Man or the Great Mother might show up in our dreams. These are the kinds of figures that have always showed up, from time immemorial, as people have dreamt their dreams. Some of their outer garb might change as time changes, but their distinctive pattern remains.

Depth psychologists tell us that in order to become whole, to realize our potential, we have to find a way to relate to this "other" inside us, to this contrasexual element. But for a long time, the animus figures in my dreams, like in the dreams of many other women, were images of men committing violent acts.

Groups of men showed up in my dreams, creating havoc, unleashing destruction. I was often robbed at gunpoint, attacked and stolen from. The female characters in my dreams were terrorized by ruthless, conscienceless men. In many of these dreams, the female characters were weak. Instead of the strong, wise feminine, like the figure of that old woman with the red coat and red hat, a different kind of woman, effectively a child-woman, showed up. She was the unaware one who could be easily captured by the negative animus.

One such dream came at a time when I was struggling to set a boundary in my personal life. It went like this. A young girl is having an illicit love affair. She tries to hide this unacceptable love from her patriarchal older brothers. She knows how rigid and unbending they are. But soon enough, she is caught. The only way for her to survive, the only way for her not to get killed off, the only way to ward off the possible "shame" and dishonor she will bring her family is if she agrees to marry someone else, someone that her brothers approve of.

In my dream, at this critical moment when she has to decide, the shadowy figure of a man steps forward. He is a minor member of the gang the brothers belong to. He is eager to marry this girl. She will increase his standing with the brothers. On her part, this woman, this still-girl, is terrorized by the prospect of total annihilation. So, she agrees to cut off the affair and agrees to this match. In fact, in the moment, she is so relieved to escape death that she almost feels exhilarated. After all, she is just a young girl who has had a brief love affair. This man who now wants to marry her is not so bad. She is elated by his interest. She is almost happy to be with him.

In this dream, I am a fly on the wall, the observer. I know, beyond any doubt, that this girl is naive. She is convincing herself with all kinds of possible arguments that this new arrangement is better for her. But I know, for sure, that this will not end well for her.

This dream comes to me at a crucial time. In the past few days, an issue I need to confront has come up. It is something I care deeply about. I need to say no. Am I going to protect my boundary or give it up? I don't put this choice in so many words. What I feel instead is a shakiness, as if I am not inside my own skin. I am agitated, not paying enough attention to what is going on around me, not listening to conversations I am a part of. I feel threatened, scared of what might become an ugly confrontation.

At the same time, I feel angry with myself. Why can't I protect my space? Why do I have to still need others' approval? What I want to do might make them angry but so what? Why can't I be sure and secure? Why does this always take up this much energy?

It's when I am struggling like this that the dream comes. As an observer, I am acutely aware that the easy choice won't work out for the girl. She is naive to believe it. When I think about the dream, this girl reminds me of a part of me. I am often giving in way too easily. Like a child, I think *"If I play nice, I won't be hurt."* But this is not always the case. In reality, sometimes, the safer choice is to confront issues. It's not to cower in fear or to give up your space.

It feels like the dream is summing up my situation and giving me its suggestion. In the next few days, I make the choice I have so agonized over but wanted to make. In the end, I have followed through. It goes over a lot more smoothly than I had expected although one person is miffed. The catastrophic thoughts that had overtaken me for all those prior weeks don't come true. Life simply moves on.

I know that both the girl as well as her brothers are parts of me. I have internalized the rigid, authoritarian conditioning that beats down softer and undeveloped aspects of myself. It's up to me to look at this dynamic. It's up to me to not follow along obediently, no questions asked. It's up to me to stand up to contaminated beliefs that show up as brute forces.

Now, whenever I have such a dream, I take it as a sign that I am bowing down to some rigid idea I have internalized. Often, it means that the masculine-on-crack values that I have inside me are making my feminine side cower. I may be discounting all I have been doing, rushing on relentlessly, treating myself like a machine. I might be willing myself to power through when I desperately need to rest, when I need to just let things be for a while. These kinds of dreams signal that I am getting tired, that I need to be aware that a negative, still-living belief has been activated and that I need to take better care of myself.

Over the years, as I kept looking into the mirror of my dreams in this way, I have also noticed more and more how the inter-relationships in my dreams changed as I changed. In the first three or four years after the move, there were different concerns tugging at me. I was struggling to become more of the essential me, a process that had already been going on for many years. But here in America, every choice felt like voting for my new identity. Here, there was a different kind of space, of both openness and shakiness, as well as a chance to do things differently. Or not. In the end, it was up to me to decide the balance between the old and the new.

In my confusion, at first, the seesaw went up and down rapidly. Although I felt uprooted and wanted to stay connected to my past, sometimes, it also disturbingly felt like parts of old, patriarchal India were still alive and kicking here. A friend told me, for example, of Indian women she knew who didn't go to the temple on the days when they had their periods. This bothered me a lot. It took me back to an old space and reawakened an early memory.

The incident had happened when I was a young girl, maybe twelve or thirteen, visiting a small town in North India for a family function with my parents. Many extended family members had gathered here. One day, during a break in the festivities, some of the women decided to go together to the nearby temple. I had gone along with them. One of them had her periods that day and told us she would wait outside while the rest of us went inside and paid our respects. I still remember how deeply disturbed I had felt. I also had my periods then. I had just kept quiet and tagged along inside with the other women. But I had also felt an intense longing to belong to this group of grown-up women, to be like them.

Afterwards, I had felt like a rebel. I had also felt like I had done something wrong. Even then, especially then, I had felt the deep unfairness of this norm, the subtext that there was something dirty about women's bodies, that they were somehow impure. In my small, little life then, I had already seen enough to deepen a sense of injustice. But there was also a nagging doubt. Could I be wrong?

That little girl had doubts even though she felt she was

doing the right thing. She paid for her choice with guilt.

Now, when I looked back, I had compassion for that little girl. I knew she wanted to be loved. I knew she felt things deeply and suffered because of her constant weighing of what was right and wrong. Now, when I heard of these same things still happening here, in one of the world's most forward-thinking places, even though decades separated me from that little girl, I still felt her intense feelings. Is this all the progress we'd made? Is this all the progress I'd made? It was almost as if I was in that little girl's body.

This came up at a time when I had again been feeling extremely homesick. On the one hand, I liked that we lived in a housing complex with a mixture of different nationalities. This was unlike the Indians living in silos that happens in some localities in the Bay Area. But I also felt that break of being transplanted. I feared I would lose touch with India completely as time went by. Neither Rohit nor I were religious in the traditional sense of the word, but in the middle of my pangs of homesickness, I couldn't help but wonder: Should I start doing things differently? Should we go to the temple regularly here even if I hadn't done that in India? Would I become sundered, without a place to belong to, if I didn't change my ways?

There was a strong attraction to the familiar in this new place that was still becoming home.

For years, I had been struggling with my relationship with God, so this presented an even bigger problem. A part of me was always a seeker and would always be one. But I no longer believed in the Gods of my childhood. Feelings of skepticism washed over me every time I thought of going to a temple. Was there even a God? What did that word even mean? Besides, I wasn't interested in going to a place that denigrated women.

I kept going back and forth about going to the Indian temple. There was one walking distance from our house, just minutes away. But I wasn't sure. Rohit told me I was confusing God and religion. But that was only partly true.

Of course, it was also the tremors in my identity that made this such a heavy choice. Around me, I could see what felt like two choices that people had made. Indian immigrants seemed to fall into two groups. There was one camp that clung to tradition like it was the very air they were breathing. It was a way to hold onto their old identity, a way to be sure of themselves in a new place with completely different ways of being and new challenges.

The other camp was made up of those people who had made a decided break with India. There was not a lot they missed about India, definitely not its chaos, its noise, its traffic, its inefficiency. When they talked about India, it was as someone once removed from it. They were definitely not pining for home. Instead, they seemed to be cutting the past away, as if it was a shameful secret.

I felt like I belonged in neither of these camps. Was I going to become an in-between person? Was I going to remain unfinished somehow? How could I hold on to the past? How could I become someone new?

It was only as the years passed that I realized these two choices were false choices. There was a third choice. I didn't need to get into a tussle with my roots. I couldn't cut them off. I didn't want to cut them off. I could put everything in its assigned place. I could do some things without thinking I was caving in. Something changed inside me.

It was then that I decided to go to the temple on my own. Rohit still wasn't very interested. But now, going no longer meant I accepted everything the temple might stand for. It simply meant I could see how deep my beginnings were, how much I needed them. The incense in the temple, the stories embedded in the images of the deities, the way I put out both my hands to take back the sweets from the priest, the *prasad*, these were all a thread back to home.

I could remember picking the *madhumalti* flowers from the garden in my uncle's home and gathering them in my skirt to take to my beloved maternal grandmother, my *naani*. It was a special task to be done for the *pooja* every morning, as she, as together we, prayed to the Gods. In those childhood vacations, the air was perfumed with magnolia. She would shape the cotton into wicks for the earthen *diya* she would light. The altar itself was on a shelf in a cupboard filled with household items.

Through ups and downs, through all the different things that life had thrown at her, my *naani's* faith wasn't burnished. She still lit her candle. She still offered those flowers. It was a faith that was woven into her everyday, a faith that swirled around her and the God I am looking for is that God, the God who lived on a shelf in a cupboard, a God we wholeheartedly loved and who wholeheartedly loved us back.

Where had this loving God gone? That connection had stretched thin, run taut over the years. My wicks had burnt out. The oil had run low. No longer was there that comforting warmth, that heartwarming fire.

As I had grown up, a harsh internal voice had become the voice in my head. In Delhi, in my work at a multinational company, something unbending, something unforgiving had driven me. I had to do good, be good. I had to try hard. Even when my body did not want to go one more day to that job, even when it physically resisted, even when it was an overriding impulse not to continue like this, I had still gone. I was being flogged by something inside me, something that didn't even care about me. I was the artiste contorting her soul to fit into a mould.

At that time, while I had hankered after the kind of success that looks good to others, I had never quite made it. My heart was never in it. Even before my move to the States, for many years, I had been on my own inner journey. In Delhi, I had done my first writing workshop. I had started freelancing while working. With the move to the States, there had been a stripping away of another layer that wasn't me, and it was in my dreams that I could witness my psyche changing.

When I looked back later on at the "wedding dreams" I had had in the first year after the move, they felt positive. In them, different combinations of the masculine and feminine had joined together in completely new ways. These weddings often had men as lead players with qualities very different from the controlling, dominating masculine energy I had often associated with men. In my own life, Rohit was a different kind of man. He was thoughtful, kind, and very patient, patience especially not being a virtue I usually associated with men. These new men in my dreams reflected the re-shaping of the masculine inside me.

Over the first few years, as I changed, my dreams had transformed as well. In a hopeful dream, someone I know in my daily life, someone very patriarchal, appeared as an even older version of himself. He looked weak and lost as he fumbled around, looking for his slippers. It felt as if the negative animus was growing weaker and weaker in my psyche.

The positive animus also showed up more often in images like that of my brother who is quite different from the stereotypical masculine. He is more thoughtful, more open and less prone to throwing his weight around. There were also many months when I had multiple dreams featuring gay men, signalling a different kind of masculine, one that could contain different energies, emerging in my psyche. All these different positive animus figures felt full of possibility, as if a new, enlarged concept of masculinity was taking hold in my soul.

It isn't that I magically got rid of all my negative associations with men or the unhealthy ways in which I related to my own masculine energy. There were still beliefs inside me that needed to be snuffed out. Even now, I still slip into old patterns. The negative animus still shows up in my dreams. But now I know it feeds and gets fatter and fatter on the choices I make. It grows stronger when I give in to my conditioning. Now, alongside the negative animus, my dreams are also filled with more positive masculine figures. They promise that change is afoot.

Like all change, at times, this process has felt like two steps forward and then one step backward. During one period, more and more animals appeared in my dreams. Some of them such as dogs and horses seemed to be animus figures while others seemed like pure instinct.

One dream had a vicious-looking Pomeranian dog come barking at me. In this dream, he tries to bite me while I swat it with a rag. But it still does not give up. A man tells me I am not doing a very good job of it. In another dream with an animal, I look from a cobra's perspective as he watches two men walking over his wild terrain. Then, my view in the dream shifts, and I am the observer looking at this scene. I know that if the men look at the cobra in the eye, it will be the end of them. In this dream, almost in that instant when I am thinking like this, just when it feels like it's finally safe, one of the men quickly looks towards where the cobra is and meets his gaze for a second. But then, nothing happens, and I breathe a sigh of relief.

The men are able to board their plane. At last, I think they are going to be safe. They will escape after all. Soon, the plane rises slowly up and the two men are skyborne. But then, out of nowhere, the cobra, like all those omnipotent creatures that live in our dreams, comes flying and crashes through the windshield.

To my conscious mind, this dream means I am flying too much into my mind. I think I can do away with my instincts and pretend that the cobra is not a part of me. But the dream is telling me that I am fighting a losing battle. The two men seem to symbolize my mind. My body is the snake. I have a fractured relationship with it, and it comes biting, hissing when all I pay attention to is my mind.

The dog in the other dream feels like the attention-hungry, needy part of me that grows ravenous when it doesn't get my attention. All these dreams seem to be saying that I don't know how to pay attention to my animal nature, locked up as I am in the flights of my mind.

Other dream animals also show up during this time. There is a gorilla creating ruckus in a building in one dream. Something feels uncaged. In another dream, an armadillo patrols the perimeter of my home. Later on, I read that armadillos symbolize boundaries in certain mythologies. It seems miraculous then, as if there really is a pool of common mythology that I dip into when I dream, as if all the things I don't know personally, I know somehow.

With the coming of these animals, all sorts of hungers, instincts and needs also show their face. I can't classify them all. I just sense their energy. Some feel trampled upon, these messed-up, ragged-looking creatures. Some animals are fierce and powerful. Some of the wilder ones even feel like something good happening inside me, as if a less cultivated part of me is waking up.

During this time, there also comes another kind of dream. It's the kind of dream I have read about, but never thought as something I would experience soon. My everyday life feels so routine, so wrapped up in the mundane. But then here comes this dream with a cosmic element in it. In this dream, I am on some sort of a ride, in some cosmic theme park, and the stars, the very universe, are spinning right past me. It feels absolutely beautiful and exhilarating as well as a little scary. I get frightened by the experience and close my eyes. But I do experience some moments of unadulterated beauty. With this kind of a dream, it's almost as if some specks of moonbeams filter through into my day-to-day life.

In another dream, I also experience a moment of lucid dreaming. This is when you know that you are, indeed, dreaming while you are in the dream itself. When I had first come across this concept, it had felt frightening. But the few seconds of awareness in my dream, when it comes, feels completely natural. I don't feel scared. I haven't done anything specific to have a lucid dream. Just paying attention to my dreamworld has led to this moment. Afterwards, I don't try to intentionally make this happen again or learn more about lucid dreaming. Already, I have enough to work with. The more open I am, the more dreams fall onto the page than I know what to do with it. It's almost like I can't quite keep up with them.

As I continue working with my dreams over the years, many times, just as before, I don't understand a dream right away, as soon as it comes. Then, I wait patiently with all the pieces I have gathered till it finally makes sense. But then, there are also those other times when dreams come that are not as mysterious, not as incomprehensible. Sometimes, these dreams even offer direct opinions.

At a time when I am cycling through anger, a character in my dream says: *"Maybe, you are feeling sad, not angry."* In my waking life, it's as if I have been taken over by anger. But something inside me thinks the real feeling is sadness, not anger. I am forced to think about this. Anger does feel like a more powerful, more comfortable emotion than sadness. It feels much less vulnerable, much more in control. Although I don't quite manage to implement the dream's suggestion in real life fully because feeling sadness is still very hard for me, more and more, the wisdom inherent in my dreams feels apparent.

In dreams, I have come to know, new doors like these are opened all the time.

There *is* something to this. There *is* something in me, something in my unconscious, something in the collective unconscious that knows more than my conscious mind. It has an intelligence all of its own. Working with it is like working with myself, and yet not with myself. It feels both amazing and confounding.

Working with my dreams over the last few years is one of the best things I've ever done. Moving to the States prodded me to open the door on to this world that was within me all this time. In my dreamworld, I can look at parts of myself split up into multitudes and projected into different forms. I can look at the ebbs and flows of my life and witness the telling of many stories, stories that have ended and stories that are still being born.

This is a world teeming with creatures, some nuzzling contentedly and some ravenous with hungers. In it, a creative intelligence connects the dots and seems to know what it is talking about. It is I who have to continue to learn its language.

My dreams have helped me connect to a deeper creative layer, something there is no other way to touch, no other way to know except through them. They are the bridge that I can walk on, on both starry and moonless nights. They take me closer to something beyond words, something that plays in images, something that makes up things.

In this journey into my dreams, it's been like going into the inky ocean with a boat, for the very first time, believing there was nothing inside. But in the folds of the night, when my boat tipped over, I found wondrous, fluorescent creatures floating by. It was almost as if they were pulled out of the darkness to show me that I don't know a whole lot. It now seems like the darkness is not a curtain or a void, but, in fact, fertile soil. In it, the soul grows.

When we dream, it's our essential self, fragmented in countless images, that flowers up into our consciousness. It gives us its invitation. It asks us some questions. Will we risk the descent down into our unconscious? Will we risk looking at our dreams? Will we risk going through our twisted-up desires and our repressed angers in the hope of finding pieces of ourselves that we have been so desperately looking for?

In the music of our dreams, in the dance of their stories, we can find these lost fragments. We just have to risk beginning the adventure, with its frightening, snarling creatures, with its breathtaking cosmic vistas. We have to decide to ride its crests to see where it takes us.

We don't know exactly what all these images are. But then, we also don't know exactly who we are. Maybe, the adventure is to find out.

Maybe, in the images of our soul, in the deep, dark, stormy ocean, in its waves and in its tides, we will find the energy that takes us inside itself to tell us our own story.

Chapter 3

Calling for God and Finding Symbols

When I first moved to the States, I brought with myself an impacted relationship with God. As a little child, I had felt part of the whole. I had taken in the coolness of the shade. I had gotten burnt in the sun. I had felt part of the greater universe, a star in the fabric of time. But then, things happened, very early on, and with them came the pain that comes from feeling all alone, flung by the winds, here and there, randomly. The universe had changed.

It was no longer kind. It no longer made sense and with that feeling, the experience of being connected to the sun and the moon and the stars had disappeared. There was no longer that God, that feeling of being part of the whole. There was no longer that voice that said: *You are not alone. You can tap into the energy that runs through this world. You belong.*

That feeling of home was both a memory and a gap.

Once upon a time in India, when I was trying to seek answers, I came upon the work of the mystic Gurdjeiff. I didn't know who he was, but something I read about him has stayed with me ever since. Gurdjeiff's teachings says that we carry within us, not one but many different people. There is the glorious, robed one inside. There is the part dressed in tattered rags. There is the madman going crazy. Sometimes, I think, that's what hurt does to us. We start off whole, but then we are cut off into all these different people. Some of these parts with their gaping holes break off from the core. They roam inside us, reminding us of our own poverty.

This is what my own different parts felt like. There was the seeker, the one who believed, the one who lived on, even through periods of not believing. There was the injured one, licking its wounds, howling in pain. There was the frozen, suspended one. It looked behind and wailed: *Why me? If there was a God, why me? Do you really exist God? Do you?*

Throughout my twenties, these different parts showed up at different times. Sometimes, the seeker appeared. I would then take a few steps forward towards the mystery. But then, something would hurt terribly, and the wounded one would show up. I still didn't know how to bandage its hurts, how to clean and disinfect its wounds, how to take care of it. What else could it do but rail against God, fling itself against walls, and hurt itself even more?

It was a schizophrenic existence, first believing, then not believing, following, then turning back, trusting, then not trusting at all. How could you know for sure there was a God? How could you live without not knowing?

When I moved to the States, I brought all these different pieces with me, wrapping up the jagged-edged ones with those that glowed with a ruby-light. Once again, I would look at them. Once again, I would try to fit them together, make them reconcile.

When I set up my new home in the Silicon Valley, I made a little shrine on a shelf next to the kitchen counter, just like the countless home-grown altars that exist in almost every Hindu home, rich or poor. I was not very sure about it, not very sure about God, not very sure what exactly I believed. But I couldn't not have it. It was a link in the chain, a piece of my past.

Even after it had been set up, with a framed photo of Radha-Krishna, the divine lovers of Indian mythology, a little Ganesha idol my sister had given me and other sundries, I hardly ever used this space. I didn't say any prayers. I didn't light an *agarbatti* or ring the little brass bell I had kept on the plate.

Then again, it wasn't as if I had ever prayed before in any ritualistic way. I had grown up in a home where there was again that taken-for-granted shrine, but most of us didn't pray there every day. Only once a year, during Diwali, the festival of lights, did our entire family form a semi-circle around the altar. We would then recite the few *aartis* we all knew, led by my mother, breaking up and giggling when we came to the parts we didn't remember.

Obviously, just setting up my new shrine would not make me pray.

But in my new home, in this new place, I would sometimes think, maybe, I should start praying. The little shrine seemed to chide me. What was the point of having it? But then, the very next minute, I would feel deeply irritated with myself. I didn't really believe anymore in all these images of God I had assembled. Why was I still complying to them? Wasn't I a hypocrite, a coward?

All the stories of my childhood felt null and void. Krishna, playing his flute, up to some cosmic prank, didn't pull me anymore. Shiva, meditating in the mountains, the ascetic, the ultimate *yogi,* no longer had that magnetic attraction. Where had those stories disappeared? When had the spark that animated them died down? Why was I still holding on to them? Was it just that I couldn't trespass the idea of God that I had been raised with? Was it just that I couldn't go beyond it, that I was scared?

This push and pull kept me suspended. For the first few years in the States, I only engaged with my shrine a couple of times a year, on festivals. The rest of the year, it was just there. It picked at me, getting into my eyes, reminding me by its very presence of something that had disappeared. Rohit wasn't very religious either. So, it was only once in a long while that we made our way to a temple. There was even a small temple down the road from our house, dedicated to Krishna, the flute-playing God and Radha, his divine consort. It was a five-minute walk away but even that was too much for us.

Sometimes, I would think, if we didn't make some kind of an effort, wouldn't we lose touch with all our Indianness? Wouldn't I lose touch with all my Indianness? Rohit had grown up in different countries outside India and he joked that he didn't really have a home. But me, what about me? Already, it felt like the tide was shaping my life differently. Already, it felt as if the ground had shifted. In what direction would things go if I didn't make some effort to connect to the past, to string together some chain? Still hesitant, still ambivalent, I would suggest to Rohit that we *should* go. *Why don't you go?*, he would counter *Well. Maybe, I would.*

But then, I would double down. It didn't feel authentic. Why should I start going to the temple here when I didn't do it living in India? What exactly was I trying to connect to anyways?

Some months before I moved to the States, I had taken another gulp of those pulsating, beautiful, ugly, pockmarked waters that now made up the experience of Hinduism for me. I had accompanied some relatives on a trip to different places in northern India, some vacation spots and some other places that were centers of the Hindu faith. Two of these, *Badrinath* and *Kedarnath*, perched in the mighty Himalayan mountains were two of the four *Chota Chaar Dhaams,* some of the holiest-of-the-holy pilgrimage sites for Hindus. Just like people wait all their lives to visit Mecca or Jerusalem, devout Hindus hope to visit these ancient temples in many different corners of India at least once during their lifetime.

But I hadn't gone along on this trip of a lifetime for the good karma I would be accumulating. I had gone because soon I would be leaving India, possibly for a long time, possibly forever. Who knew when I would get a chance to do this again? Who knew how much I had missed experiencing of my own country that I might never see now, not feel, not sense, not be a part of? It was noticing something just before you left it, trying to hold on to it a little longer, an ode to a place that existed inside you.

This trip, the gift of a beloved uncle, had been both beautiful and evocative and dotted with little troubling incidents. In one famous temple, we had waited in a long line till one of my relatives bought some *prasad,* the offering of flowers and sweets you carry to the Gods and then also gave a bigger donation. We had been amped up straight to the head of the line to enter the temple. Things like these were commonplace in India. The logic went that in a country of more than a billion people, it was not the Gods who were tainted, but those who made a business around them, the business of selling the flowers and other offerings, the business of running the temple towns that had sprung up around these sites. That was just how it was.

Growing up, experiences like these had disenchanted the idealistic me. For years before, I had hardly ever gone to a temple. But now, seduced by the knowledge that this might be my last chance to see and experience these places, at last, here I was.

Badrinath was the last big temple we had visited. Nestled in the Himalayas, Badrinath is also a place from where several mountaineering expeditions into the Himalayas begin. But its beating heart is its ancient Vishnu temple, situated on the banks of the thundering Alaknanda river. It was evening by the time we had made our way to the temple for the *darshan*, the viewing of the deities in the inner sanctum, in time to be part of the evening *aarti*. The *aarti* was a beautiful collective prayer sung out, fragrant with roses and incense, resonant with the chiming of bells.

It had felt as if our prayers wafted upwards easily, in swirls of heady perfume. The ringing bells had chimed inside my soul, striking some pattern embedded deep within. Afterwards, it felt as if something had been joined, as if something had been made whole.

As we got out that day, behind the temple, framed by the snowy mountains, the mighty Alaknanda was carving its way ahead. Mist had been rising from it when we'd reached the temple. Now, outside, in the trailing darkness, all I could hear was the torrent of its overflowing waters.

Here, cupped in the arms of an ancient mountain, with an old river that had seen generations come and go, it was easy to believe in God. It was easy to believe in all those myths that had risen from rivers like these as they curled and pounded their way across the Indian subcontinent. There was Vishnu here in these mountains, the Preserver and Benefactor of the great Hindu trinity of Gods. He was keeping a watchful eye on the billion or so people who depended on him.

Somewhere in these colossal mountains, there was also Shiva, the Destroyer of the trinity. He meditated, eyes closed, as the mighty river Ganga flowed out of his matted ascetic locks, as a serpent coiled around his neck. When his third eye opened, all old forms would be destroyed. It was then that Shiva would dance his dance of destruction. Everything, as we knew it, would burn to ashes. But then, from these old crumbled forms, another cycle of creation would start anew as Brahma, the Creator, would create the world again. Once more, the wheel of cosmic time would begin. Once more, life would open its tendrils.

In the music of Vishnu's conch, in the rhythm of Shiva's drum were the rhythms and undulations of the world, the source from which everything rose, the source into which everything falls.

But, and here was the big but of my life, did I believe in this anymore? I knew I did not believe that these were actual people living in some mountain, orchestrating our fates, like I had done as a child. But were they even personified forms of energetic patterns that weave through this world? Did their stories, glimmering like fireflies, come from some deep encounter with the world and its energy, as some ancient people met these mountains, met these rivers, met the changing seasons? Or were they embroidered wishes, hopeful but delusional, a way to give meaning to meaningless life?

What was the real essence of these tales that had been sung for so long?

In Badrinath, I felt as if I had touched again on that deep hope, on that missing connection. With our spirits glued together by the *aarti*, afterwards, we had made our way from the temple area to the surrounding town with its bustling marketplace. Here, we had come across something that now just stemmed my hope, made me halt in my wish to forge this connection again. Gathered together were a group of *sadhus*, holy men wearing saffron robes, smoking *ganja*.

It was hard to believe that these *sadhus*, smoking weed, would find God before any of us did. Who had come up with these convenient ways to be with God? Did they even believe in their path? Were they getting closer to God or were at least some of them just charlatans, like those characters in R.K. Narayan stories, ordinary men pretending to be holy?

I had felt disillusioned. One minute, you could feel connected. The next, it was back to life as usual.

Before Badrinath, we had visited other temple towns. The first of them had been Rishikesh, on the banks of the holy Ganga, punctuated with one temple after another on the river bank. In Rishikesh, we had done white water rafting, an activity which was increasingly popular with the chic Delhi crowd. In the evening, I had seen a resplendent *aarti* on the river banks. The harmonics of the prayers had rung inside me as I looked at the countless lit earthen lamps that had been floated in the river. With their shimmering star specks gliding on the deep, dark river, they had also kindled something inside me.

It was easy to see why people from all over the world came to places like this. The ceremony - the light and the sound and the color - they all drew a portal through which you could walk into another world. As an artiste, I felt the appeal, this drawing of a picture, this swelling of a sound, this invitation offered and received. There was something so beautiful, so incandescent about these rituals, this transformation of the mundane into the mystical. Hinduism is often about the trance of the beloved. Unlike Buddhism, another great religion birthed in India, it's often not about detachment, but about attachment, about that feeling of living inside the divine.

In the States, when I have thought about it, I sometimes feel as if the creation of an idol, an image of God, an idea that people often question, is very similar to an artiste creating a painting and pouring something beautiful inside. It's this beauty that we pray to. It's this feeling that makes a deity out of rough stone and wood. Before it got corrupted and wrapped up in outer trappings, maybe that's all this was, an impulse which nudges us to give the formless a form.

It's this allure, this creating of a bridge with ritual that so resonates with me. It's what I miss touching and feeling whenever I doubt the existence of God. They live and dance inside me, these experiences that I grew up with. When this place is struck with a fragrance, a sound, or a chant, it's easy for it to harmonize and sing along.

During that trip, up from Delhi and winding north into the mountains, it was as if there was one sensory feast like this after another. After Rishikesh, we had driven a long day so we could get up early the next to make our way to the Kedarnath shrine. We were here just before it closed for the season. This was going to be the most inaccessible of all the shrines.

It had taken a seven-hour climb (including riding on mules for the last few excruciating hours) up the Garhwal Himalayas to get to Kedarnath, with its ancient Shiva temple. I was hardly in shape for the climb, but it was as if a feeling had carried me upwards. We had made it just in time. It was the last day the temple was open. The next day, everyone in that temple town would make their way down to the little village where the regulars stayed in the freezing winter and from where tourists left. Then, the temple would turn inwards for the winter. Maybe then, from those steps in the mountains, Shiva would descend and meditate there.

It was a magical, otherworldly place, like visiting a different planet, this temple town surrounded in a haze, with a mystical river flowing near it, with all its last-to-leave people who would say farewell to it together.

This evening, just before the temple closed for months, we had our *darshan*. We also met teenage sadhus, ascetics or yogis, who had taken vows to earn Shiva's graces. Huddled under a tea shack, as the rain washed down the landscape outside, one of them, a teenage boy, talked about how Shiva was a god you didn't find easily. You had to show him you meant business. After all, this was *Hatha* yoga, a yogic practice of taking a stubborn vow, a vow that showed God just how much you wanted him. Shiva had to be propitiated, had to be shown that you were just as stubborn and determined as him. While climbing up to the temple, he had come to know of a sadhu who had taken a vow not to speak till he met Shiva. He had been silent for decades.

Later on, I would think about this teenage boy, so much

younger than me. I understood the attraction. Shiva, the God who lives alone high up in the mountains, the ultimate meditating yogi, calls to something in all us stubborn souls. Unlike Vishnu, who is a God of the household, granting boons, Shiva is aloof, doing ascetic practices, not paying attention to the world as it turns. It's his followers who have to make their way to him. It's his followers who have to show him that their faith doesn't waver, that they can literally climb mountains for him.

In the States, when I tried to learn more about my own culture, everything I had missed learning in India, I thought about that teenage yogi when I came across a reference to hatha yoga in which hatha was roughly translated as "Sun Moon" yoga, yogic practices that integrate the body's solar and lunar energies.

I couldn't help thinking that was too simplistic. "Hatha" really was hatha, like that yogi had said, being stubborn and deciding that you were going to find God, at all costs, whatever it took. Hatha was what that sadhu in the Himalayas was attempting to do, deciding that God just couldn't turn him back. Hatha, I knew Hatha. I understood it. I could take stubborn vows too, although I had never taken one to go and find God.

That day, listening to the yogi speak, with all his youthful belief, as the rain calmed down outside, I had thought, would he give up some day? Or would he die trying? At least, he was not double-minded like I was. At least, he had decided something. Here I was, with all my intellectual arguments, believing, then not believing. Not believing, then believing.

What good did that do?

The Krishna Temple in Silicon Valley, Synchronicity and Jung's Famous Case of the Beetle

Around six months after meeting this teenage yogi, in mid-2012, I moved to the States. In the coming few years, whenever I got lonely, I wished I didn't have this sceptical streak in my believer's self. I wished I could be more like him. I wished I could make that wholehearted, complete offering that dares to call God up from the mountain down to where you are standing.

My fragmented relationship with God continued. After an initial visit to the temple down the road, I wouldn't visit for a few years. Once in a while, we would go to the Sunnyvale temple or the San Jose Sikh Gurdwara. With its hymns in Punjabi, the language that flew along the Ravi and the Beas, the language that made the waters of the Chenab sing, the Gurudwara reminded both Rohit and I of our childhoods, of our grandparents' homes, and we went to it, just like we had to similar Gurudwaras as children. For me, it was another sanctuary, another road back to home.

When a few years had passed, when my little shrine had chided me for long, when I had been through the shaking of that home place that happens for all immigrants, for everyone who leaves something behind, finally, finally, I would make my way down to the temple down the street. The years would change me, if only a little, and I would try to reach for something that felt familiar.

This temple down the road is dedicated to the flute-playing God Krishna, an incarnation or *avatar* of Vishnu. He is Vishnu come to rid the world of all its growing suffering. It also has, like all Krishna temples, his beloved

Radha. The temple building doesn't look anything like the triangled buildings that house temples in India. It's just a two-storeyed building, much like any other normal building. The temple area is downstairs and a library of religious texts is housed upstairs.

That day, when I went in, I could see that there were no priests in attendance all-the-time, like they were in the nearby popular Sunnyvale temple. At least, none that I could see. What looked like a volunteer sat in front of the door to the inner hall. He had religious books laid out on the table in front of him for purchase. We greeted each other with Namastes and I stepped in. There were chairs laid down. I sat in one.

The temple had been done up imaginatively. It seemed as if apart from the main statues, they changed things up for different holidays. Little scenes in Krishna's life had been set up using materials that would appeal to a child. There was *gota* and *kinari*, golden-tassel worked clothes. There were clothes with mirror-work and sequins. Lego bricks had been used to depict a scene in Krishna's village. In another scene, it was spring in Vrindavan. All the different seasons, the different *ritus*, the changes in mood and environment were depicted. In most of them, Krishna danced with Radha, his divine consort.

There was all the color and emotional life of India, and I could feel my energy flowing down to the ground. Krishna is a God you can love. He is a joyful God, a God full of cosmic pranks. In one of his beloved stories, his mother Yashodha finds the child Krishna and accuses him of stealing and gobbling up her hand-churned butter, yet another time. She orders him to open his mouth, and if she finds any traces of the said butter, he is going to be severely punished.

Like any willful child, Krishna says No till finally, Yashodha makes him do it. It's then that the child Krishna opens his mouth, and his human mother is astonished to find that her divine child has in his mouth, not her butter, but the entire cosmos revolving in it, the sun and the moon and the stars. Planets spin around, in eternal time, marching to a cosmic beat. The immortal aspect of God is revealed, too gigantic to be beholden.

Seeing this, Yashodha faints. But when she wakes up, she does not remember what she has seen. Once again, Krishna is her beloved, naughty little child, always up to some prank. She loves him dearly and is also continually exasperated by him.

Krishna evokes this kind of human love. You love him as a little child, up to one inventive prank after another. In some of his statues, he is shown in this child-form, with butter smearing his lips. In fact, Krishna's birthday is celebrated with these images of his childhood every year. Little boys dress up as Krishna. In temples, the baby Krishna is placed in little decorated cots.

In Krishna's beautiful stories, when he grows up, he is so enchanting that all the women in the village are in love with him. Shining like a moon among them is Radha, who loves him with all her heart. Their love story is one of the great love stories of Indian tradition. It is an enchanting tale set in an idyllic place, fragrant with roses, in a place where deer and peacocks roam freely.

Like all great love stories, it also has a separation. Krishna is, after all, a form of Vishnu. He has come to the world to right wrongs, to balance the scales of justice. When he goes away, Radha longs for him. Nothing is beautiful anymore. She sees him everywhere, in the rocks and in the trees and in the faces of everyone she meets.

Wherever she looks, there he is.

There is a heart-quickening quality in the stories of Krishna, a poignancy. Here's God, mesmerizing and pulling towards him all of creation. It's the God you might find in the buzzing of honeybees, in the fragrance of white *mogra* flowers, in the lake when the moon is dripping low. It's a heady, ecstatic kind of love, a love that cools you, a love that might set you aflame.

It's this sensory quality, this pulling of the imagination that animates Krishna-Radha temples. More than any other God in the Hindu pantheon, Krishna is the enchanter. Radha-Krishna temples are drenched in color, in music, in beauty.

When I let myself feel this pull, I feel enveloped in memory. In the little sanctum of this Silicon Valley temple, I think of going to the temple in Baroda with my beloved naani. I think of the peacocks that came to the lawns of my maternal uncle's house in that refinery township. I think of times encrusted like crystals, times that now feel fragmented, lost to me. Being in this temple is like pulling a thread through and sewing, sewing, till it comforts my heart.

It's not that I don't question. There is no stopping that. One time, I go to the temple and notice again that the statue of Krishna is in the center. It is flanked by one of Radha and one of a devotee sage. That is unlike other temples where Radha and Krishna stand together. Why is it always the man at the center? Why is it always the woman pining for her beloved? Why is God never a woman? These are the same old questions that make me not want to come here again, for a very long time. Their truth freezes me. Is this God? Or is this the God we've made up?

How can this God take care of me? All lies, all made up stories. Obviously, there was never a Krishna. I take one step forward, pulling the threads of old tales together. Then I hit a snag, and I unravel the whole thing.

I am still learning to hold these two opposing ideas in my own self. I still feel too brittle. This concept that you can feel two conflicting ideas, ideas that enlarge you, is something new to me. It's something I have come across in the works of Jungian therapists. They talk about how you don't have to polarize yourself. You don't have to pick up the baton of the rational and sacrifice all your ideas-that-don't-make-logical-sense. Neither do you have to give up rationality to follow the pull of something inexplicable that tugs at you. I don't fully understand this.

How can you be two opposite things? How can I both believe and not believe in these Gods?

What I do come to understand, by and by, is that I need to create space for both sides. There is no doubt about how nourished I feel by being in a space like this temple. It's up to me to let it be a part of me, to not hastily cut a vein, to not throw everything to the wind when I find God confused with all these different trappings.

Looking at the past means picking out a few beads and keeping them. Maybe, I will find new beads, and then string them all together. I judge a little less, both the people who follow rituals as well as those who don't. Things I was a hundred percent convinced about, like looking at the operating cost of this temple, advertised on a screen, asking for donations and then thinking about what a waste it was and how hypocritical - how many people in India could be helped by this much money - these thoughts are a little tempered now.

I understand a little. At any rate, no one is asking me to donate. I can donate to anything else I feel like, and I also get to come here, to a place where something inside me finds a home.

In the past few years, I have also been following different threads. I feel a new interest in learning about India, far as I am from it. I read about the spiritual meaning behind the images of Gods and Goddesses. I go to Native American sound healing concerts and drum circles and talks by Shamanic practitioners.

I have also started painting and making art, and images are coming up from a deep spring inside. I have always been a creative person, an artiste in the broadest sense. But one sense I had always felt was lost to me was my visual sense. Whenever I heard of people who could see in images, it felt like they had access to a way of being that was blocked for me.

Only once, during a brief interlude in my life, had this part of me awakened.

It was when I was working with some design software in my twenties. Then, there had actually been days when I looked at the world and saw it in lines. I had heard of how there were two different kinds of painters, one group who saw the world as patches of colors while the other saw the world as intersecting lines. For a short time, I had spontaneously started seeing the underlying shapes of things, how lines intersected, how they created the foreground and background, how they shaped our perspective of the world.

I could trace with my eyes, the lines of the cars parked on the street, the lines that made up these streets, the lines of the surrounding world that framed them. For a little while, I could draw these quite easily on a piece of paper. I could see how you created a three-dimensional world on two-dimensional paper. It felt like a little miracle. I loved artistes and was always reading books about them, about Raphael and Delacroix, about Rembrandt and Vermeer. This felt like the opening up of a world I longed for, the opening up of a new way of seeing.

But that opening had only lasted the duration of the course. I didn't quite climb down through the hollow. I didn't quite drop deep enough. Looking back, I see how much I struggled with owning my identity as a creative person. Was it even okay to *want* to be a creative, an artist, a writer, a painter? Was it even allowed? How could I even know whether I was any of these things?

I also had that curse of having more than one love. Was it writing I wanted to do? Was it dance? My guru, my classical dance teacher, a leading proponent of the Odissi dance form, had once commented that only one percent of people who learnt dance from him could do what I did. He had been teaching for decades, and was, in fact, involved in the revival of Odissi as a classical dance form. So, this praise meant something.

But the rational part of me could not figure out how I could survive as a dancer. I didn't know how to make my way through it. Classical dance also involved dependence on others. You learnt from certain people. You were tied to a specific form. There wasn't enough scope for expression. Maybe, what I *really* wanted to do was write.

I went back and forth, thinking about these options until it felt like I was just potential, echoes upon echoes of decisions not made, paths not taken. My 20s were colored by this feeling, by not deciding to follow an artistic path, by feeling like I had betrayed my true self, by trying to be a "normal" person working in a normal job. I had an immense resistance to naming myself an artiste.

But in the end, after seven years of corporate work, the deep discomfort I felt living in this box I had myself climbed into became the catalyst. While still working, I started freelancing on the side. It was also during this time that I did my first creative writing workshop. It seemed as if my days, which had been crumbling into sameness, were now wakened from a dead slumber.

By the time I met Rohit and then got married and moved to the States, I had created a little more hard-fought space to be myself. *Was I an artiste? Was I?* Looking at the ticking clock on the wall of my office, feeling the moments trickling away, I had often asked myself that question. How did you know? How could you be sure? How could you bear to take that risk, to find out? But now, I had finally answered the question I had been asking myself for so long.

Was I an artiste? Was I?

Yes, I was.

Just the fact that I had spent years agonizing about this question, twisting and turning it, feeling my breath getting squeezed, feeling my real self getting cramped should have been enough of a hint.

In the States, I had followed some more of this path unfolding in front of me. Quite soon after the move, I found writing workshops at *The Grotto*, a writer's collective in San Francisco. It was an entire floor full of small rooms that writers could rent out as offices. The idea behind the collective was that professional writers needed community.

If you were working on a book or a screenplay, it would do you good to be in a space with people just like you, people who knew your struggles. The community would give you both a structure to do creative work as well as function as a place to exchange ideas. In addition to the shared office space, *The Grotto* also hosted numerous writing workshops with published authors of all stripes - short story writers, journalists, experimental fiction writers and so on.

Once I had explored enough alleyways in different workshops, the next step had been to put my work out there in the world. It was then that I had started my blog. While I had workshopped some material at *The Grotto*, I was still searching for that elusive thing that writers talk about, my "voice." My expression was still tremulous, tentative. It was at this point, when I was practicing expressing myself, that I stumbled upon an article that talked about how writing by hand was qualitatively different from typing away on a laptop. That seemed simple enough to experiment with, so I started doing some writing by hand, to get a sense of what the difference felt like.

One day, as I wrote out some playful writing exercises, I had the experience of images popping up. They came up swiftly, as if moving my hands was striking something in my psyche. A stream had appeared where there was none before. I was no longer in my mind, thinking things up. I was in my body, pulling things down. I was practicing a movement I had forgotten. It was a similar experience to what I had felt during the multimedia course. A gate had opened. Images were bubbling up from an invisible cauldron.

Whenever I wrote by hand, I had this experience. Pictures appeared. Associations unwrapped. I had found an easy way back into the world of images. With my experiences with dreamwork, I was now even more attuned to symbols and pictures. As I wrote by hand, as these images streamed forth, my curiosity got even more heightened.

Over the next few years, everything that was coalescing inside me found a home either on the page or on the canvas. I did writing exercises. I painted. I did mixed media. I pulled out little tufts of images and glued them together. I pulled at thin slivers and lengthened them. When some images fell, almost fully-formed on the canvas or when they smoked their way across paper, I was struck by the ideas they seemed to talk about.

At one point, spontaneously, I started drawing a lot of spirals. They came from some feeling inside me, a feeling that nudged me to draw them, to explore them. Even in the outer world, wherever I looked, there they were. In true Jungian fashion, synchronicity struck one day when a friend and I went to see an exhibition of Impressionist painters at the Asian Art Museum in San Francisco. As we roamed through the different rooms, looking at the Monets and the Van Goghs hung side-by-side with works by Japanese painters that had inspired them, my friend found a wire earring someone had dropped. She handed it to me. Should we find someone to give it to? It was shaped like a spiral.

116

What should we do? What would I do?

It felt as if some energy had been invoked, as if these images were literally falling at my feet, calling to me to pay attention.

I thought then about Jung's most famous case of synchronicity. He was working with a female client who one day, told him of a dream in which she was given a costly piece of jewelry, shaped like a golden scarab (beetle). This woman was highly educated and intelligent, but she had been resisting dealing with her feelings during therapy. She was always coming up with rationalizations and intellectualizing her emotional issues.

On this particular day, as she recited this dream, Jung heard a faint tapping on the window from the outside. When he opened it, in flew a scarabaeid beetle. Jung is said to have plucked the beetle out of the air and handed it to his client saying, "Here is your scarab."

Somehow, at a pivotal point in the therapeutic process, the universe had brought this woman what Jung calls synchronicity, a "meaningful coincidence." Literally meaning "falling together in time," synchronicity occurs when a thought or experience in the mind is mirrored by an external event to which it has no direct causal connection.

Jung articulated his concept of synchronicity after many years of experience with his psychotherapy patients and after conversations with two great scientists, Albert Einstein and Wolfgang Pauli, the Nobel prize-winning theoretical physicist who was one of the pioneers of quantum physics. In fact, it was his discussions with Einstein during the early days when Einstein was developing his first theory of relativity that got Jung started with thinking about a possible relativity of time and how synchronicity might occur.

Jung believed that synchronicity served a similar function as dreams in a person's life. When some meaningful, striking coincidence occurred, it helped shift the person's egocentric thinking. In the case of the woman and her beetle, the beetle had helped shake her one-sided view of the world. The world was more than what could be understood by the mind. There was a mystery in it. Events happened that you couldn't explain away easily.

It was interesting that this woman's unconscious had thrown up the symbol of the beetle, an ancient symbol for transformation and metamorphosis, the very experience she needed. Not only that, her inner symbol had also showed up quite miraculously in the outer world. The beetle tapping on Jung's window was not a common bug in those parts of the world. In fact, it was somewhat of a rarity. But just when she needed it the most, there it was, offering her a moment of communing with the possibilities of the world.

Jung's concept of synchronicity shares similar characteristics to what people of a religious bent think of as grace intervening in a person's life. This is one of the reasons why it's often said that people who are more "religious" (whether or not they believe in organized religion, they believe in something bigger) gravitate towards Jungian psychology.

Because of its truthful and daring attempt to look at all those things that are actually hard to quantify and measure, the practice of Jungian psychotherapy and the number of therapists trained in its practices are not as common as other schools of psychology. But Jungian thought stands as one of the great psychological schools just because it dives deep into this complexity of the self, just because it goes to the heart of what ails us as people, just because it shows us that what might heal us often lies within.

The Symbols of the Spiral, the Snake, the Crocodile and the Spider

When the universe handed me the image of the spiral, it felt portentous. I tried to find out more about the symbol and gradually, started stumbling across many different potential meanings. Some books on Shamanism talked about how spirals combine the form of the line (the linear, the masculine) with the form of the circle (the feminine, the circuitous). Doing that, they embodied a new way of being. This meaning felt right to me, the bending of the line into a circular path. It felt like a symbol for where I was in my own life.

It felt, in fact, like a symbol for my own being. All my life, I had had the feeling of walking sideways. I had pretended to keep beat to a music I didn't understand. I had rejected my own rhythm. I had often felt like there was something wrong with me, wrong with the way I did things.

But now, with the spiral in my hand, as I looked back, I could see how my intense discomfort at different times in my life had been because of how very hard I had tried to be "normal." I had tried to religiously follow the linear path. But my way had never been a straight line. My path had always been a spiral. It seemed like a talisman of my very being, of my own nature as an HSP.

This is a nature that combines different elements. This is a nature that does things by moving in closer and closer circles towards the center. This is a nature that values the feminine qualities of feeling and sensing, even though they are ambiguous, even though they cannot be objectively controlled.

The more I read about the spiral, the more it felt like it was asking me something. Would I return to my own self, a self that curved inwards? Or would I keep bending down to the "one true way" of doing anything?

Even in writing, this was my path. I naturally followed a circular process I often discounted. But now, I could accept this process instead of making it into something that was not me. As I started experimenting with combining the linear and the circular, I could see how to use this concept. For longer pieces, especially nonfiction, it was good to have an outline with the points clearly laid out. That gave me a way forward. This was the objective bit of it, the structure bit of it. But when I started writing and working through different drafts, it was then that I moved in tighter and tighter circles till I landed right into the heart of the material.

While it was good to start with an outline, with a map, during the actual writing, I could also veer off the outline. I could add more points or flesh out different topics than what I had started out with. For me, it felt that writing was never a linear process, even though it had *some* elements of linearity.

These were just some of the associations I found for the spiral in my own life. As I kept myself open, more meanings started coming up. I stumbled upon another reference that talked about the spiral being the symbol for

Kundalini shakti. In Indian yoga philosophy, Kundalini *shakti or* Kundalini energy is the creative potential that lies dormant at the base of the spine in the human body. This untapped energy is symbolized as a coiled snake, hence the name *Kundalini*, the coiled one. Practitioners of Kundalini yoga try to raise this energy up through the body to the top of the head from where it can merge with universal energy. These Kundalini experiences, the merging of the untapped energy inside us with the energy of the world, are said to be ecstatic.

This waking up of energy sleeping inside the body and its merging with universal energy also means heightened perception. When you look at images of Indian gods like Shiva who is shown with a coiled snake around his neck, this is what it symbolizes, the fact that his energies are at their peak. Shiva's third eye, in the middle of his forehead, is not a physical third eye, but symbolic of the gift of true sight that can see inside the reality of the world.

The reason why I had started reading up about Kundalini energy in the first place was because I had had what felt like some small Kundalini experiences. I knew about Kundalini experiences cursorily from reading about Yoga. But my experiences hadn't been anything like the blissful experiences that yogis aim for, that ecstatic merging with the universe, that ecstatic spinning into the divine. In fact, mine hadn't felt spiritual at all.

Instead, they had felt like forceful, powerful energy rising up from the base of my spine. This energy almost seemed to be pulling me out of my roots. They had felt very uncomfortable, as if something was forcing me right out of my skin, as if my whole self was overcharged. Only one day, for some fleeting seconds, I had a taste of that bliss and had felt as if a spark had been ignited. But mostly, it was a physical feeling of something powerful yanking me up from my roots.

When I read about it, I found that while Yogis aim to consciously awaken untapped creative energy through Yogic practices, sometimes, given the right conditions, it was said that Kundalini energy could awaken on its own. I was not sure exactly how it had happened for me. Maybe, something had shifted energetically inside me because of all the changes coming through my life. Maybe, it was something else. But the feeling of huge discomfort, the sensation of being physically pulled right up, like a tree in a storm, scared me quite a bit.

Yoga gurus talked about this. They told tales of how dangerous raising Kundalini energy could be if you were unprepared, if you didn't have someone guiding you through the process. It was like overloading a system with energy that it simply wasn't ready to handle. That definitely seemed true for me. Obviously, I wasn't ready for this experience. At that time, I also felt like I wasn't too keen to follow this trail. Maybe, someday, when I felt ready, I would find the right Yoga teacher and explore this for myself.

In time, these months with their mini-Kundalini experiences petered down. The small waves disappeared back into the ocean. What remained with me was the discussion around Kundalini and how it was conceptualized. This untapped creative power was thought of as feminine in nature. It was part of the energy of the body. It could rise up to meet a field of consciousness, which was itself conceptualized as masculine.

Unlike the passive role given to divine feminine energy in

different cultures and even in many of Hinduism's Goddesses, Kundalini, the creative potential, was the activating principle. It moved things. Without it, consciousness, the masculine principle, was considered inert, immoveable. Of course, there was also the other side. Without consciousness, this creative energy was disordered, aimless, like one gone wild. Each was a part of the whole.

Was this why coloring in my coloring books had felt so therapeutic? Was it because doing that had given me a conscious channel for moving my creative energy? This whole discussion of untapped creative energy rising up to meet consciousness reminded me of the Chinese Yin and Yang symbol. In each system, there were two paths, both of them inextricably linked. In each system, there were two parts that created the whole.

As I continued to engage with the spiral, it was as if it spilled open a treasure chest. The image of the snake had also been showing up in my dreams. I could come up with many different meanings for it. Sometimes, I was sure it symbolized the shedding of my old skin.

Sometimes, it felt like it was telling me about the rising of my own creative energy. I was being more creatively productive than ever before. Sometimes, it felt like the symbol was saying that creativity and sexuality were two sides of the same coin, of the same moving, slithering energy. It was almost as if the same energy could be shifted in different ways. If I used it in creativity, in making art, it rose and almost filled up my heart and nourished it.

As these images of the snake came up, I also got the chance to try an idea inspired from my Shamanism explorations. Somewhere, I had read that one way to engage with a symbol was by interacting with it in some tangible, physical way. I put this into practice when Rohit and I went to the California Academy of Sciences in San Francisco one weekend. The Academy had an aquarium and a planetarium as well as several other sections. In the piazza, I stood in line behind some eight and ten-year olds and waited to pet a snake. Thankfully, the woman holding it didn't raise an eyebrow. The snake itself was small and thin. It was green in color and, of course, non-poisonous. It almost looked cute. When my turn came, it didn't feel anything like the rubbery, slithery texture I'd imagined snakes as having. It felt cool to the touch, like a jewel. I posed, and Rohit took a picture.

The hooded form of the snake also raised its head in the outside world. During a visit to Mexico in 2015, Rohit and I visited Chichen Itza, the remains of a large pre-Columbian city built by the ancient Mayans. Usually, I am the kind of person who reads a lot about the places I visit. But I had been distracted this time and didn't know anything of its history.

As we walked through the sprawling grounds, listening to our guide, he told us that the step-pyramid in the center was a temple to Kukulcan, the Maya feathered-serpent deity. All around me, it felt as if images and carvings of snakes had sprung up and multiplied, as if the something inside me and the something outside me were part of the same continuum. It was a moment of pure delight.

It turned out that during the spring and autumn equinoxes, the sun's rays created a shadow across this pyramid that even looked like a serpent slithering down a staircase. The world fluttered in hope that day as I looked around me. Later on, I would buy a cool, black obsidian carved into a snake as a reminder to follow my curiosities and to remember that there was a home everywhere I went. In Mexico, I felt the thread that connected me to the surrounding landscape. There was that same sense of looking at the world and finding it touched by the sacred. There was that same sense of seeing the sacred in countless forms.

When we returned back to our home in the Valley after the trip, I imagined the orange groves that had once existed here before they were sacrificed for this modern settlement I now lived in. But ancient ideas still reverberated in the air around me. They lived in the little creatures that breathed in and around Coyote Creek as it flowed past my house. They were my roots into this new home, whose topsoil might be sanitized, but that had a fecund, moist layer underneath it, teeming and turning with life.

When I had first engaged with foreign-sounding words like Shamanism, I had only thought of the "backward" connotation at first. But now, it felt as if it was a vast, mixed-up field. Now, when I thought of a Shaman, I thought of a liminal experience, the kind where doors between two worlds opened. It had little to do with superstition. A shaman, I thought, was anyone in the world who heals the soul.

They don't call themselves by that name, but a therapist calling back fragments of the soul lost to trauma was the latest in a long line of shamans. So was someone whose medicine was creating something beautiful that bewitched and enraptured, that replenished our soul life, or someone who suggested a way forward by creating a tarot or other card deck. The magic was in the process, in the ritual, in the falling into another dimension of meaning.

Engaging with the spiral also showed me that symbols could be unpacked almost endlessly. Over the few years after it first came up, more and more associations kept coming up for the spiral. I had to be careful to not try to fix its meaning too closely. This was something that dream workers also sounded a caution about. Symbols were imbued with meaning, they said, but they also came from a different world. It did us no good to pin a symbol down, to reduce its meaning to just one thing. Doing that suffocated the symbol, drained it of life. What we needed to do instead was to hold the symbol lightly, like an enchanted dragonfly, with the utmost care. We had to play with its possibilities. We had to let it open us up and add to us.

Of course, this is easier said than done. In exploring symbols, I have often felt like I have gotten the "right" answer as soon as I interpreted something one way. This happened once for one symbol that crawled up from my dreams. It was the image of the crocodile. It was an unusual image and my conscious associations with the crocodile were somewhat sinister, influenced by all those tales I had heard as a child. It had definitely not come from a T.V. show or something else I had watched, which sometimes happened when dreams picked up images from actual life. Instead, it felt like a symbol that had come up from some deeper layer of the unconscious.

It came up during a time when I was having a kind of identity crisis. Sometimes, I tried to copy Americans I knew, which meant I tried to be direct. But coming from me, that came across as brusque. It didn't suit me. Then, feeling off, I would switch back to my Indian ways. It was as if I couldn't quite find the correct way to be, whatever that was. I kept flip-flopping, no longer sure what the true norm was, no longer sure who I really was.

It was during this time that the dream with its crocodile showed up. I jumped to the most obvious conclusion. I thought the dream was telling me that I needed to grow a thicker skin. Change felt so hard for me. I let everything get under my skin. I let everything irritate me. I was always noticing some new cultural faux pas I had made and registering other people's reactions. Again, I felt that caustic sense of faultiness coming up. It wasn't enough that the outside world kept saying it. Now, my dream was taking a dig at me too. *Toughen up. Don't be so soft. Grow a thicker hide*, it seemed to be saying.

But this had felt impossible to do, especially now that I had discovered what it meant to be an HSP. It was a Catch 22 situation. How could I have my thick armor up and still be myself? How could I grow a thicker skin? What did it all mean? What was my dream trying to tell me?

It was frustrating to puzzle out, so I just set aside this image for some time. It was only months later that I came across another meaning of the crocodile in a book describing symbols from all around the world. In it, amidst the triskelion and the ankh, there was also the symbol of Denkyem, the crocodile. In Africa, and specifically in Ghana, it said that Denkyem was regarded as a mystical creature because of its dual ability to stay in the water as well as move on land. Traditional healers considered it a totem animal for greater flexibility and endurance.

This was a very different suggestion from my first thought of needing to grow a thicker hide. In fact, it was pointing in the opposite direction. It was telling me *not* to become hardened, but instead to become flexible. I had interpreted the symbol the first time around through the lens of my own not-good-enoughness. It had seemed to come jeering and laughing, echoing the negative voices in my head. But *this*, this was different. I could see the value in the suggestion to become more flexible, to have the ability to move with ease in different worlds. It would probably take a lot of trial and error, but I could figure it out. This was a much more helpful showing of the way than bashing my head in, trying to follow the supposed suggestion I had first arrived at.

Engaging with the symbol of the crocodile, I also came closer to an ancient part of my psyche. It felt like it had come from a deeper layer that contained the history of all humankind, experiences that other people might have had or actual things they might have encountered. My own nature was built on a pre-existing matrix. Something inside me knew to use an ancient symbol to tell me about the exact quality I needed at the exact moment in time. Here again was an invitation into mystery.

So I kept on following this path into the woods, making art, writing down my dreams, observing what called to me. I let myself paint, even when no high art was happening. It was okay to make things without knowing exactly what you were making. Sometimes, I made do with just the ends of some shape that was coming from inside me. Sometimes, images fell fully-formed onto the paper.

Seals appeared. Koala bears hung on trees. Beavers burrowed up. More than ever before, now when I went out into the world, I was conscious of my attraction to things. Was I drawn towards horses painted on a bag? Why had peacocks, an image I had always loved, come up for me again? Who was I meeting in my dreams? What synchronicities was I encountering in day-to-day life?

In a group meditation during this time, the image of an elk popped up. When I came back home, I realized I already had, resting behind my bedroom side-table, a walking stick with an elk head. I had bought it on a trip to Yellowstone National Park a few years ago, picking it out from a host of other sticks with different animal carvings. I had hardly noticed it over the years. But here it was, the symbol of the elk, guiding my path. The elk is an animal often associated with the Goddess.

Then, there were the spiders that often showed up in my path. For one of my photography classes, I took picture after picture of spider webs. I had always loved spiders, and now I came across them all the time, very close to my home. Sometimes, I found them under the bridge that ran over the thinned-out waters of Coyote Creek. Sticking my head underneath, looking at their intricate thread work, mesmerized, I was immediately part of their world.

It turned out that in the Native American tradition, spiders were the keepers of the primordial alphabet. They were considered a talisman for writers. Shaped like the number eight and with eight legs, their bodies symbolized the infinity sign, the endless possibilities of creation. They spin their webs from the raw materials of their body, much like writers weave their creations out of the raw material of their own imagination and experiences.

As these images and symbols rushed forth, a word kept coming up for air again and again. I would catch it for a moment. Then, it would slip away again. But then, I would catch hold of it once more. Goddess. *Goddess.*

It felt slightly heretical. I came from a culture with a multitude of Gods and Goddesses, but when I thought of the divine, I first thought of God, not Goddess. Just saying the word felt transgressive. Yes, spirals and circles were frequently connected to Goddess worship in ancient times. Yes, Radha and Sita were Goddesses. But were they God? *Goddess.*

The Feminine Word for God and the Turtle and the Hummingbird

When I went to metaphysical bookstores during this time, books with words like Gaia were my last bastion. I was accepting the word "alternative" for myself more and more, but this was where I stopped. Gaia, what nonsense, I would think. What a new-agey word to use. I even turned away from YouTube channels where some poor soul, non-Indian, had decorated their walls with images of Indian Goddesses. Did they even understand what they were talking about? Wasn't it a bit like people calling themselves yogis just by going to yoga studios and practicing physical postures?

But then again, wasn't I, myself, attracted to different things? Everything that spoke to me, *aartis* with their heady incense, Sufi poetry, Native American dreamcatchers, the Sikh temple with its Punjabi prayers, they were the same idea split into different sounds and pictures. Now, these pieces seemed to be coming together, joining together in some completely new way. *Goddess.*

Goddess. Why did the word feel so uncomfortable? Why was it so hard to say?

When I thought of God, I first thought of Krishna, playing his flute. I did not think of Radha, pining and yearning for her beloved. When I thought of God, I thought of Ram, another *avatar* of Vishnu, steadfast in his duty, living in exile for fourteen years. I did not think of Sita, his wife, his divine partner, who accompanied him in this exile.

It wasn't that Radha and Sita were not important. They were, in fact, *very* important. You don't say Ram without saying Sita. You don't say Krishna without saying Radha. In the temple town of Vrindavan, said to be the place where Krishna grew up, you won't be greeted with the usual Hindi *Namaste,* but *Radhe-Radhe,* a chant of Radha's name. You cannot remember Krishna without remembering his beloved Radha. Then, there was Sita, the ideal of Hindu womanhood, the dutiful wife who faithfully followed her husband into exile.

In the States, when I first heard of how Catholic women were expected to be modest and virtuous, I thought of Sita. This was probably a flawed comparison but to me, both seemed to embody the same qualities. They were chaste, self-sacrificing, compliant. There is probably a little bit of Sita in the majority of Indian women, this internalized expectation to be a receptacle for others' energy, to be someone who waits patiently, waits eternally, and who gives without thinking of the cost to her own self. There is probably also a little bit of Radha, drunk on love, with her longing, her yearning to be one with her beloved. Both Radha and Sita are steeped somewhere deep in our psyches, imprinted indelibly on our souls.

The only problem was when I thought about them, I hesitated to call them God, even though they are considered divine. They were not the principal actors. Hindu philosophy even talked of things like Radha being a symbol for the soul, yearning for union with God, which Krishna personified.

Of course, there were other Goddesses in the Hindu pantheon a little different from Radha and Sita. There was Durga, a fierce warrior Goddess, who rode a lion, who slayed demons with her many hands. She is the archetypal figure of the Great Mother, both a benefactor and a protectress. Durga is highly revered in North India where I come from, but I didn't remember many parents who told their daughters to be like her.

Then, there was Kaali, an even more problematic and less popular image of the Goddess. Kaali is like Durga, but even more fierce. She personifies radical anger, the kind of righteous rage that breaks through rigid lines, that subverts and changes. In her images, she is often shown wearing the skulls of the demons she has slayed, strung together in an intimidating necklace.

Kaali gets rageful. She dances on the heads of the demons she has slayed, her tongue out. If you were to look at an artist's rendering of her, you would be repulsed. The closest image I could think of for her energy was rockstars with their tongues out.

Kaali energy is energy that challenges the system. It lives on the fringes. It bends the rules.

As a child, I knew Kaali only faintly. She was the Goddess who lived on the perimeter of our lives. She wasn't very popular in my "normal" milieu. When I thought of Durga, on the other hand, I thought of the great mother you worshipped but who you couldn't be like. After moving to the States, at a time when I was struggling with embracing a more powerful femininity, the image of a friend from India kept popping up as she

132

danced with abandon in my dreams.

This friend is someone I think of as both feminine and strong. She also comes from a state in India where Durga is the principal deity. At that time, I had thought of how she had a very different image of the feminine embedded inside her as compared to me.

This is the feminine that can take up arms, that doesn't capsize in front of stronger forces. This is the feminine that does not grow like a vine, wrapping itself around something. It is a tree in whose shade other things grow.

In my own life, I had briefly encountered the energy of these warrior Goddesses. I thought of Kaali as the personification of the thunderous angers that brought clarity, that mete out justice. It was this kind of energy that had helped me stand up for myself at times when everything inside me was quaking, trembling, falling away like leaves. Kaali was the hot tongue of anger I could sometimes barely hold, that could scorch and burn, but that could also be used like a torch.

When I looked back at those angers and learned more about these fierce goddesses, finally, I could see how anger was also a part of the feminine range. The feminine was not just Sita, the gestator of life. It was not just Radha, yearning for completion. It was also Kaali. It was also Durga.

When I searched my memories for why these Goddesses were so absent from my makeup, an early memory stood up. It was one of my earliest childhood memories from Delhi. It went like this. One day, when I was very little, maybe four or maybe five, my parents told me to go along with a group of girls, some older than me. In this big group, we went from one house to the other in our neighborhood, all of whom had opened their doors to us this day. This was the end of *Navratri*, the auspicious nine nights when Durga is venerated.

At each of these houses, we were asked to sit on the floor. Then, our feet were reverently washed with water. A red scarf woven with golden threads was placed on each of our heads. We were given the meal specially made on this day - earthy brown chickpeas fried with cumin, poofy ballooned-up *pooris* for bread, and a sweet raisin-studded *halwa* for dessert. In our little plates, a few coins were placed with devotion. The enthusiasm, the love even, of the women doing this ceremony and their husbands fondly looking on was infectious.

We went from one house to the other like this, and in each one, we were greeted in this same way. I remember feeling so special, so tended to, so cared for. It was one of those memories that you want to hold close, that you could wrap yourself in.

But then, after many years had passed, there had also come a time in my teens, when this yearly ritual was over for me. Only pre-pubescent girls, girls who hadn't gotten their period, were considered the living embodiment of the great mother. Only they were part of this ritual. Then, it had felt as if the Great Mother's spark didn't shine in me anymore.

When I picked up the tarnished pieces of this memory, I finally understood my ambivalence about this ritual. It had a bittersweet aftertaste. It had added something positive to my feelings of being okay, very different from the not-good-enough feelings I collected later on in my life. But it had also snatched away my connection to my own potency.

What would have been different if that wonderful feeling of being touched by the divine hadn't been contaminated? Isn't this what we were all looking for as women? Isn't this what we suffer from not having? It was a soul wound, believing that the Great Mother had left me.

Decades later, as I resistantly stepped closer to this memory, I hoped that it would become like mulch. Maybe, broken down, it could add to my nourishment. Maybe it showed me my guardrails, the shapes of my beliefs, the statement of everything known that I rejected. I stayed with it, mourning for something lost a long time ago.

I felt. I sensed. I made art.

Just like the spiral before, something else had been bubbling up for some months now. I had started spontaneously drawing another symbol. At first, I was not exactly sure what I was scratching in when I took the end of the paintbrush and made marks in layers of gleaming red and green paint. It took me weeks to realize that I was making the marks of the treble clef, the musical symbol with its "and-like" shape.

I had been feeling my way to it, often using just my fingers to paint, letting them guide me, long before I realized what exact shape was coming through me. From some rainbow well-hidden underneath an old door, from which crescent moons and heady stars had been falling onto my canvas for some time, there had now come these gliding musical notes. It was only when they fell sweetly for quite a long time that I thought, finally, of her, that most important Goddess, at least for me, the Goddess I had almost forgotten, but whom I could also never forget. Saraswati.

I grew up in a household in India, similar to many others, where when you dropped a book on the floor, you picked it up immediately. Then, you touched it to your forehead or kissed it. You did not disrespect Saraswati, the Goddess of learning, the one who gave knowledge and discernment, through whose agency you could know things.

Saraswati, literally translated as "the one who flows like a river," is the Goddess who gives the boon of flowing inspiration. She is ever-present in Hindu consciousness, even though she is not as popular as Lakshmi, the Goddess of abundance and wealth. Maybe, she has taken her leave from a world mesmerized by Lakshmi. Maybe, she just doesn't care, absorbed as she is in learning, in becoming even more skilled, even more refined.

My journey with the word Goddess had brought me right back to her. There is a great deal of Radha and Sita in me, but there is also a great deal of Saraswati, the connection to this Goddess of all arts, including the art of writing and music. As someone who has always loved books and their flights, and whose imagination has often saved her, I am a follower of Saraswati, whether I consciously pray to her or not. Now, here she was again, calling me back.

When I turned to her myths, they often talked not just about her but her relationship with the Goddess Lakshmi. In Indian tales, Saraswati, the Goddess of learning and Lakshmi, the Goddess of wealth, are often shown as having a complicated relationship with each other. Often, it's said that when one is present, the other does not stay around for long. Some stories even talk of how very jealous they are of one another.

So, when I first read about them, it seemed like it was a choice between one or the other. It was either Saraswati or Lakshmi. Their divide seemed like the gulf between pure art and commerce. But then, as I read more, other tales appeared. They talked about how following the path of one Goddess did not necessarily exclude the other. So, following Saraswati's path, the path of learning, did not exclude Lakshmi, worldly success. But it did mean that both Goddesses urged their followers to choose who exactly they were going to put first. Who was more important?

Was it Lakshmi, glowing like a queen bee, the one who granted fame and fortune? Or was it Saraswati, riding on her swan, the one whose path required a certain amount of rigor but who gave the inspiration that turns time liquid?

At first, as I meandered my way through these stories, *this* felt like the difference between Saraswati and Lakshmi energy - success through learning and depth of knowledge versus success that comes from understanding the dynamics of the market. In one, you are immersed in learning something for its own sake. In the other, you are also creating and learning, but the learning is not an end in itself. It's a tool. It does not call you as deeply. It's less immersive.

But then, just as I thought I had figured it out, there were mentions of yet other stories. There were myths connecting both Saraswati and Lakshmi to Durga, to the same Great Goddess. In fact, these said that both of them were just two aspects of the same divine mother, two different faces of the same exact energy. This was typical of the way Indian stories morphed and multiplied. There was no way to catch them in one shape. There was no way to pin them down.

At first, my analytical side feels frustrated with this game of smoke and mirrors. Are they different? Are they the same? What's the meaning of these different stories? Did anyone even know? But then by and by, I feel like these are stories split from one main story, as if they both are the same energy, arranged in different ways. I decide then that what this means is that all kinds of creative energy is available to me. It's not this or that, but both.

Still, the distinctive form of Saraswati speaks to the deeper currents in my own soul. With her, I touch upon a kind of womanhood very different from the conventional. In her stories, she is the consummate scholar who loves to have intellectual debates with her husband, the creator Brahma, who sometimes wishes he had a more docile and uncomplicated wife. She is often lost in her thoughts, detached, a little away from relationships. Something else calls out to her, absorbs her, pulls her attention.

A Saraswati woman, it seems to me, is someone so absorbed in learning that she needs a lot of space to grow and unfold. The divide inside my own soul feels clearer then. There is often a tug of war between the Sita inside me and the Saraswati. Sita is partly my conditioning of what it means to be like her, to be good, to be virtuous. But I also resonate with her deeper qualities. She is the imprint of higher ideals, the resting space in which things grow. But sometimes, her image veers dangerously into passivity.

Then, there is Saraswati. A deep artistic impulse dances in

my soul. It wants to be free, to be by itself, to follow its yearnings, to look inside the forest and behind the curtain. To do this, it needs a certain detachment. It needs to be a little on its own, a little away from relationships, especially those that demand Sita-like qualities, where you become the facilitator, the one whose energy is intertwined with others. But with Saraswati, you have to lay down that giving movement. You have to risk aloneness, failure and doubt. In a way, it's an even harder path than the sacrificing path of Sita, this peeling back the layers, this not knowing what you will find, this not knowing who you will become.

Maybe, that's why I've neglected Saraswati, I think.

But as I continue to do more art, as it nourishes my very heart, another thought occurs to me. Maybe, Saraswati's discipline is not so much discipline as love. It's Degas painting with failing eyesight. It's Michelangelo freeing human forms from blocks of marble. It's people working long, working hard, searching for something till they find it, till they become conduits, the instruments through which Saraswati sings. Through them, new forms are brought into being. The mundane world falls away. This is why we pursue Saraswati, for all those moments when we sway in the music and the music sways in us, for all those moments when we are whole and holy.

With these Goddesses, I touch upon all my beliefs about the feminine. I try to take apart what I automatically think. I try to include all these different energies.

I get a miniature statue of Saraswati and place it in the *pooja* thali in my altar. I change the arrangement of the plate, put her in the center, and arrange the other little statuettes around her. I also include a crystal lotus my sister has given me. The lotus stands for many qualities, but in my mind, it stands for Lakshmi. It symbolizes how important beauty is to me, how deeply it calls my soul. With Saraswati at the center, my little altar feels awakened.

Bit by bit, it collects other objects, talismans of my journey. It welcomes a dragon in the shape of an incense holder. The other pictures huddle together to make space for a colored drawing I make. This contains a two-tusked elephant living at the bottom of the sea, butterflies rising from the waves of a celestial ocean from which ideas come, and a spider-bird swooping down amongst many other things.

I have colored most of this drawing except for a few bits and pieces of the creatures that are still being formed in this celestial ocean, still being created by a divine energy. In the center is a circle with a lotus and an Aum on one side, the primordial sound vibration from which everything is said to be created in Indian mythology. At Christmas time and long afterwards (because now I have taken a special affinity to trees), a red and green spiral-growing Christmas tree finds a new home in my altar. The aum sounds an amen. A silver vessel I fill up with water and float candles in during Diwali holds sage and sandalwood incense from day-to-day.

My sister, when she visits from India, tells me this is an artiste's temple. She means it as a compliment. It *is* an artiste's shrine, even though I have often tried to shake that dreaded word from my sleeve. But now, I think, it's a good thing to be an artiste. Artistes combine things. They look at the hawk flying above them, and think of the messages he brings. They pick up life that has gone to dust, dried flowers and leaves, and paste them on to scraps of paper and make something beautiful. For them, Grandmother Spider creating the ancient Native American world and Krishna holding up a mountain on one finger are tales from the same mythology.

The temple is at home. I feel more at home, more at ease with it.

It's not that everything has been magically resolved. I still doubt. I still question. Even making these little changes, I wonder if I am doing something wrong. Am I praying in the wrong way? Am I crossing some religious line? But can you ever pray in the wrong way? Aren't the lines I am crossing only the lines of my conditioning? Isn't this the real Hinduism, the one that chants the thousand names of the divine because you cannot contain something so large in just a few words?

Isn't mine the real Hinduism, the one that preaches that the soul has no gender? Why then, would it think that loving someone of the same gender is unacceptable? Isn't my own path just like this religion I grew up with, the one that can expand to fit in everything, that in its ten *avatars,* its ten incarnations of Vishnu, also counts Buddha? Stories within stories within stories.

Isn't this what God is, the same light split into different colors?

In this new-to-me country, I find more veins, running like silver in the belly of the earth. I learn about Celtic symbols, read more poetry by Kabir and Hafiz, and think of how they are all part of the same vocabulary, letters of the same alphabet. They are all yearning for that same thing we can't name, that same thing that reminds us of home.

141

As I finally make the changes to my altar, it also feels like the year gone by has built some things up but also broken some things down. I have taken many steps forward, but by the end of it, I am also exhausted. Writing is like mining, and like being in a mine, sometimes, you can set off explosions. Towards the end of the year, it feels like I have written my way back to my wounds. In fact, I have struck them hard.

They are howling and crying and lashing out in pain. It's been an adventure for some time, but now, I fall into a dark night of the soul. The little faith I have been stitching together all year trembles under this weight. Everything feels hopeless. Nothing seems to make sense any more. All the things I used to think would make me happy are no longer enough. They seem meaningless, gone to dust. Why this? Why now? When everything was going so well. Through all of this, something in me is also saying, *Surrender.*

Surrender? That's something I won't do easily. As 2016 draws to a close, I feel a gnawing depression. I try to walk on willfully, put things together for a writing fellowship. I get together all my letters of recommendation. I manage to not self-sabotage. I submit in time. But all this effort during a time when the fog falls heavy brings me down to my knees. Some days are dark as tar.

Then, one night, a wondrous dream appears. In it, I am driving a car I am losing control of by the minute. I careen this way and that, nearly hitting the people walking on the roadside. The car veers off the road, crashes and then goes into a free-fall, straight into the river. But then, something wonderful happens. Instead of falling into the river, the car lands on dry land. I am on an island. It's safe. I see a giant tortoise as it rises up from the deep bowels of the earth and moves slowly forward.

When I get up in the morning, I can't quite remember whether the island was an actual island or whether I landed on the back of the tortoise. But I am suffused with the feeling from the dream. I feel deeply touched. It's as if something has held my wounded, broken self. I feel a physical sense of grace.

But this sense of being held doesn't last long. The day rocks me here and there. My mind takes hold. The game of surrendering and not surrendering begins. But still, the tortoise or the turtle (I can't decide which one it is although turtles seem more natural in the water) has come, from the depths of an invisible ocean. I later learn that in Native American mythology, the turtle is the symbol for the earth. In fact, I find similar stories that appear in both Hinduism and Native American culture, of the great turtle on whose back the world rests.

Maybe, I am being invited to slow down, to look within, to create my own sanctuary. Maybe, I am being told that I am getting off center, ungrounded. Is the dream telling me that moving slowly is the right rhythm for me at this moment? I think of how I am not very patient at the moment, and I am not sure exactly what the symbol means. But I do know that it means a lot. This is the most positive, comforting dream I have ever had. It feels like being encapsulated in love.

One day, soon after this dream comes, I am strolling near Coyote Creek on one of my "beauty" walks, slow walks in which I look at the flowers and the sky and the birds flying above. I peer down from the overpass into the water, looking at the geese. A swaying rope looks like a water snake. It's been raining in torrents these past few weeks, and the creek is full. The world looks washed over with gray paint. Just then, a turtle swims and puts its head out of the water. He is directly beneath me.

He seems to be looking at me just like I am looking at him. I hadn't realized there were turtles living here, I think, and a feeling of happiness takes over. Then, what I imagine as the mamma turtle joins the baby turtle, and they swim along. They look both clumsy and graceful at the same time. It feels like my dream has found its place in the world.

This dream is like an interlude in a dark symphony. In my day-to-day life, it's as if the hurts I've stuffed in the cracks in the walls have gotten infected. It's as if I have left something precious out, and it has gotten pummelled and ravaged by the storm.

One day, when I am feeling unbelievably down, in my tiny balcony that overlooks the hills, I watch as a spider weaves its web. I have been feeling disheartened, as if my heart is contorted, as if I cannot take in life. But now, here is the spider. For the past few minutes, it has been pulling threads, weaving its web, making its medicine. The world hurts me hard, and because of certain experiences, I have a habit of giving up hope easily. But something about the spider kindles my heart, creates a hearth inside. The sun shines on the threads she is spinning. The light fragments inside the dewdrops into pieces of the rainbow.

My attention is consumed by this little spider spinning. I am part of her world. It's like a poultice across my heart. Over the next few months, I let the spider webs grow in the balcony. I know I will have to get rid of them at some point, but they are a portal into magic, into a world where a spider follows its instincts and weaves magic. When I look into the outside world like this, from behind her lacelike curtain, it is subsumed by energy. There are worlds within our worlds, spinning life, dancing their own ecstatic dance.

It was also here, in this balcony, that the hummingbird had come. Another day when I had been hurting, feeling all alone. I had wanted to believe, but it was hard. Again and again, it seemed like I kept repeating the same pattern, just with different people. Now, at this stage in my life, it was people I was trying to be friends with. Why did I keep getting entangled, keep getting enmeshed? It was as if we were all beggars in this world handing out our hands for caring and love, and no one was filled up enough to give from a full heart.

I had thought that day of all the things that were hurting me, the deep lacerations of always being the misfit, the odd one out. It was maybe because I felt in so much trouble that I started praying that day, something I hardly ever did, even with all those alterations to my temple. *Please help me God. Please help me,* I called out to the scrawny trees outside the perimeter of the colony. *Please help me God. Please help me,* I called out to the chirping birds whose names I did not know. *Please help me God. Please help me,* I called out to the dull blue sky.

Almost immediately, within a few seconds of that fervent thought, that day, something had happened. A hummingbird had come, almost as if it had heard my silent prayers. First, it had hovered in front of me. Then, it had stopped in the middle. Finally, it had flown from one side of the balcony to the other. It had kept this on for a bit, as if trying to distract me, as if trying to pull me out of my miserable thoughts. Then, as swiftly as it had come, it had flown away.

145

Maybe, I had been in such a blackened mood and my prayers had been so sincere that it had heard me. The wind might have carried my message, or it might have tuned into a different layer of the world where you could hear more things. All I knew was that I had called, and something had listened.

It hadn't just listened. It had answered.

In that moment, I had felt as if I had been given an infusion of energy. But then, as the day had gone on, once again, my sceptical mind had pushed this aside. This was quite normal. Nothing so great had happened, I had told myself, almost as if something answering me as soon as I asked for it was an everyday occurrence.

But then, something more happened. The same experience happened again. It was another day. Again, I was letting myself pray. Again, just as before, the hummingbird came, within seconds, as if it could hear my prayers, as if it wanted to talk to me. Again, it hovered in front of me and danced here and there. But then, once again, after a moment of complete belief, I ran back into my rational mind.

For the next few months, whenever I walked near my house, a hummingbird would come. It would coast over my head for a bit before flying away. Sometimes, on our morning walks, I would stop and point one out to Rohit, till he grew used to it, and started pointing them out to me. I didn't know whether all of them were the same as "my" hummingbird, but now it felt as if all of them were mine.

In true Jungian fashion, soon after these visits began, I saw a flyer at the library for an upcoming talk on hummingbirds that was being given by a local photographer. Attending it solved one mystery. It turned out that not all hummingbirds were migratory birds just passing through. There was, in fact, one species that did not migrate to the Bay Area, but that actually lived here all year round. These were permanent residents.

That's why I had seen them over so many months. The photographer also talked about how hummingbirds were very intelligent and even remembered the flowers they had last visited for nectar, so they knew which ones had already been sipped empty. The tiny hummingbird's heart was huge, she said. It was relatively the largest of all animals at two and a half percent of its body weight. Hummingbirds were also, of course, the only birds that could fly backwards.

In the talk, she told us how we could make a mixture of sugar and water for our bird feeders to entice these enchanting creatures. My random thought about unnaturally fattening up some poor little bird was resolved when she told us that hummingbirds burn sugar so fast, they need to keep eating throughout the day.

Later on, when I looked up their shamanic meanings, there was mention of their ability to cover large distances, their adaptability and endurance as well as their staying power. Hummingbirds also have a unique hovering pattern that draws out the infinity sign, and so they are again connected to infinite possibilities like the spider. They also have a special affinity to flowers, and while I hadn't consciously registered it before my hummingbird came, I had been increasingly drawn to learning about flowers and their energetic properties.

After this talk, I ordered one of those red hummingbird

feeders from Amazon. Maybe, I could make greater friends with my hummingbird, I thought. Then, one day, something peculiar happened. Rohit and I hadn't gone on our morning walk that day, and I was prepping for breakfast. As I walked through the house, I suddenly saw my hummingbird. It was just outside the living room windows. It flew in front of the house, to one side and then the other, a little ribbon in the air. For some time, it carried on like this, till it finally realized that I wasn't coming out. Then, it flew away.

Something about this made me very uncomfortable. Was I going to be responsible for my hummingbird, responsible for feeding it? Something about it made me very resistant, as if I was not comfortable with such intimacy.

Over the next few weeks, I still went for walks, sometimes on my own, sometimes with Rohit, but more and more, I felt like staying inside. Slowly, most of these walks petered out. I stopped seeking the hummingbird. Soon, it stopped coming for me.

In the stream of life happening around, I let the magic slip. What was that burden I felt? Was I afraid of opening up to more relationship, more responsibility for something else? I was always trying to relate to people or rather trying to take care of them, and to get them to like me. But now that something had started relating back to me, it had become more difficult. It was now all up to me, and I wasn't sure what to do.

The hummingbird slipped out of my hand. I was disappointed and a little ashamed of myself.

But still, with all these encounters, something changed.

The feminine was still sprouting, still growing talons. In time, in the study, on top of a bookshelf, there now stood a resplendent statue of Saraswati. It was bigger than the one in my little shrine. It had called out to me in *East West*, Saraswati, resplendent in her iris-blue saree, playing the *veena*. The first time I had looked at it, I had stopped myself from buying it although I felt such a pull, such a feeling. I am a magpie, always collecting things, and here was another. But then I regretted it and went back, hoping it was still there. It was. I bought it and enthroned it on top of a bookshelf.

Statuettes of deities are normally kept in a separate shrine, but wasn't the bookshelf a kind of shrine as well? Wasn't this Saraswati's natural home? I was a little hesitant about bending the rules, but then I decided to put the statue on the top. I liked it there.

This making up my own rules in the last few years has felt freeing. I have thought again and again of how the first people who made images of Gods, carved *murtis* and statues of deities, were probably artistes giving form to a feeling. It was probably a long time afterwards that rules and regulations about how to pray and how to relate to these images codified. When these rules for relationship become claustrophobic, I think it's then that a new religion comes up, which again shatters the old forms, shatters the old rules, and starts again, starts with the word, starts with the sound, starts with the mystery.

It feels like a never-ending cycle. Nothing we make is quite perfect. We have to keep making and re-making even the way we think of God. But there is something in us, and it's always been there, that wants to give shape to the shapeless. That's what these *murtis* are to me, forms of ideas and thoughts and feelings. The colors that adorn them are the colors of some quality, like the purity of the white associated with Saraswati's clarity or the fullness of the red and gold associated with Lakshmi's abundance.

In Saraswati's flourish, in Sita's faithfulness and in Radha's allure are little mirrors I can gaze into. The feminine has always been there. It has rested in the lazy afternoons of my childhood, in the winds scented with mango trees, in the fragrance of the heady *agarbattis* lit for prayers, in the bright orange marigolds in my grandparents' garden. In the nights when the power went out, and all of us kids were excited and animatedly searching for candles and flashlights, in those ink-black nights, the breeze made the trees sway and the moon glowed silver. The dark, the rest, the peace, the gliding light, that's where the feminine was. In it, all the world hung like a pendulum, moving, swaying, breathing, cradled in being.

Now, in the linear choppy rhythms of learned life, decades between me and the child that I was, the one who looked at the moon, knowing and dreaming, I long to hear that breeze, long to hope for time broken open like flowers. I want to see once again that I am free, that child who roamed in her imagination, who was connected to the marrow of the world.

That's what I try to find in my God, that freedom, that sense of being loved, that feeling in my feet as they touch the bare ground, that aliveness that is like growing on a vine or falling like cotton on a piece of moist land next to a river.

What I want from my God is my connection to me.

But I also know that I have a sceptical, rational streak. It has stood me well at times. But it's also something that keeps me from jumping headfirst into the mystery of things. But maybe, falling headfirst has never been my way. Maybe, I am one of those who light a candle, who listen to the breeze, who dream in the day as well as in the night, and who slowly invite themselves to be changed. Going headlong only scares you, while going slow gives you a chance to breathe.

In my two steps forward, one step back, there are only a few things I know for sure. I know that feeling in my heart when it opens. I know that feeling when colors become an unfolding road, when words glide over each other. Then, there is that ease we all look so desperately for sometimes. Maybe, the challenge is to live inside this feeling, instead of trying to figure out, for sure, whether there is a God or not. Whatever that God or Goddess might be, it lives in my own spirit. It helps me sing my own song. It is what I pray to, to help my wounds close up. It is what helps me start once more, all over again.

The Native Americans say that if you have stopped singing, if you have stopped dancing, your spirit leaves. As someone who loves to dance, but doesn't dance enough, this appeals to me very much. It tells me that I can search for God not through circling inside the maze of my mind but through remembering that I cannot be separate from what I carry inside.

It's through blowing the dust off my own being that the dancer and the dance become one.

After all, why would it be so hard to touch God?

Chapter 4

Re-Drawing the Meaning of the Word "Empath"

The word "empath" jumped up in my awareness a few years after I had already been in the States. When I first came across it, it felt so woo-woo and new-agey that the "normal" part of me balked at it. It was hard enough to own being a Highly Sensitive Person, words that had research backing them. But this empath thing, this was taking it even a step further. It veered off into ambiguous, questionable territory.

In fact, when I had first stumbled across the word online, trying to find a way to understand a part of my sensitivity that being an HSP didn't quite encapsulate, I hadn't even thought that it could possibly have anything to do with me. But the more I listened to other people's stories, the more I followed the breadcrumbs, the more it started feeling that although the words that people used to describe their empath experiences were foreign, what they were talking about was essentially my own experience. It was just that some of these people connected that experience to belief systems I didn't always resonate with while some others wrapped up the word in explanations that felt like the making up of a false story.

But slowly, I could see that at the heart of it, beyond the cloak of words, beyond the different interpretations that people gave, our experiences felt similar. Like these so-called empaths, I often felt flooded with other people's feelings. Their curiosity, worry and frustration jumped out at me. This often made me feel like I was walking through emotional minefields or collecting new feelings like you would collect scraps of paper.

Going back to India after moving to the States, each time, I was stuck by how much all the little daily interactions, packed tightly in one day, which were part of my parents' Delhi household, affected me energetically. Living in suburban America, I had often found the quiet too much. Then, I had thought nostalgically about India. Weeks could pass here without anyone so much as ringing the bell to our house. But it seemed like I had conveniently forgotten the other side of the story, forgotten how overstimulating Delhi had always been for me.

There was, of course, the familiar sensory overload all around - the continuous honking of horns, the laborers working noisily in the house next door, the continuous ringing of the bell as different people came and went - the *dhobi* taking the clothes for ironing, the *koodawalla* come to pick up the daily trash, the delivery boy delivering groceries from the neighborhood *kiraana* store. But apart from these interruptions, inconveniences and overstimulations, there was also something more.

In Delhi, every day, more lives touched mine in a day than they did in weeks in America. Going back, I could see, clearly for the first time, how much this sensory overload cost me and how much other people's feelings leaked into mine, so much so that I almost felt them in my body. I could see that the *koodawalla,* the one I had always liked, the one from some kind of a "lower caste," had changed in these past few years.

He was angry now, unlike the calm resignation, almost acceptance he had carried inside him before. His anger seemed to jump out at me, as if he thought I was part of a whole tribe of people who had kept people like him down for years, who had relegated him to this lower caste, who had only given him the permission to do "dirty," degrading work, like collecting the trash.

I could see why he thought so, even though I didn't believe in the caste system, even though when people asked me about it in the States, I gave examples of inter-caste marriages and told them I had lived in India's capital, not in some small town or village. India, itself, lived in different centuries at the same time, I would explain to them, paraphrasing lines by Arundhati Roy, the celebrated Indian writer.

But now, here was the leaping flame of the *koodawalla's* anger. I had felt both singed by it and a little ashamed. He was part of my story too. I wondered what had happened to him in these years, what had shifted him away from compliance. It was probably a better place to be, this twisting and forming in anger rather than trudging along obediently like a workhorse. I knew that. But didn't anyone else see his anger? Didn't anyone else feel it? When he went house to house every day, when someone opened the door for him, didn't they experience the burn of that flame that seemed to leap out at me? Didn't they feel as if they had stepped right inside a circle of fire?

Each day, every day, in Delhi, it was as if there was yet another interaction like this, yet another example of my emotional porousness. After months of relative peace and quiet in America, this melding and chaos seemed to underline the fact that at least some of my emotional tumult was not because of my own feelings, but because of absorbing someone else's feelings. Walking in the neighborhood one day, I had purposefully ignored one of the neighborhood "uncles," as we are taught to call them in India.

In one of my earlier visits, he had expressed outright surprise that I had put on so much weight considering how people in America were so into fitness. He had been to New York to visit his son, so, of course, he knew all about Americans. He was right, about the weight, at any rate, but I had been offended. This time, I had decided not to engage with him if I came across him in Delhi. Like the *koodawalla*, the last few years had sharpened the edge of my anger. Maybe, this was why people thought they could say anything to me. It was because I took it. I was too open, too "nice." This time, I wouldn't have any of it.

Later on, when I had come to know that this uncle, someone I hardly knew, had developed cancer, I had thought back to this interaction, about how I had noticed his resentment, the way in which he, himself, had changed over those years. Even then, when I had pretended I didn't see him, he had looked different. His domineering anger seemed to have changed into curdling resentment. He had always had that thing that made him want to attack everyone. But he was no longer young, no longer someone people listened to because they had to. I had felt that flash of anger when I had also ignored him.

That day, I had thought about how difficult it was to set boundaries, even such small ones, when you registered everything, when you felt the intensity of someone's feelings in your own body, when you could see what else they might be struggling with underneath the mask.

Had it been wrong for me to ignore him? I knew I wasn't responsible for his underlying resentment or for his cancer. But was I responsible for always taking care of every uncomfortable feeling that I ever saw or felt vicariously? Was I responsible for always being the nice one, the one who put others' feelings first? Was I not learning about my own feelings, about the boundaries of my own giving, about the resentment that was curdling inside of me?

These were difficult questions, especially for someone like me, so invested in being nice. I wanted people to like me. I didn't want to be responsible for hurting them. I felt guilty even when I thought about people like that Delhi uncle, so far removed from my life, people who had been outright rude to me, but who seemed to infringe into my life so easily when I started feeling like I had done something wrong. Intellectually, I knew there were limits to my responsibility. But on the level of feelings, I was still struggling with my boundaries.

It was frustrating, this bashing of my head against the same kinds of traps over and over again. Even here in the States, while trying to make friends, I thought I was doing the right things, like listening before I expected to be listened to. But more often than not, things would take a nosedive. Again and again, I had repeated this pattern of giving and listening and then becoming dark with resentment. Sometimes, after a certain point, I would completely cut off from people. It seemed like this was one pattern that was common amongst empaths. Why was it that I was creating the same kind of interaction again and again?

But it wasn't just potential friendships that were affected. It seemed as if I was constantly finding people, even strangers who wanted to tell me things about themselves. At first, when someone opened up to me, I was genuinely interested. I genuinely cared. But then, once again, as my own energy tumbled down, it seemed as if the dynamic would get skewed. Again, I would start feeling, not like the "good" person I was trying to be, but like a dumping ground, like a receptacle for waste.

Slowly, I had started seeing that this venting that other people did with me, that I let them do with me, more often than not, didn't even really help them. It didn't create anything of lasting value. It was as if I was giving pieces of myself away, but in the end, it amounted to nothing. All it did was give temporary relief and then for that other person, it was usually back to square one. It seemed like I couldn't really help them. It seemed like I should focus on myself and create something of value myself, instead of feeling ill-used half of the time. I was the common denominator in all my experiences, and it was up to me to build better boundaries.

But it was a task that felt fraught with difficulties. It was as if a part of me that was undeveloped as my own caretaker was trying to build better fences but failing again and again. In my dreamworld, helpless little children often showed up. In one such dream, it was the middle of the night. A teenage boy was in a room with three or four children he was looking after. I knew he was doing his best. He really was. But even with all his sincerity, this was all too much for him. He was trying to take care of the infant screaming in his arms while he also tried to impose some order on the other children milling around.

In the dream, it goes like this. The teenage boy is feeling overwhelmed by all these demands. Then, all of a sudden, he hears a noise. As the observer in the dream, I instantly know that these children are hiding from some very dangerous people. But this boy, even though he has tried his utmost, done everything he could, has made a grave mistake. In all this confusion, he has forgotten to lock the main door. Now, as he hears the enemy move outside the house, his heart jumps in his chest. He desperately tries to gather the children and get them to an inner room.

When I woke up the next day, this was the extent of the dream that I remembered. Would this boy be able to protect those little kids? Would the enemy overpower them? Why had he made such a basic mistake? Why had the situation gone so wrong? In my day-to-day life, the little child in me had been flailing harder and harder.

Now, whenever I listened to someone over-long, I could feel myself getting more and more antsy. I could see that I wasn't an inexhaustible source, that I was not all love and light, that I was also a person with needs and limited energy, who needed to have some energy come back to them, who had to pay attention to the little child who screamed inside when she wasn't listened to. I had to develop the self-protectiveness that seemed to be lacking in that teenage boy in my dream, who I knew was doing his best but who sometimes also forgot the most fundamental things, like locking the front door.

The threads of real empathy and people pleasing had gotten confusingly jumbled up for me. I did think there was truth to the empath bit even though other people discounted it. They didn't quite understand how someone's anger or fear could enter my bloodstream. They couldn't understand how permeable I felt to catching other people's feelings, almost like you would catch a cold.

But maybe, there was also some truth to the fact that at least some of this had less to do with me being emotionally sensitive or an empath and more to do with feeling responsible for other people's feelings. Maybe, this was the co-dependent bit, the explanation that some people gave when I tried to find out more about so deeply feeling other people's feelings. They thought it was emotional entanglement, not empathy, that I was suffering from. Could that be true? Why else would I feel almost like it was an emergency to help people?

How could I untangle my mess of beliefs? How could I not give in this compulsive way? How could I empathize with that part of myself that had learned to be a shock absorber for other's feelings, whose natural sensitivity got complicated by the anxiety the little child inside her felt. This little child felt so anxious and like it *had* to take care of other's feelings. This little child believed that if it didn't do so, something terrible would happen.

How could I have compassion for this little child, this overwhelmed part of me that caused me to sometimes isolate myself? When the burden of feeling all sorts of different feelings threatened to topple me over, it felt like I had to get away from people to protect myself, to be a separate, cohesive person.

How could I deconstruct this confusing system that seemed to feed on itself? Like other empaths in those online forums, I often dealt with the danger of getting swamped by preempting other people's feelings. I took care of them. I made nice. I morphed clay-like into whatever wouldn't incite any strong feelings towards me. I took responsibility for feelings that people carried inside them, even if they had nothing to do with me.

It almost felt like just because I could sometimes see their feelings so clearly, peeking out or oozing and festering, that I was responsible for taking care of them. It was as if the very empathy that at first attracted people who were in need to me, that often affirmed I was a "good person," was actually full of holes, full of worms and maggots crawling out to eat me. Soon enough, I would find myself collecting those same tokens of resentment. Soon enough, I would start feeling taken advantage of all over again.

Why did these things keep happening when I was just trying to be a "good person?" Why did I end up getting so resentful when I was following the so-called golden rule? Was I wrong about what empathy was? Could there be such a thing as too-much empathy? Could there be such a thing as inappropriate giving? Or was it that I was not discerning enough and that I was discounting red flags because of my strong desire to have friends?

What exactly was I doing wrong?

As I built up my new life in the States, I would have to learn to soothe the little child, dismantle the rescuer and really think about what this whole empath thing meant. The new context I found myself in, being in a completely new place where everything I was creating depended on my own energy, became a catalyst for learning about my own needs, my own energy and my own boundaries.

Life as an Emotional Empath

In the beginning, when I first started thinking about what it meant to be an emotional empath, an incident that had occurred in my last workplace in India bobbed up in my awareness. It told me how I had framed picking up on people's feelings for myself and just how trapped and burdened I had often felt. At that time, it had felt like something was wrong with me, as if I was this weird person who caught on to odds and ends that just weighed me down.

But now, when I thought about this incident, it felt like a little opening had been created. Maybe, there was more to being an empath than just feeling cursed or burdened by feeling too many feelings that I didn't want to feel.

The incident had happened during the interview process for a new job. As part of my written interview, I had sat answering test questions on a desktop computer in an open office space. I had started typing out my answers but soon afterwards, my energy had started dipping low. It felt contracted, as if it was being pushed down, as if it was being tightened around me.

By the time I had finished the interview and gotten out, I had the beginnings of a splitting headache. The beating Delhi NCR sun and the noisy traffic had just added to that feeling of being locked up in a confined space. By the time I had reached home, though, my energy had somewhat stabilized.

This kind of thing often happened to me. I had chalked this up to picking up on someone's mood or energy in that office, something I was prone to doing, even though at that time I didn't know there was an "official" name for it. All I knew then was that this was another one of my weaknesses, this catching of other people's energy, this tumbling down into some new pit that could open up, anywhere, anytime, without any advance notice, without my being able to control it. The only weird thing was that this didn't *always* happen. I didn't *always* entrain with other people's energy, even when it was strong or overpowering or loud. But I *often* did.

Even in my home in suburban America, far removed from overwhelming Delhi, in itself the size of a small country, I still sometimes felt that same sense of overwhelm I had felt that day in that office when I "caught" some feeling. It could be something innocuous like taking the VTA train to get around in the Valley and being seated in front of someone who was feeling a strong feeling. It would then feel like I had caught the energy of that feeling and it was dragging me down.

In one such ride, I got on the train and made my way right to the back, like I often did, and sat in front of an Indian woman. As the ride progressed, I could feel her curiosity jumping out at me. I felt distracted from what I was thinking, as if the energy was knocking on my back. The feeling was so obvious it was almost like an underlined statement.

One of our running jokes was how some Indians seemed so surprised to see another Indian here in the Valley even though there was a significant Indian population here. But on a more serious note, in this case, I thought about how this woman was probably someone new to this place, someone who might have recently relocated. There was nothing inherently wrong with her curiosity.

The only thing was that whenever I came across a person like this, someone intensely curious or someone lonely and wanting to talk or someone angrily speaking on the phone, I would feel myself getting pulled into their emotional world straightaway. It was as if we lived on a continuum, as if there was no separation, none of that *"know where your feelings end and others' feelings start"* that books on boundaries talked about.

It felt like such an impediment. Could I not go through

the world in peace, just dealing with my own feelings? Could I not again stumble onto something that other people were trying to hide but that seemed apparent to me?

But at least now, knowing that I was an empath, I had a little more self-awareness. I had been trying all the little suggestions I had come across about protecting your energy and space. One of these methods had talked about not sitting directly opposite someone whose energy you didn't want to pick up on. It was better to sit on their side or with your body slightly angled away. I think I came across it in some books on *Chakras,* including one by the noted psychic Sonia Choquette.

These books also talked about how crossing your arms in front of you was a way to stop energy from invading your personal space, from getting into your solar plexus chakra. This was an interesting thing for me personally because somewhere in my teens, I had decided to do exactly the opposite.

In some rudimentary book on body language, I had read how crossing your arms was a defensive position. To me, it had seemed like the mark of a closed person, not open to things, not willing to accept something new, and in my naive teenage surety, I had decided that I wouldn't close myself down like this. Now, reading this different perspective about a quite basic way to guard yourself, I felt immensely silly. That undiscerning openness had not just been embedded in my posture, it was also embedded in a corresponding belief that said I shouldn't judge in any way, that I should be indiscriminately open to people and situations.

But now, with my new knowledge, it was time to be more

discerning. Now, when I came across people around whose energy I felt uncomfortable, or on days when I felt tired and couldn't simply remain centred in myself, I physically moved away. If someone was angrily talking on the phone in the train, for example, I started giving myself permission to move instead of sitting there and pretending it didn't bother me. It did. I had two options. Either I could try and stay centred. If I wasn't able to do that, it was better to have a physical boundary.

Another thing I had learnt during this time helped me take another small step in my empath journey. On a visit to an energy healer when I was feeling really down, almost out of nowhere, she told me that I needed more sleep than normally recommended. It was a good idea to sleep longer, even for nine hours or more. She had just given me a very accurate reading of my energy and my challenges, so this suggestion made an impression on me.

I was already someone who slept well and relatively long, very different from people who often talk about needing less sleep almost like a status symbol. But I had always been vaguely ashamed of this fact, as if it made me somehow "less than," less grown-up in some way than others who could so easily sacrifice sleep. In contrast, sleeping fewer hours always made me irritable and left me snapping at everyone around me.

But now, this implicit permission, this someone telling me something so specific about my needs felt like another step forward. The mystery of why I felt so sleepy after I had engaged in draining conversations was also solved. That had always made me feel like I was weird, an anomaly, as if "something" had come over me seemingly out of nowhere. But now, I could see that this signalled that my energy had been drained. It was a *tell*, a way to notice which interactions were costly energy-wise.

This process of accepting myself as an empath was similar to the little pieces of self-acceptance I had strung together when I realized I was an HSP. The fact that I got startled by loud noises, for example, had no longer meant that I was a scaredy cat. It just meant that I had a sensitive nervous system. It indicated responsiveness, not fear. This was rewriting some of the stories I had heard and that I had told myself about my sensitivity while growing up. One that stood out was an early memory from childhood.

In our summer vacations, at my *naani's* place, we were allowed to go to the neighborhood park on our own. With its swing sets, origami-looking painted concrete ducks on which little children could sit and a mighty giraffe with a ladder at the back on which older children could climb, it was a far cry from the mostly barren patches of green that were part of my Delhi neighborhood. Every summer, right from the time when I was quite little and someone tried to get me to climb those stairs to get to the top of the giraffe's back, every summer, I would think that this was going to be that year, the year when I finally did that impossible feat.

Every year, often alone, I would go by myself and try to climb those stairs. Just a few steps would make me feel scared and I would cop out. Every year, I would try to be bold and fearless, just like all those other children who scrambled up quickly. Every year, I would tell myself what a coward I was for being so scared to fall, of being so scared to get hurt.

It was a little thing but one of those little things that my childhood was full of, times when other people labeled me sensitive or weak or shy or, worse, times when I incessantly scolded myself for being this sensitive and this weak and this shy. In time, any one of these words had started implying the others. Sensitive meant weak. Shy meant weak. Sensitive meant being unable to bear hurt. It meant being vulnerable. It meant that people could push you around.

When I was seven or eight, I remember another incident in this same park when two little boys around my age roughed me up. They hadn't looked like they belonged in this self-contained little township that mostly housed engineers who worked in the nearby refinery. They had looked like street kids. I think I had tried to fight back but I was a little girl and they were aggressive. Afterwards, for days, I had been scared of even entering the park. I had felt that hurt of not just being physically weaker but also someone who didn't naturally take to fighting.

Very soon in that unprovoked scuffle, tears had stung my eyes. I had tried my best not to cry but tears seemed to come easily to me. But to cry also meant that you gave away your power. In this case, at any rate, I had obviously come out one down.

It was after many days that my *naani* had ferreted out the secret. As luck would have it, those boys had been in the park when we went there together. After they had been given a dressing down, they had never bothered me again and after some days, I didn't see them ever again. Afterwards, I had felt both relieved and a little guilty when I thought they had been scolded because of me. I had known they were trying to get power, in one way or another. When they had been talked to, they had looked little, just like me. They had been dressed in tattered shirts, and I knew they had it much worse than me.

But this was one of those few childhood experiences where I had actually told someone and they had come to my aid. But there had been other incidents. I knew even then that children bullied you to feel good about themselves. But there was a certain shame in being the weak one, the one who got bullied, the one who could be easily dominated.

As a quiet child who was often on her own, I was also an easy target. But that sense of not knowing how to deal with those more aggressive than me, even those whom I understood on one level, is something I still carry with me. It would also take me many years to peel off that label of shy, that label that is put on sensitive children who just like to observe.

Just as looking back with my new knowledge of being an HSP had helped me have compassion for that little sensitive child oscillating between self-awareness and self-criticism, thinking about this new empath bit had started to give me a little more context. It was telling me something more about the background of my life.

Now, when I looked back on my experiences, like in that office in India, I had a little more compassion for myself. Maybe, as a result of this compassion, I could now also think of another explanation for what had happened that day. Maybe, just maybe, the fact that my energy had dipped so low didn't only mean I felt other people's feelings in my own body and got overwhelmed. Maybe, it was also one more thing. Maybe, my body was also telling me something important about *my own reaction* to the energy of that place.

In the initial interview, my body had actually picked up on things that later turned out to be true. My experience in that workplace had turned out to be exactly like that energy I had first experienced there. I had felt cramped, hemmed in. I had felt my energy getting depleted and running low. As time had passed, I had learnt the dynamics in that office were heavily politicized. The rules were ambiguous, sometimes deliberately so. When I had finally left that job, it had been like stepping into open air and finally being able to breathe.

My body, in that initial interview, had been like a barometer that gave me an accurate reading.

If this was true, then it also meant that I needed to pay attention when my energy see-sawed. I needed to realize I was picking up on the energy of a situation. My sensitive self acted like a ringing warning bell whenever I was going to walk into something wrong for me. But I was often so preoccupied with feeling the negative weight of whatever it was I was feeling and so preoccupied with believing that something was wrong with me that I just couldn't see this.

I couldn't see that I intuitively picked up on energy. I couldn't see this had a good side.

Maybe, this jumble of feelings that we can't quite sort out is what makes life so hard sometimes for emotional empaths. At first, maybe for a long time, it's hard to know when is it that you are sensing and absorbing other people's feelings and when is it your own body responding. It's almost as if our bodies feel so much, we have to first become really comfortable with the entire dictionary of feelings. Only then can we sort these feelings out.

Maybe, we also get lost because some of us are turning

away so hard from our giant feelings that we expend all our energy trying to keep a tight lid on them. We can feel as if our feelings are an enemy that is constantly turning against us and as if we, ourselves, are a big, unsolvable problem. Maybe, because our feelings feel so strong and we don't know what to do with them that we instead turn outwards and become an expert at other people's feelings, so we can control our own.

But maybe, as I did, when you look back, you will see that a lot of the things that you thought were wrong with you, a lot of those ends that you wanted to trim right off so you could finally fit, were only things that *felt* wrong because you were looking at yourself through someone else's eyes. You were making a superhuman effort to become something that was not you, that was, in fact, the opposite of you. We have all felt the sting of people's words. We have all thought that feeling so much, all the time, really *is* problematic. So, it's easy to imagine how we can start believing other people know more about us than we ourselves do.

With years of abandoning myself behind me, I could now start seeing that maybe, just maybe, some of my problems were because of the fact that I was the one constantly turning against myself. I was the one who didn't listen to my body and its warnings, who couldn't stitch together the meaning of the information it brought me. I was the one with such little self-trust that I often gave up my own sense of things and abandoned my intuition. Maybe, I could start making friends with both my body and my intuitive sense. Maybe, that would make my new world easier to navigate.

Learning to tune in to my intuition also felt like a way to cut through my overwhelm, to zoom out and focus on the bigger picture. Sometimes, I noticed so many nuances that it was counter-productive. I just got overwhelmed by all this noticing and seeing. It was only when I put these disparate details into a context that they finally became helpful.

This is what had happened to me while noticing differences in American culture in the first few years. Until I had a context, until I gave credence to my noticing and contextualized the subtle nuances I had picked up on by consciously learning about cultural differences, my experience had been like sitting under a pounding waterfall. Something powerful was happening. But that power was just pounding me down. But as soon as I could fit things within a framework, as soon as I could objectively say which things were caused by cultural differences and which were simply personal differences, it had gotten much easier. Then, it was like standing in the river downstream where the water flowed slowly and softly, where life was calm and understandable.

As I started reading about empaths on the one hand and honing my intuition on the other, it felt like I had found a way to both connect to myself as well as others. In online forums, many empaths talked about experiences that resonated with me, such as how they avoided crowded places like malls where they were inundated with people's emotions.

Some even talked about how they often knew something deeply personal about someone without even knowing them, such as if a person had been abused in some way. It was as if emotional subtext was the actual text for them, the writing on the wall, as if many of those things that are considered hidden weren't hidden to them.

Like them, I had had many experiences in my life where I had known things about people without being told. These weren't little things. Later on, when I had come to know that person, these "knowings" had been verified. Some of these intuitive experiences were just resonance. It was a bit like how someone with a certain experience can recognize other people with a similar kind of experience.

But there had also been other not so easily explained away things. Sometimes, the knowing was something basic like feeling there was something "off" about someone's energy very early on. This was usually when everyone around me was telling me otherwise, when there was no "logical" reason to feel this way, when I was almost a little ashamed of being judgmental.

At these times, it had been hard to hold on to my own inner sense. I felt invalidated when other people didn't see what I was seeing, and I questioned why I was having such intense reactions. But by the time I had reached the States, time and experience had shown me how often, my feelings had been spot on. There was something to be said for validating my own intuition. Maybe, I caught on to some things because I was "sensitive" or intuitive. Maybe, I sensed some things because as a child, I was always on the outside, looking in. Being an outsider means you become an expert at others people's feelings.

Whatever it was, something inside me, something I frequently abandoned, knew things that could help protect me. I think this was the first time I thought I was "so different." While I had always thought of myself as an outsider, I had never realized I sometimes picked up on details that many people didn't even notice. With this realization, my journey into learning about my intuition began.

But on the way, more questions came up. One of the big ones was that life-long doubt about whether feeling this much was even a good thing in the first place. Yes, feelings were important. But feeling this intensely about other people's feelings, was that good? Was this really a gift like some people said or was this just an unhealthy adaptation?

The Difference Between Being an Emotional Empath and Being Codependent

In the beginning, when I first started calling myself an "empath," a weird thing had happened. It was as if the numbed down parts of myself came back to life. After years, the sensitive self I had buried under my rational mind seemed to have awakened. I felt acutely open to everything around me. Even if I just saw a movie in which someone fell or had an accident, I felt their pain. No wonder so many empaths talked about how hard it was for them to see shows with violence.

That hadn't quite been my experience. I had gone in the direction of "toughening myself up," in whatever little way I could. But now, all of a sudden, because I wasn't numbing myself any more, it felt like my sensitivity was causing even more pain than it already did.

At first, it had almost felt good to be more sensate again, as if I was calling back an abandoned part of myself. But now, another thought struck me. The more I considered what was happening, the more problematic it felt. When I watched a T.V. show, for example, in which someone fell off a building, I felt a wave of pain run through my body. But obviously, the people in the T.V. show or the movie were not actually hurt. They were just acting. But I was reacting intensely to this made-up feeling. This meant that anyone who was affecting a feeling, who was putting it on, could con me.

Being an emotional empath or sensing feelings did not mean I was living in someone else's body. It did not mean I could pull back the covers to see their intentions or their belief systems. Even if someone was actually fearful or angry or sad, that could be tied up to beliefs or value systems I didn't believe in. I was simply hyper-sensitive to changes in feelings, but the origin of those feelings could be anything. Hadn't I met enough people who tried to intimidate others by appearing more forceful, more domineering, and more angry on the outside than they actually felt?

That was something commonplace in my corporate life. As someone who blamed herself easily all too often, I had encountered many such people. At some point, when I had started cleaning out this part of my life, when I had stopped taking on blame when it wasn't my fault, I had seen how easily some unhealthy managers turned from me to someone else in the team, someone who also felt over-responsible but who I could objectively see wasn't actually responsible for whatever mess we were in.

This meant that registering feelings so immediately didn't always serve you well. Feelings were not an accurate map of what someone *really* felt all the time. Even when the feelings were "real," the person behind them had reached them through their own pathway. When I responded to them because they felt uncomfortable, I was often selling myself short. I was subscribing to thoughts, beliefs and ways of thinking that were part of someone else's value system.

Feelings were just one part of understanding someone. They were just one part of responding with empathy. They were not the be all and the end all.

Also, sometimes, when I was responding to people, it wasn't empathy at all. It was enmeshment or not being discerning enough when someone was going "poor me." At other times, it wasn't empathy but sympathy, when some kernel of the other person's experience touched some issue inside me. I couldn't club all my problems with boundaries under one thing or say they *all* had to do with being an empath. I had to pull all these different threads apart.

When was I getting overloaded by the intuitive information I was picking up on? When was it co-dependence and my acting out unhealthy emotional patterns that were deeply entrenched?

Once I had started exploring the empath arena, I had gradually also started reading more "alternative" stuff by thinkers and writers with a more spiritual perspective, even though I still read them in hiding, so to speak. It felt like a way to think about *why* I picked up on all the unexplainable things I did and a way to find a purpose for them.

Some of the first alternative books I had read were those by Rose Rosetree. In one of them, *Become the Most Important Person in the Room*, Rosetree had talked about how empaths were different from other people. For "unskilled empaths," their own self disappeared in a haze because they were so acutely tuned in to other people's emotions. Unlike other people, empaths were *not* the most important person in the room, even to themselves.

This was definitely how I often felt. My own self got fogged up with other people's feelings. My attention seemed to go towards whatever the loudest feelings screaming in that room were, even if no one had uttered one single word. This, of course, felt grossly unfair. This always losing my space in my own life, this finding it hard to set boundaries because I could feel the red-hot tail of someone's anger flashing out at me when I said No. This left me bouncing around with other people's feelings.

Just as Rose Rosetree had so picturesquely described, I noticed many details I didn't know what to do with. I noticed everything from the person standing around in the corner being passive aggressive to someone outrageously flirting with someone even when they thought they were being subtle to someone feeling extremely lonely. Of course, all this noticing and feeling was not *always* gloom and doom. With people who felt like kindred spirits, sometimes, it also felt as if my energy was entrained. Then, it would ring clearly like a bell. But more often than not, it was that other experience that prevailed, the feeling of being overwhelmed, the feeling of not knowing what to do.

In her work, Rosetree talked about different kinds of empaths. When I read more books like hers, it seemed to me that "empath" was a catch-all term, the best we have right now, for many kinds of intuitive experiences. One person who calls themselves an empath might have a very different experience than another empath. It turned out that some empaths felt other people's feelings in their body, just like I did. This ability was called *clairsentience* in spiritual circles, clearly sensing something in your body.

Another kind of empath could be someone who feels other people's *physical* way of being in their body. So, if someone they know has a headache, for example, they might develop a headache as well. I had not experienced this myself, but I could think of at least one person I knew like this.

People like Rosetree had the worldview that while being an empath was challenging, especially when you didn't know what to do with it, it was also a gift. It was a way of knowing things outside the realm of the five senses. It was a way of knowing things deep inside your body. It was a way of being that could help you and carve out a path for you.

This was not the first time I had come across the word *clairsentient*. But it was the first time I had consciously paid attention to it. If clear sensing was a way into my intuition, into trusting my own judgment, then I wanted to learn more about it. As I thought about where else I had come across the term, I thought about my copy of somatic therapist Anodea Judith's book *Eastern Body, Western Mind*. It was one of my favorites and a modern classic on emotional healing. In it, Judith connects the Chakra system, which comes from Yoga philosophy and talks about subtle energy, with different modern Western schools of psychology.

So, with great excitement, I had leafed through the dense book to try and find the place where Judith had mentioned clairsentience. But when I found it, it was clear that Judith didn't talk about clairsentience in the mostly complimentary way that the other writers had. Instead, she mentioned how this ability to sense other people's emotions came from being too other-focused and not grounded enough in your own body. A little clairsentience was a good thing. It made you sensitive to others. But a lot of it separated you from your own self. It left you open to being tossed around in a sea of other people's feelings and reactions, which, obviously, you had no control over.

According to Anodea Judith, this overdeveloped sense of others' feelings could be traced back to childhood experiences. If you couldn't genuinely express your feelings as a child or if your more forceful feelings were vilified, you didn't get a chance to form a separate identity that was based on your own emotional experience. You were almost trained to morph into whatever was most pleasing to others. At that time, because you were genuinely dependent on your caregivers, you became a shapeshifter, acutely attuned to others' feelings but out of touch with your own.

Reading this perspective made me feel disheartened in the beginning. Here was another person, someone whose work I had long admired, who thought that my entire way of being was an adaptation, something to correct. It wasn't that I didn't see the truth in her perspective. Part of this feeling other people's feelings business *was* unhealthy.

It was as if, at some point in the past, I had learned to be a shock absorber for other people's emotions, and now, there was a complicated criss-cross of beliefs and emotional trenches that still made me act like this emotional lightning rod. When I acted like this, I was letting people's energy run through me. I was the conductor through which it passed into the ground. But I, myself, was fried.

But the good news was that if some of this was simply an emotional pattern, then something could be done about it. I could weed out the inappropriate over-feeling. I could look at my beliefs about *why* I needed to take care of others emotionally. This held promise.

But was this all? Was this just an unhealthy adaptation? Even though I realized the truth in Judith's words, some part of me still felt the drip-drip and acid burn of this way of thinking. Was all the feeling-too-much, all this sensing nebulous feelings and subtle details all for nothing? Was all this heartache for nothing? Was it just a gnarly thing that grew out of my past?

Could it be that the others were right too, that there might be the seeds of an actual gift inside, if I could strip away the unhealthy part that Judith had talked about? Inside the morass of people pleasing and hiding my true opinions and playing nice and playing dead, was it possible that there was something good about this new word I had discovered?

Clairsentience. Clear sensing. Clear knowing?

Might it actually be tied in to something more, to some higher purpose? I wasn't a hundred percent sure but I knew I *did* still want to learn about my intuition. I had turned away from it too many times in my life and paid the price afterwards to know that I had to stop talking myself out of it. This was the only silver lining from all those wrong turns. Now I knew there was a way of knowing that came from a deeper place inside me. I had to learn about it and honor it. The word clairsentience felt like one door into my intuition, one clue that might lead to finding some buried treasure.

One of my latest "teaching" experiences about my intuition had come in one of my writing meetups. I had become friendly with someone on whom I had pinned quite a lot of hopes. I had thought she would be one of *my own* friends here in the States apart from all of Rohit's friends whom I knew. On paper, we had a lot in common. We both liked to talk about books and book-related topics. We wanted to write. We were both introverts.

But on that day when we had first met, when I had sat alone on the table with the meetup group's sign, the rest of the people still to show up, when she had stood paying for her coffee and before we had ever exchanged a single word, before all of that, the first thing that had come up for me was: "*She is self-absorbed.*" It was a very clear sense, not some voice I heard but just a clear knowledge. It wasn't loud or emphatic. It didn't have that caustic lick that comes when we make a quick judgment about someone. It was just there.

But then, as soon as we had started talking, and later on, as we had become friendly, I had discounted that first sense, that first feeling. How could I even be sure? There was no logical proof for it. Besides, our friendship was going so well. What could possibly go wrong? Even when the cracks had started showing up, quite soon afterwards, I had doubted myself. Even when I had listened and listened and she didn't seem very interested in listening to me, I had still felt unsure. After all, wasn't it right to give first and then expect to be given back to? After all, wasn't it selfish to be counting and tallying up all the time?

But then, as this dynamic had repeated itself, as I had tried to insert myself into one conversation after another and wasn't met with any interest, as I had thought again of why I kept on "attracting" the same kind of thing, with one person after another, one day my energy had dipped so low that I wanted to find someone else and just lash out at them.

But then afterwards, I had a little space in which I had thought that maybe, just maybe, I was again discounting my feelings. They were information as well. It wasn't unreasonable to want to take my turn. It wasn't unreasonable to want an energy exchange that felt fair.

Didn't I already know that you didn't really "attract" the wrong people? Before I had met Rohit, in some first and second dates I had, I had met people who seemed to jump right into saying one sexually inappropriate thing after another. Like other women, I had felt like a victim and wondered if I was the one doing something to "attract" people like these. Was I giving out the wrong vibes? What was I doing wrong? How could I control this? But with time and some really great resources, I had figured out that I wasn't "attracting" the wrong people.

It was just that when you put yourself out there, you will encounter *all* kinds of people, some right for you and some not. What I was doing wrong was not putting out some wrong vibe but rather not seeing the reality of the person. I was personalizing it. But I didn't need to get disheartened. I didn't need to believe there was no one out there for me. All I needed to do was cut my losses and move on.

In a similar way, it wasn't that I was doomed to keep "attracting" people who were self-absorbed. It was just that unlike other people with better boundaries or more self-trust who would have expected a fairer interaction, I was locked into a pattern. I was either discounting the reality of the other person or feeling pulled down by sunken beliefs that still chimed inside me, that said I had to keep on giving and giving before expecting anything at all in return. I had made a blanket value out of "giving," with beliefs that said things like "Nice people act like this" or "Good people put others first." But fairness was also a value, a value I seemed to have lost sight of completely.

All my different beliefs about being "giving," or "good," or "a nice woman," were, first one, then another, tripping me up. That's why these situations felt so hard. Often, it was about feeling "bad" when I did something to set a boundary. Then, an active, thorny belief often showed up. My identity was wound up tight in being a "giver." After all, if I wasn't a "giver," who was I? The truth was, without giving, I was lost, not knowing where to get my sense of self from, not knowing who I was, what I wanted, and what I felt.

These little pinpoints of clarity slowly started emerging during the time when I had started reclaiming my creative self. It was when I consciously decided that my new identity was going to be "writer" that some more things started to shift. The empty space left behind by taking apart the "giver" was a little bit filled by this new word. I could see myself as something different, acting as someone new. I said the word "writer" for myself in every new interaction, when I wrote a new guest post or when someone first contacted me for an interview for an expat forum.

At first, I didn't believe it. But the more I wrote and the more people emailed me when I wrote something that spoke to them or commented on a post, the more the word solidified. In the beginning, I had held onto it like a life raft. Now, it felt like it grew around me and that I, myself, was growing inside it.

I didn't have to be the person I had always been, the one who defined herself by what she did for others. I could be this other me, the creative me, the me who loved to explore, the me who had strong opinions underneath the half-truths I said to please people. I was still a giver in some ways and to some people, but now "giving" didn't always mean such a great thing. Sometimes, giving to the wrong people just encouraged bad behavior. It didn't work out like some idealistic movie in my head, where if you do good for others, they do good for you. In reality, the "good" people gave healthily and gave their share right from the beginning. It was not something for me to earn.

Now, as I attempted to work through these faulty beliefs about what it meant to be a "good person," I also threw my hat squarely in my intuition's corner. I would learn to trust it, experiment with it. I wouldn't question it just because I hadn't come up with rational, logical explanations. Of course, I would test it out, but in ambiguous situations, I would listen to my intuition.

Why was it that with my "friend," the exact information I needed about the exact thing I was struggling with was the first thing that had come up in my mind? Next time something like this happened, would I just sit and try to talk myself out of it? Or would I listen to this wiser part of myself?

Later on, as I explored my intuitive sense, I would learn that the word *intuition* comes from the Latin "teuri," which means to guard and protect. Intuition was a protective force, a force for good. It was something that nudged us. But it wasn't exactly like every other feeling. If I was feeling angry or disturbed or fearful and these feelings were driving me to act in some destructive or self-destructive way, that was *not* intuition. Intuition was always a protective shield.

It was like a clear feeling telling me of impending danger, its voice like that of the guard outside the door who kept watch. Even if it showed up as fear, that fear did not propel me towards a destructive action. It always protected me. But all this cautious guard could do was come and warn me. In the end, I seemed to have the executive power. I could listen to the guard. I could override it. It was up to me. Maybe, if I had been more discerning before and listened to this voice, I could have prevented all those caustic, murky feelings from flooding me.

Just like my dreams, my intuition came from some bigger part of me. Like them, it had an intelligence all of its own. It was my conditioning that I had to counter, the conditioning that slayed any evidence that didn't have to do with the mind. But the mind was not all there was. After all, even the mind is just a thing which had to be created by something else. Something more.

As this understanding coalesced, I went through any material on intuition that I could find. I read books. I went to any talk with the word "Intuition" in the title. I did any exercise that said it might help increase intuitive awareness. A lot of my creative expression, the art I did, also felt useful. It cleared the gunk of old feelings, which gave a chance for something clear to arise.

An insight I had come across informed this search. It said that while you couldn't directly *make* yourself have intuitive insights, you could make it *more likely* that intuitive insights occurred. Basically, you could create a more welcoming environment for them.

A big question for me was that although I felt I was a highly intuitive person who could tune into a lot of undercurrents and while I had often been quite good at predicting certain things, I had also often felt almost wholly disconnected from my inner guidance. Why had I been ruled not by my inner sense but by my chattering mind? Part of the answer came when I attended a "New Age" concert in the Ananda temple in a city called Palo Alto in the San Francisco Bay Area.

How Our Intuition Helps and Protects Us

Although I had heard of it described as a "temple" and dedicated to the Indian spiritual *guru* (master) Paramhansa Yogananda, when Rohit and I had walked into Ananda, it had looked more like a tiny church than a Hindu temple. Later on, I would come to know that Yogananda, whom I had only known before as the writer of the spiritual classic *Autobiography of a Yogi,* had come to America in 1920.

He had been the first of India's yoga *gurus* to make their home in the States. Over the next three decades of his life, he had lectured tirelessly, extolling the virtues of the yogic path. He had also emphasized the underlying unity of all religions and taught the mystical teachings of Christ. So, all in all, the Ananda temple with its pews and its stained glass was, in fact, a befitting place to be named after someone like him.

That day, as we had sat down in one of the pews in the middle, my first thoughts had been about the church attached to my Convent school in what was then called Bombay. A film of nostalgia still covered my feelings when I thought about India, and I was constantly discovering patches of familiarity wherever I went.

The hall had filled up quickly in that temple-church, and the growing excitement in the air was palpable. The program for the evening was a musical collaboration between David DiLullo, a drummer we had heard before and Steven Halpern, a Grammy-nominated musician considered to be one of the founding fathers of New Age music. As the buzz around us had crescendoed, someone behind me had talked about his recent trip to China and how surprised he had been to see all those skyscrapers there. Rohit had sat checking emails on his phone while I had hoped he wouldn't be bored.

Soon enough, a man I thought had to be Halpern, from the thrill of excitement that shot up in the crowd, made the rounds and stood speaking to some people he seemed to know in the front rows. Dressed in pants and an embroidered Indian *kurta,* he looked the part of the "alternative, new-agey" person he was supposed to be. The hall was now filled to the brim, and the concert soon began on the tiny makeshift stage. We had been to a few drum circles that DiLullo facilitated, and I had been looking forward to his beautiful percussion. Music like that always sent my energy right down to the ground.

At first, both the musicians jammed together. Then, it was time for Halpern's solo performance on the keyboard. He played several instrumental pieces, and I couldn't quite pinpoint when the shift began and exactly when it felt like something had changed. But it was as if a door had swung open inside of me. There was that same feeling of being connected to something bigger that I used to have as a child, that feeling that seemed so hard to find nowadays. The waves of music washed through me, through the build-up of all the messy, thorny feelings, and then it felt like a new door, a door beyond the room of feelings had now swung open.

I was still me, but me without those clogged-up feelings. I could see them in perspective, see they were just a part of me and that my entire self was something bigger. This new feeling was familiar, grounded, connected. I had felt like this once. I had lived here once. It wasn't like visiting a new place. It was more like I had misplaced the key to this part of me.

I wished the music would last forever so I could keep on feeling this timelessness, so I could keep on feeling connected instead of falling again into those now familiar feelings of being fragmented and suspended. The music seemed to have transformed the space from a little church with its blue-covered altar and its wooden pews into something touched by the sacred. Just like the *aartis* and the incense that cast spells of enchantment, this was music that struck deep strings, strings unstruck for long. By my side, Rohit had actually fallen asleep. He was quite an insomniac. Every night, sleep was a struggle. But the music seemed to have snatched away his phone and lulled even him to sleep.

Like all good things, soon, the concert had ended, much sooner than I had expected. It had felt like taking a dip in a cool lake, shaded by giant trees. It had felt like everything was right side up, in its proper scale. I knew this door would close again, as something in my mind, something that liked to control things, startled awake again. But this feeling of remembrance, this feeling of connection would be something to hold on to, something I could consciously enter again.

This concert was my first experience of brainwave

entrainment music, music that alters brainwave frequencies, which results in a different state of consciousness than what we are used to in daily life. What Halpern had played were pieces from his wonderful album *Deep Alpha*, music that induces the Alpha state, a state of deep relaxation and creativity.

Alpha is a state we can enter naturally, without any aid, when we are relaxed and at ease. Now that I had a taste of it, I thought it was the kind of state that had been easy for me to enter when I was younger, when I had carried the world of my imagination in my arms, when I could set it up anywhere I went.

Alpha, it turned out, was exactly the state we tend to get out of touch with the more "adult" we become. In our normal, everyday lives, we are usually in the Beta state. As it goes, Beta is a good state to be in if we want to accomplish things, problem-solve or do cognitive tasks. But Beta is also the state associated with stress and overload. While it's a good state in the right context, it's not a good state to be in *all the time*.

It's in the other states like the Alpha that we have access to something more than our linear, boxed-in mind. It's in them that we can bridge the gap between our conscious thinking and our unconscious self. There are other brain states apart from Alpha that are fecund for this kind of bridge-making as well. Monks who learn to meditate deeply, for example, can even slow their minds to be in the Theta state, when our brain waves move at an even slower frequency.

The rhythm I had encountered in Alpha seemed to be the rhythm that I had lost by trying to jam myself into the "normal, productive" slot. There hadn't been anything wrong about being productive, per se. But in my many years of corporate work in India, I had force-fitted myself into work that didn't bring the engagement that can also be part of Beta, work that only added to my stress, to my sense of meaninglessness. Day in and day out, all I had were the feelings of "not good enough," weighted down under the impersonal nature of my work. I was just another peg in the corporate machine, not creating lasting work that was my unique expression, something my artistic soul longed for.

In those years, it was as if I was running with the box of my overwrought mind perched precariously above my disjointed body. I had been so filled up with odds and ends that my sensitivity hadn't felt either helpful or useful. It just felt like it cluttered everything up.

There was also just too much stimulation in that workplace, one reorganization after another with corresponding shifts in management and a feeling of being out of control. There was also my sense of not being one of the "loud" ones, a sense of being the one whose work got covered under her quietness, inside a cloak of invisibility. At that time, instead of having compassion for myself, I had tried to shove myself inside that box.

Instead of realizing that I struggled to do things mechanically because I had a certain kind of talent, I had compared myself with others who didn't seem to find the corporate grind half as hard. In this frenetic, rushed, chaotic mind, always feeling like I was lagging behind, always trying to be more "normal," I had inflicted more wounds to myself. In such a forced, pushing state, how could there be a connection to something bigger, something that was separate from my struggle to prove my worth?

Maybe, that's why the connection to my intuition had disappeared all those years ago. I was so soaked up in stress, so occupied with trying to make myself into something else that I couldn't enter into that liminal state where things weren't so hard, where they could flow easily.

This is why the Ananda concert had felt like such a homecoming. I had heard of brainwave entrainment music before but had discounted it and thought it was nothing much. It was only when I had finally let myself be more of my real, "alternative" self that I had tasted it experientially. Then, I had found that it worked. The music worked.

But the real breakthrough was that I had started letting myself follow my curiosities instead of neglecting them, instead of abandoning them. This time, instead of letting the denigrating charge sometimes associated with the words "New Age" scare me away, I had let myself experience it for myself. Now, it felt like words could be so many things. They could be labels to stick on things for blanket dismissals, or they could be new ideas that could help you pry open your very self.

Later on, I would think about how artistic movements like Impressionism and Fauvism had used the same words to describe themselves that had been thrown in their faces like an insult. Fauvism, for example, literally translated as the style of *les fauves* (French for "the wild beasts"), was an artistic movement that owned the derisive word thrown at it by its critics. The painters of this school *did* have this quality of the wild in them. Their work *was* instinctive, charged with brilliant colors and writhing lines. Maybe, it was the ones who called them "the beasts" who were a little too tame.

In a similar way, the name *Impressionism* stuck when an art critic saw an exhibition in which one of Claude Monet's paintings called *Impression, Soleil Levant* (Impression, Sunrise) was displayed. In his review, he dismissed all the paintings in this exhibition as just that, basic, rudimentary impressions. While he had uttered the label, what was later to become the Impressionist group of painters took this discount and wore it as a badge of honor. A new way of painting, a new way of looking had been born.

For me, this was what "alternative" felt like. It was not just the opposite of "normal," that thing I had always strived to be. It was also a way to belong, a way to draw out new lines, figure out new forms. In their most positive interpretation, words like alternative and New Age implied people like Halpern, a kind of renaissance man, combining music and science to create an accessible way into a relaxed state that many of us try to keep forcing our way through. He used sound to tap into the bigger world of the soul. If this was alternative, I was on board with it.

This was the bigger world of the self. It included states like the Alpha, which were those spaces in which you could access your intuitive self, in which you were connected to your own harmonics. In them, your mind was running deep inside your body, not fragmented from it. As I thought about this and learned more ways to get into a more creative mindspace, I also stumbled upon the work of Dr. Lester Fehmi.

Dr. Lester Fehmi of the Princeton Biofeedback Center was a pioneer in the field of biofeedback. He had created something called the *Open Focus* training, which had tools and exercises that you could use to shift into the Alpha state at will. As scientists sometimes do, Dr. Fehmi had begun his experiments by trying to train his own brainwaves into the Alpha state. But at first, nothing he tried had seemed to work. Then, one day, after a lot of frustration and confusion, in a moment of surrender, he had decided to stop trying, to just leave it be since no solution was forthcoming.

To his utter amazement, the monitoring equipment he was still hooked onto had suddenly registered a great deal of Alpha activity at this moment. His tension seemed to dissolve. His arthritic symptoms disappeared for a bit. He felt amazing. He was in Alpha when he stopped trying to be in Alpha. There's a Zen koan for you.

But Dr. Fehmi still couldn't articulate what exactly had shifted. Yes, he had let go. Yes, he had surrendered. But how could he do this again, at will? That was what he was after.

It was only after years of experiments and observations that he finally realized that what had changed was his *attention*. In his words, what changed was, "*not what I was attending to, but how I was attending to.*" Because Dr. Fehmi was a scientist first and not a spiritual seeker who might have stopped at this insight, he kept on looking for ways to produce this creative, insightful Alpha activity. After many experiments using different methods like relaxation exercises as well as sensory stimuli like perfumes, he found that none of them worked well enough to get you straight into the Alpha state. But finally, finally, there was one thing that did work.

It was paying attention to space in different kinds of

ways. If you were to stop doing what you were doing and just pay attention to the physical space you were in, for example, the shift in that attention seemed to also come with a shift in your actual bodily experience. Some of these exercises were effective enough to put you in a relaxed state where intuitive insights bubbled up to the surface.

The specific exercise I had come across from Dr. Fehmi's work had to do with a particular kind of space, the space inside my own body. I practiced this while sitting out in the sun, whenever I felt ungrounded, whenever the fear of being rootless came up again. Just as the instructions had prompted, I paid attention to the space between different parts of my body.

I let my attention roam freely in the space between my eyes. I paid attention to the space between my ears. I imagined the space inside my throat, between my shoulders and between my hips. I expanded my attention so it filled up the area between my ankles and my knees. My attention was open and diffuse but still contained as I imagined the space inside my spine.

This kind of exercise was very much up my alley, a kind of visualization exercise, very much like the visualization exercises I had sometimes used before. It had no specific goal. There was no right way of doing this. The only thing I was trying to do was to pay attention in a way that was both directed to a specific space but where it could also roam freely within these confines.

Images often popped up when I did this exercise. An image of sand shifting and moving and changing its form came up when I moved my attention across different points in my body. This was similar to how images popped up when I wrote by hand. Just like writing had felt physical and embodied then, instead of something you do only with your mind, this seemed to be another way of bringing up things from the imaginal realm.

It was also just good to feel how intertwined my body was. When I focused on one part of the body, some entirely different part also relaxed. I wasn't in pieces and my body wasn't a thing I carried around with me. My attention was inside my own body at these times, instead of roaming around like a phantom in my mind.

For months, I had been searching for these new ways to connect to myself, to find something inside me that would help show me the way. Every so often, in the middle of this transition, I seemed to come to a grinding halt. Even when there was so much good in my life, someone like Rohit who supported me so much, I was so busy handing out my energy in bits and pieces that I would come crashing down again and again.

Then, I would find it hard to take care of myself, fill myself up again. The mothering principle, some active thing that took care of the little child inside, seemed to be missing in me. This learning about intuition was a way to take care of this little child inside, to trust my own judgment and draw boundaries that were good for me.

In my day-to-day life, as I started taking my intuition seriously, I also started checking out big and small nudges. If I had a sudden curiosity, I let myself check it out instead of dismissing it as irrational. Often, these were little things but they were all ways to build more self-trust, instead of locking up my life in the closed fist of my mind. One day, while visiting Rohit's office, I was hanging around near the gift shop on the ground floor for a bit. It was close to Christmas, but there was nothing left to buy. I didn't really window shop, except if there were books involved.

I had never even been inside this shop that seemed to be filled with seasonal gifts this day and stocked with flower bouquets outside that you might take home to some neglected spouse. That day, all of a sudden, a really strong feeling that I *should* go into the shop came over me. It was pronounced but there was no logical reason to back it up. So, for a bit, I tried to talk myself out of it.

But I had been experimenting with my intuition and so, finally, I let myself go in. Soon enough, I had found a few things I liked, amongst them a set of two Christmas-themed earrings with little snowmen and Christmas trees that I could wear to a party. When I took everything to the counter, it turned out that the card-swiping machine wasn't working.

By the time I had rummaged through my bag and located only a few spare dollars, it seemed like the lady serving me, whose shop it was, had decided that the money didn't matter. I didn't have to give up the earrings. I also didn't have to come back with the extra cash even though I told her I would. She would just take whatever I had in exchange for everything I had picked out. Even as I asked her whether she gave me these purchases for almost free because it was Christmas, I knew that wasn't the case.

I knew she was just a generous person who would have probably done something similar even if it hadn't been Christmas. But more than just bringing me a few things for free, most importantly, my intuition had given me a chance to connect. This was December 2016. In the new political climate of America, as the color of my skin felt visible for the first time, as some old fear activated inside me, that deep, sometimes unwarranted fear that early trauma primes you for, here was this so-called "white" lady, who was, like many Americans, hard-working as well as kind.

What she did was just an everyday thing for her. But for me, this was a vote for trust, a vote to have more faith. Things were chaotic right now. It seemed as if both my own shadow as well as the collective shadow were rising. But there were many people like her, who by their very presence made my world safe.

Little experiences like this encouraged me to keep on learning about my intuition, to keep on being interested in it. One of the first questions that had come was how to know when it *was* my intuition and when it *wasn't*. With time, it seemed as if one of the big clues was whether I had an opinion based on something that my senses could measure, for example, how someone looked or not, or whether the information came from outside the realm of the five senses.

Intuition was definitely the latter. Even if I might guess correctly about the other person based on an observation, that was different from intuition. That was my intellect forming an opinion. This was sometimes true and sometimes completely off. But intuition was something beyond this.

It could show up in different ways. It could make me feel very uncomfortable when I was about to take a wrong step, just as if I were a chess player about to make the wrong move. This intense intuitive discomfort was different from other kinds of discomforts. It was something that would vanish as soon as I understood why

I was uncomfortable and changed what I was doing. I had made the assumption in the beginning that intuition was a searching curiosity, a feeling to explore an unexplored path. But it was many things. It wasn't something that always made you *feel good* right in that moment. Sometimes, it was just discomfort.

After months of these explorations, tiny experiments and getting a feel for my intuitive muscle, I got another chance to exercise all I had been learning. As chance would have it, it was at another writing meetup. The initial social, interactive part was over and everyone sat with their laptops or books out. This was a busy day. Lots of people had showed up. In fact, there was no more space on the one long table that had been joined together from two.

A few late-comers had already spilled onto another table right next to my corner seat. As I moved my pen across my notebook, an Indian woman around my age walked into the cafe and settled down at a chair at this table. I glanced up for a microsecond. I hadn't seen her before. All around me, everyone else kept on typing and writing away, as we did when people were late.

As a little trickle of time passed, I found myself getting more and more uncomfortable in my corner seat. I felt as if I was being pushed, as if my energy was drawing back, tamped down by a more aggressive energy. Even as I tried to not get distracted, even as I tried to pretend to myself that I wasn't affected, I felt a mounting discomfort.

Nothing outward had happened. There were at least a few new people who showed up every week but never had I felt like this. Even with people I didn't quite connect with or the few I didn't quite like, I had never experienced this. Usually, the group energy was up. It felt like being around people who spoke my language, even if not all of them were kindred spirits. So, this was different.

As the writing period came to an end, different parts of me felt the dilemma as one person after another started leaving. I didn't just get up and leave even though I was getting more and more uncomfortable. A part of me felt annoyed with myself for having such a strong reaction, such a decided feeling. I had wanted to stay and write a little longer, like some of us did, beyond the prescribed group time. Did getting up, leaving and moving to another cafe mean that people could just sway me from my place? Was I just weak and easily ungrounded?

Soon, more people left and I was alone at my long table. There were only two people left at the other table, including the Indian woman and someone else I didn't know. As I sat with my eyes glued down, I could sense the unspoken expectation in the air, that at some point I would interact with her. After all, we had both been the only Indians in the group.

But the more aware I grew of what I wanted, the more I realized that I didn't want to engage. I had only recently been taught another lesson about not listening to my gut feeling. Now, something in this person's energy was speaking to me in a very specific way.

The social norms of the group went like this. Often, depending on how well you knew someone, people got up and left without saying a Bye, not interrupting whoever was working. So, at last, instead of deciding to stay on, instead of trying to come up with some objective way to back up my feeling, instead of criticizing myself for not being "nice," instead of questioning whether I was being weak, that day, that's exactly what I did.

It did feel a little rude. Again, it felt like it was my job to take care of any expectations I sensed or imagined. But instead of doubting myself, instead of asking myself how I could be so sure and whether I was being judgmental, like I had done in the past when I asked myself questions like *"How could I be sure if someone was narcissistic?"* I realized there was no way of verifying everything, for sure, right there at any given moment when you have to decide.

My energy was telling me something. I had to trust my own energetic response.

Maybe, I would see this woman again some other day when there were more people around, and I could observe from a distance. Maybe, I would never see her again. But whatever the case, I had to break the unsaid, unformed "nice" rules in my head that I often complied with such as automatically talking to someone just because I felt it was expected. Instead, I had to learn to trust whatever my body was telling me, and learn to read any warning signs I came across.

As I got up, I could sense her surprise, even though I didn't look at her. I still hadn't let go of the caretaker in me, so I felt a charge. But what was more important was that I could now change my behavior instead of waiting for all my feelings to change first. I didn't have to do this perfectly. It was important to not just take care of others, but also to take care of myself. It was important to protect my energy and guard it so it didn't leak all over the place.

This was more important than merely being "nice."

This was more important than waiting and waiting to make up my mind, discounting the gifts my sensitivity often brought me. The parts of my sensitivity that worked for my benefit carried tufts of unsaid feelings and lifted subtle nuances out of the air and handed them to me. It was upto me to respond to them.

This was just one small interaction in which I let myself develop that sense of self-trust in what I sensed and felt. Another experience that had felt insightful and that had nudged me to practice this had come during one of my sister's visits from India. In fact, it had not just felt insightful, but almost like a test from the universe. Was I really serious about trusting my intuition?

That evening, we had both gotten ready and were waiting for Rohit to come home so we could go out for a special dinner. As we had sat talking that day, our conversation had been interrupted by the ringing of the bell. At first, I had disregarded it. If it was a parcel, they would leave it by the door after ringing the bell once. We weren't expecting anything that needed to be signed for. But then, the bell rang again.

This was an unusual occurrence, especially for this time of the evening. So, instead of walking down the few stairs to the front door and peering through the peephole, I opened the living-room window to look down to see who it was. It turned out to be a young man, of slight build, well-dressed, probably in his early 20s.

At the sound of the window opening, he looked up, said *Hi* and told me that he was my neighbor from down the street. He then made some remarks about the neighborhood, and the impression I got was that he was someone who had just moved in who had come over to introduce himself. We talked for a minute or two, or rather, he talked and I smiled and nodded. Then, within a couple of minutes, he asked me whether I could lend him some cash. I was left with the confused impression that he was a neighbor stuck in a jam although the reason why he needed the cash wasn't clear.

For a minute, I had thought of how I could say no. I had also thought that maybe he really needed the money, and I should give it to him. Feeling caught up in the rush of polite conversation, I had told him I would check whether I had any money in the house at all. This was a plausible excuse. After all, like most people here, we almost always used credit cards. It was wholly believable that unless we needed it for something specific, we wouldn't have much cash lying around in the house.

But this evening, I knew I wouldn't have to look for cash. I knew I had some in the house. After making my excuse, I had walked back from the window, out of this young man's line of sight. I looked at my sister then, who had been hanging around in the background, out of his view, listening to our conversation. Her back was straight. I could see that she was on alert. *Should we give him some money*, I asked softly. She shrugged. This was my turf, and she didn't know if this was normal. After all, this was not India where we were used to having people knock on our doors asking for donations, sometimes for completely worthy causes and sometimes running little scams. Was this a scam? Was this genuine? She couldn't tell. It was up to me.

I was still hanging back. I was still waiting, not sure for what. Both of us were not in his line of sight although I could see him clearly from where I was. As I stood waiting and considering, I saw him move towards the door of the house next door. I saw him ring the bell. Unlike the picture of suburban America with its single, detached houses, our home in this gated community shared a wall on either side with two other homes. This was a community with rows upon rows of these houses. So, my neighbour's house where he had rung the bell was right next to ours, its front door just a few steps away, plainly visible to me.

In just a few moments, I saw the door opening. I couldn't see who it was. They spoke softly, so the voice didn't carry over. But I could clearly hear the young man speak, as he looked at whoever opened the door, and immediately said: *Sorry, I have the wrong house.* As soon as he uttered those words, instantly, in a flash, I knew beyond any shadow of a doubt that it was the man of the house who had answered the doorbell. Instantly, I knew this young guy had rung the bells at several other homes and selected our house deliberately.

As soon as my neighbor's door closed, this guy sauntered back and took his position in front of our house. I gave him a second. Then, I went to the window and told him I didn't have any money in the house. It was almost as if a switch had been flipped. Instead of being charming and pleasant like earlier, he immediately turned petulant. He needed the money, he said now, because he was in college. He needed to pay his fees. In fact, he *needed* the money, and I *had* to give it to him. He offered me another option. I could write him a cheque. But now, I knew. All I said was *Sorry, I don't have the money,* and shut the window finally.

As I retreated back from the window, we waited for a few suspended moments before we heard this young guy's footsteps receding away. It was only then that my sister and I looked at each other. This was a test from the universe, we both said. We had only recently been talking about how we needed to listen more closely to our intuition. We had only recently been talking about how often we had paid the price for not listening.

Later on, when I thought about this incident, I had felt slightly stupid. I knew most people would have said no to this guy right at the beginning. After all, he was a stranger. That was the right thing to do, wasn't it? But it was never that simple for me. How many times before had I thought that I shouldn't be naive? How many times before had I thought that I shouldn't lead with trust? I knew the reason I had considered giving him the money was a mixture of different reasons.

Some of it was my empathy which made everything complicated. Some of it was actual confusion about what the situation was all about. But some of it was also just my driving need to give whatever was asked to whoever asked for it.

In the end, I had gotten plain lucky. This guy hadn't been a slick operator. He wasn't smooth. It was relatively easy to figure him out. He had hardly been sophisticated when he changed his story the second time around and made his ask. He had shown belligerence. He had practically demanded I give him the money, as if I owed it to him. He had also rung the other doorbell in the minute or two he had been waiting for me. He hadn't even had the slightest amount of patience or restraint.

But in his unsophisticated, clunky way, this young man had still used many of the same techniques that successful con men (and women) often use with their victims. Before this incident, I had been rereading security specialist Gavin De Becker's book *The Gift of Fear* in my effort to learn to distinguish between helpful cautionary fear and the overworkings of my mind. Some of the techniques this guy had used were classic textbook, ones that De Becker had described in detail.

One of them was talking too much and giving too many details. He had told me he was a neighbor, commented on some construction work in the neighborhood, talked about the weather and given me a host of random details in the minute or two of our initial conversation. Just as De Becker had said, it was as if all the details were a cover-up, a distraction from the actual reality of the situation, the fact that he was a stranger who was soon going to ask me for money for no clearly discernible reason. Like other liars, this young man had been aware of his lie and kept on talking to divert from it, to throw a fog around it.

He had also used another tactic called "forced teaming" during our interaction. He had used the word "neighbours." He had given me the impression that we were part of the same group of people, a group that *should* help each other. He had even used the word "we" as he talked to establish our commonality.

He had also, from whatever I could make out, sought out a woman specifically. He had retreated quickly when my next-door neighbor had opened their door. Why wasn't he being as neighborly to them? Was it because it was easier to get sympathy from a woman?

Although our interaction had lasted just a few minutes, maybe three or four in total, he seemed to have deployed multiple tactics that De Becker talked about in his book. When he had used "too many details," it had blurred the context for me for a minute, the context that De Becker says is most apparent at the beginning or the end of an interaction, not when you are caught up in the rush of conversation.

For me, the context was that this man was a total stranger. For a minute, I forgot that in the past three or so years, none of my other neighbors had ever rang my doorbell asking for cash. No one had run out of it, and then needed to borrow it urgently. Even apart from neighbors, no one asking for donations had ever come to my door. In fact, it was rare to even have someone ring the bell at this time of the evening. On many levels, this person didn't fit into what was my usual experience.

In his case, I had been able to keep all of this in mind. I was no longer as "nice" and as gullible as I had been years earlier. Although I had found it hard to say a direct No and felt a little ashamed at even doubting his sincerity, I had come up with an excuse even as he had made his ask. My awareness was also heightened because of all I had been learning about fear and intuition. In the end, it was a combination of my awareness, my intellect and my intuition that had kept me safe.

I had listened to my doubts. I had registered my initial hesitation at believing his story. So, I had paused to assess him. I hadn't dismissed that initial doubt summarily. His own newness at this game and his own showing of his hand many times had confirmed my suspicions.

When I later thought about him, I thought of how while this was a tiny interaction, these kinds of tactics were also used by other manipulative people much more smoothly, with much more finesse, and in extremely serious situations. Now that I was paying attention, I could register them more and more. Now, instead of getting lost in the minute details of a person's behavior and doubting myself if they did *some* things right, instead, I let myself look at the overall pattern. I looked to see how everything fit together. I listened to people's actions much more than to their words.

Now, for me, experiences like these have become reminders about why it's important for me as an empath and HSP to become more discerning. If I give the benefit of the doubt one too many times and then get taken advantage of, like I've done in the past, then I feel more and more victimized. This undiscerning openness doesn't bring me any closer to people. It closes me off. I feel that I just can't trust and that I will constantly be in the red when it comes to interacting with people. But when I can be more discerning and see that I will always come across all kinds of people, then I can use my own instincts to protect myself first and then be empathetic.

Then, it's not a situation where I lose and someone wins at my cost. Then, it's a win-win. That seems to be the only way to interact in a sustainable way.

So, when something in me pauses, now, I know that I need to look. When something in me doubts, I need to ask what it's all about. My instincts, my doubts, my intuitions all have important messages for me. When I listen to them, things go well. When I don't, then my sensitivity feels like an enormous burden.

If I can stay aware of this and remain aware of the pitfalls of sympathy, I think then my sensitivity won't bring me down to my knees any longer, overwhelmed and exhausted. Instead, I think it will become something that helps me tune in to the wind as it is changing and to the tides as they are turning. It will become something that helps me pick up nuances that can then be made meaning of.

Then, I think I can meet the world as it is instead of projecting nice things onto it, instead of believing that niceness will protect me from the turbulence of the world. I am learning now that the real harbour is inside myself and that what really protects me, in the end, is me.

Chapter 5

Meeting the Dragon

As I kept on learning more about intuition, it seemed as if synchronicities were shaking things into my lap. In my favorite metaphysical bookstore, *East West*, I saw an advertisement for a class enticingly titled *Surviving a Sensitive Lifetime - Even around your Family*. It was a talk cum workshop by someone called Scout Bartlett, someone I hadn't heard of before. But Scout was supposed to be a clairsentient and that was all the elaboration I needed to sign up. This was exactly what was calling to me right now.

As it turned out, this was a talk that Scout gave every year at *East West* right before Thanksgiving. In fact, this was a kind of yearly ritual for him, talking about handling being sensitive right before a festival so fraught with touchy interactions and possible emotional meltdowns. Later that evening, he would jokingly talk about Thanksgiving being *"National Co-dependence Day."* We would all laugh as we acknowledged the truth in that.

This particular day, I was here with my sister who was visiting from India. From the time that she had told me about *The Highly Sensitive Person*, I had traversed quite a few miles from being "in hiding" to actually starting to own what it meant to be sensitive. Sometimes, I even felt good about the trait. At any rate, just the fact that I had "come out" even if in this small way, gathering bits and pieces, sticks and stones to build my own understanding of what it meant to be clairsentient, that itself felt like a shift.

I had been in the Events room at the back of the store, many times before. This was where Rohit and I had come for *David DiLullo's* drum circles when the percussion had rung in some ancient part of me. This was where I had heard Tony Redhouse's Native American music and felt it reverberate inside my bones. Here, in this room, I had also come for author events and free group readings, feeling like part of a community, part of a circle of people who were strangers to each other but who did not feel like strangers. They felt more familiar than people I met in my day-to-day life.

These were my people, my soul family.

Like always, that day, the little room was filled to capacity, with maybe twenty-five or thirty people attending. I could feel my energy entrain with theirs. Just being in a "like" environment made me ring like a bell. As always, there was an electric buzz in the air that preceded a talk like this, a talk everyone had been eagerly looking forward to. My sister and I sat down in our chairs, a little to the front. Soon enough, the evening began in earnest.

Scout, the clairsentient, did not disappoint. He looked like an everyday, normalized version of the great wizards you read about in books. He was like Merlin, just without the garb. That day, he was wearing a purple shirt and dress pants and also had purple shoes on. Later on, I would find that he had a matching purple motorbike. Bald with a cherubic face and a salt-and-pepper goatee, he looked like he was in his forties.

He reminded me a little bit of a cousin of mine who as a child, had always been up to some prank - shoving lemons down VCRs, ringing bells in all the apartments in his building complex, throwing potatoes down from our first-floor house when he visited. I could easily picture Scout doing something like that as a kid. In short, he was an imp. Later on, I would think of how he reminded me of Dumbledore or Gandalf, good guys maybe in the bigger scheme of things but having that trickster energy that nudges the poor, unwitting hero down some hard, exacting path.

As Scout talked and I turned inwards, the energy in the room, supportive and womb-like, held me a bit. He dived into the subject matter right off the bat. The first part of the evening would be experiential. He was going to work with the energy in the room and give us a taste of how energy changed as he worked with it. Pay attention to your feelings and sensations, he told us. They were more important than words.

But first, before he started changing the energy in the room, we first had to establish a baseline. He told us to notice exactly how we felt at this starting point, to register how we felt being in the room and how far his voice felt, as well as pay attention to the chattering of our minds and to details like the light level and how the room itself felt around us. As I sat next to my sister, I had my eyes shut, and I could feel his voice coming from somewhere at the back of the room. I registered what I was feeling. I was a bit tired. I felt pulled away from my body, not really in it and as if I was not paying one hundred percent attention. My energy was slow and clunky. I could hear Scout moving around.

Now, he was going to change the energy in the room. He told us to pick up our favorite worry. Worry it with all your might, he said. Notice how it feels in your body. Was it a burden on the shoulder, a drop in the pit of the stomach, a clenching of the jaw, something else? By now, he was going so fast, giving all these instructions that all I could do was to keep up. But yes, I could worry my worry. That wasn't difficult. I felt my body scrunching up, wind up tight. It was a familiar, well-worn groove I could fall into easily. *Worry. Circle around in my mind. Worry.* I worried, like Scout had said, with all my might.

Again, it was time for another change. Visualize something beautiful, he said, anything you could think of. I think he gave some corny example of rainbows. Notice what's happening in your body again. Notice what the room feels like, what being here feels like. Soon, I felt a little lifting up of the worry, felt the load getting a little lighter. Okie, so, now it was time for the last change. Pick up your worry and worry it again please. How do you feel now? Did you notice anything different?

At last, Scout had slowed down. The whole exercise had taken just a few minutes, maybe four or five. But as I opened my eyes, it felt as if my perception had shifted. Colors looked saturated. The edges of the room seemed more defined. A few people spoke up. One said the worry had felt lighter the second time around, as if you could just brush it off. Another person talked about how the second time, the worry had bounced right off them. It seemed like most of us had felt that the worry did not grip us as hard, and was, in fact, something we held lightly the second time around.

It was then that Scout started his talk. Everything was energy, he said. Quantum physics said that and so did metaphysics. He talked about his own training as an engineer before he gave that up to pursue his gifts. He talked about speaking with physicists who, sometimes, didn't agree with all concepts from metaphysics. But wasn't it true? Everything was energy. Our thoughts, our feelings, our sense of self, *everything* was energy.

I knew he was preaching to the converted. I believed in things I sensed to be true. Wasn't all new knowledge at the edges of science once? Wasn't science sometimes playing catch up to intuition? Like most people, I knew, of course, that matter is energy.

As someone who grew up with Hindu thought, it dovetailed first with my philosophy but then also with my very feeling. Wasn't this what reincarnation meant, that when you die, there is an energy that is not extinguished, there is a flame that doesn't die out but that remains, that lives on and transforms into something else? So, this was all easy to understand, all easy to know. It wasn't final death I was ultimately afraid of. It was everything in between.

The Most Consistently Held Energy in the Room

What Scout had done, he told us, the believers, was work with the energy of the room in a subtle way. At first, he was just in the room, as he was. When he had asked us to worry the first time, he had pulled his own energy inside of him. He had, so to say, squashed it. Then, when he had asked us to worry the second time around, he had expanded his energy field out through the room. He hadn't worked with *anyone else's* energy at all. He had *not* tried to change their energy. He had *not* tried to lift them up.

All he had done at the different points in the exercise was to work with and change his *own energy*. What had happened then was that as he had shifted his own energy and consistently been in that energy, everyone else had matched their energy to his. This was what Scout had to say about this dynamic and this was what felt extremely important to me as I first listened to this idea: *Everyone had a tendency to match the most consistently held energy in the room.*

We were all tuning in to each other all the time, he said. We were all empathic that way. But we did this unconsciously, without being aware of it. Whoever had the most consistently held energy in the room was, in fact, affecting everyone else's energy. This was also the reason why negative people often pulled us down. It was because, Scout said jokingly, they were so consistent with repeating their worries and fears or *Poor Mes* like a negative mantra, over and over again.

More than any happy person ever did, they held onto their negative energy for dear life. So, by default, they often ended up being in their energy in the most *consistent* way as compared to other people. But when Scout had become the most consistently held energy in the room, people had *also* automatically matched their energies to his more positive energy. It was why their worries had crumbled, dropping down from their weighed-down shoulders.

As Scout talked, I could feel a resonance deep inside me. It felt like he had said something I hadn't even realized I had been looking for. *Everyone has a tendency to match the most consistently held energy in the room.* Later in the evening, he talked about growing up in the Kansas City area, how he had been a child bouncing off the walls, not knowing why he was this way, not knowing why other people's energy affected him so much.

He also talked about working as a delivery boy, walking

into a room and instantly feeling the emotional undercurrents in the room. Like other empaths, he had then tried to make himself small. He had scrunched himself into an energetic ball. He had tried to keep himself into himself both as a defensive tactic against what felt like others' overwhelming energy and also because he did not want to be "*too loud*" energetically. He had assumed, like many other empaths, that other people were as sensitive to energy as he was.

So, he had tried to be energetically "polite" and to make sure that his energy did not intrude on others in any way, unlike their energy that kept intruding on him. But the thing was, he told us, most people just weren't that energetically sensitive. As he had learned about energy, he had realized that he could be as "loud" as he wanted. No longer did he have to shrink inside himself or make himself small.

I felt the truth of these words in my body. Long before I ever knew there was a word like "empath," I had squeezed myself into smaller and smaller balls. Everyone's energy seemed to always be intruding on mine. I wouldn't be like them. I wouldn't be the person who energetically dipped into someone else's territory. I think I had felt so adamant about this at one point that I had stopped taking up space, almost disappearing when I was around people.

But, as Scout had said, everyone did not feel other people's energy so acutely. I did not have to tamp myself down. I did not have to use this as a defensive tactic. As empaths, we were not getting in other people's way. We did not have to energetically shrink inside ourselves for some misguided reason.

With these facts established, what could sensitive people do, Scout asked? What could you do if you were energetically sensitive, if you felt other people's feelings so much that you were bouncing here and there with them, if you were a clairsentient or an emotional empath? For sensitive people, it was important to *be the most consistently held energy in the room*. That way, we could remain centered in our own energy and let other's energy just pass through us. That's what Scout had done when he had asked us to worry the second time. He had *been* his own energy. Instead of getting pulled by the strings of other people's emotions, like I sometimes did, instead of being led by them, he had simply been his own energy.

Not only that, he had let his energy take up space in the room. By doing that, he had been able to shift the energy in the room. Worry, he added, was a sign of low energy. When you were vibrating with a higher energy, worry disappeared. That had also happened with us.

As the talk unfolded, it felt like everything Scout was saying was so obvious and true. Hadn't I felt this way as a child, once upon a time, in a distant, hazy past? Hadn't I known that people's energy could just pass through me, almost as if I were transparent? I had known then that although I was moved by it, this energy didn't have to make home inside of me. Maybe, this is why I didn't completely agree with shielding yourself against energy by visualizing white light or something like that. While that could be helpful sometimes, and in the end, it was again about intention, some part of that also felt like you were always on the defensive, guarding yourself against people who were mightier than you.

But this, this felt like a more grounded explanation.

Maybe, this was why on the days when my energy was already filled up, like when I did affirmations, I did not simply match other people's energy. It was as if I was embedded inside my own energy. Or maybe, it was better to say that I was embodied and had higher positive energy. Because of this, instead of jumping out of my skin, head-first into someone else's experience, I simply remained in my own energy. When I felt good about myself, I also didn't automatically squeeze myself small as a defense tactic. I did not become a curled-up ball, scared of contracting some metaphorical energetic germ.

In these cases, I was in my own energy. I did not unconsciously match energy.

This seemed to explain why I often couldn't predict when someone's energy would affect me and when it wouldn't. I wasn't aware of how energy worked. As Scout talked, I found myself remembering. It was also interesting to flesh out some more nuances of what it meant to intuitively pick up information. Scout talked, for example, about how being clairsentient or clairvoyant did not necessarily mean that you could predict the future. That was precognition. You could be a clairvoyant with or without precognition, for example.

If you *were* precognitive, you could be precognitive in any of the different ways of knowing things intuitively - like clairvoyance, clairsentience, clairaudience and so on. It was not like the movies. Clairvoyants, for example, are people who get intuitive information visually. But they might get intuitive information simply as colors and not as the flashing pictures or scenes that we often saw mediums seeing in movies. That means that intuitive information and the capacity for intuitive flashes is much more normal than many of us believe.

Basically, Scout said, if someone said they were clairvoyant or clairaudient, you wouldn't know exactly what they did. It was sort of like if you met someone who was a carpenter, while you would know they had woodworking skills, you still wouldn't know exactly what they built everyday just from knowing they were a carpenter.

Was it tables they built or bookshelves or something else entirely? It was the same with intuitive ability. You could build different things with it. Of course, there was also a challenge that came with intuitive ability. Scout talked about his younger self, the self that felt like it had to smooth over everyone's energy, that just because he noticed things, he was obliged to fix them.

Later on, I would think about this when I read depth psychologist Bill Plotkin's book *Soulcraft*. In it, he talks about how our soul wound and soul gift are closely interlinked and how the things we have the most challenges with are also what carve out our gift. In the book, Plotkin talked about a woman named Allison who had grown up in a big, boisterous family in which she had largely felt unseen. This wound of being invisible to others was her soul wound.

In all her interactions as an adult, it was this wound that got triggered. But it was this same experience that had also honed Allison's gift. It had made her unusually observant about interpersonal dynamics and given her a great sense of when something might escalate. While she was growing up, this had served her well as a coping mechanism. But now, the weight of those feelings of unworthiness was heavy.

When Plotkin met her, Allison was ripe for unlearning

these "not good enough" feelings that were part of her old identity. She was ripe for confronting the sting of her wound. She was also learning to take responsibility for changing her own tendency to merge into the woodwork, to become invisible. In fact, she was at the cusp where if she could just shift enough, she could start sharing her keen observations with the world.

It was unlikely, Plotkin said, that if Allison had grown up with a different, less challenging family, she would have had the opportunity to develop her soul gift, her gift of seeing. But now, her gift had grown big enough. She was at a crucial juncture. She had to dare to look inside her wound, inside its pain, its dark, messy bits so that it could be transformed and healed. Only then could it become a pathway to living her purpose. Only then could she break through the shroud of silence.

I deeply felt with Allison. I also had the wound of being unseen. Many of my interpersonal problems came when I felt again that people couldn't see me. Even when it was innocuous, even when I might have explained myself better and so the other person might have understood, even then, not feeling seen had a big charge for me. But, as Plotkin had said, maybe there was a larger purpose for my soul wound. It had been intertwined with that cloak of invisibility that sometimes made me perceive more than what was apparent on the surface. Like Allison, I had to find a way to let go of the sting of the wound and instead learn to channel its gifts.

In one of my dreams during this time when I felt like I was changing a lot, I had a weird dream. In one hazy scene, there were some older women from my birth family present. There was also a related fragment in which there were feces, maybe my own. Suddenly, the excrement transformed into a shell-like, porous substance that felt foreign but beautiful. The dream felt weird and striking at the same time. It had a distinctly different from normal feel. It felt like a stunning metaphor for the things that were happening inside me psychologically. At any rate, I hoped that was what it was, an indication that something old and trashy was being transformed into something that was actually valuable.

Listening to Scout that day, I had felt a similar opening to a new way of looking at my life. He had wiped down the mirror, this wizard from Kansas who had once upon a time been an engineer. His insight about *consistently being in your own* energy was what stayed with me long after the talk even though we had also done some other experiential exercises. He had recommended a kind of meditation where you visualized sweeping energy from the center of the earth, up through your body, as a practice you could do any time, all the time to create and move your own energy. This felt similar to the visualization exercises that energy teachers often teach, such as imagining yourself as having roots that reach into the earth to feel grounded.

For me, more than any specific exercise, it was his conception of energy that resonated the most. I could use this idea. I could consistently be in my energy in many different ways. I could do affirmations, for example. Words always brought my energy up. I could do art. That nourished the very depths of my heart, the colors filling scrunched up, grayed out places. I could consciously pay attention to practices that filled up the reservoirs of my energy.

If I could just do all of this on a regular basis, I could keep my energy up. I could then be in my own energy instead of being swept away in other people's experience. Maybe, it was because I didn't do all these things enough, because I wasn't energetically filled up inside that I just tipped over so easily into whatever everyone else was feeling. But now, I could practice being in my own energy consistently.

I had found another piece of the solution to the problem of over-feeling and over-identifying.

Apart from this energetic piece, I also had to keep clearing my beliefs about what healthy giving was and what was rescuing and people pleasing. I had to bring these up into my awareness and change them. Fixing them was also a big part of the solution.

Of course, being in your own energy is often easier said than done. After that talk with Scout, I would do this well sometimes, sometimes only a little bit and sometimes, not at all. After some time passed, I would come to another dark point, when all my naked wounds would be activated. They would howl in pain, and I would tumble deep down into the dark night of the soul, forgetting everything I had been learning over the past few years.

But when the night was over and after that dark chasm had been crossed, I would once again pick up these valuable tools. I would try to practice them again, sometimes frustratingly slowly and imperfectly. After a few years, I would go to this same talk by Scout again and hear the same familiar, yet wholly new things. Maybe, this time, I would remember them better. Maybe, now, after so much falling and getting up and falling again, I would more fully know that I am the one in charge of my energy and my boundaries. I am the one who can fill myself up, and in doing that, I can deal with the world better.

As an empath, it's a continuing process of learning to give myself what I need, however imperfectly. It's learning to give importance to what nourishes me. Because I am attuned to energy, it's important to work on keeping my energy clear. Like other empaths, I like being near water. Nature soothes me. Once in a while, I sage my house or use *sandalwood* agarbattis. Scents and sounds are both evocative and clearing.

In the fragrance of *mogras*, in the hoofbeats of drums, I hold my intentions. I make a home. As I look back, I pick up more new-to-me practices from Indian culture. I learn, for example, that the mustard oil used in traditional earthen lamps also clears energy just like sage. It's all similar and different. I put together my own small rituals, rituals that have meaning for me and that are not merely things I am desperately holding on to stay connected to the past.

Over the next few years, this process becomes an unfolding journey. It also brings up doubts. What happens when you say words like clairsentient or empath? What happens if you are yourself a little more openly? All this forward movement awakens the ghosts of my conditioning. They cry out with every forward step I take. Fear rises at the base of my back. My very being feels threatened, as if I am compromising my safety by ripping off the shroud of "normal." Will people think there is something wrong with me, that I am not "normal," a notion I have been trying to disprove all my life, even though I am not sure any longer what normal even means? Will my real self unfold in safety or could it become a target for attack?

This feels like such a strong, deep fear, almost as if the fear has claws that have taken hold of my roots and is tearing them up. With this demon of fear, more muck rises. On the one hand, the rigid identity of "nice" that I have crafted for myself, consciously and unconsciously, now has a decided crack in it. But it's also as if with this permission to look, I am walking down farther into the cave of my unconscious.

There's an unexpected spin on the circle. It's as if the many unspoken, unfelt resentments that have clogged me up have now coalesced together. They have grown into a mass of putrid, fetid material that has jutted its ugly head up.

I am still not done falling.

The Meeting with the Shadow

In the same bookstore where I saw Scout Bartlett, *East West*, there lived, for a time, a wooden statue of the Indian God Ganesha. It stood in front of the water fixture that made sitting on one of the two chairs facing it so very calming. Over many months, whenever I gathered all the books I was browsing through and sat down on one of the seats, I always looked at it and wondered who had made it.

All around me, there were symbols and artifacts from different religions and worldviews, from Native American dreamcatchers to statues of Radha Krishna, from Tibetan sound healing bowls to tiny figurines of angels and fairies. They were all beautiful to look at and possessed of that quality of soul that comes when things have been made with care and love and by hand.

This Ganesha statue was well-made as well, carved by

some unknown hands, imported from somewhere in India. The elephant-headed, human-figured God stood with a snake wrapped around his torso. All the details in his clothing had been painstakingly carved. The statue was around three feet tall, one of the most expensive items in the store, and I hated it almost from the get go.

Obviously, the craftsman who had made it was highly skilled. Ganesha's face and eyes were highly expressive. But I also thought they were mean and spiteful. I imagined the artisan carving slowly and pouring all that was inside him into the statue. Wasn't that what a lot of art was? Wasn't that what I sometimes pulled out and put onto the canvas? My own emotions, my own feelings, my own self?

Whenever I went to *East West*, I looked at the statue and wondered if someone would ever buy it. Why would anyone want to have a mean Ganesha, a God normally supposed to symbolize auspicious beginnings and good luck, standing in front of their house looking spitefully at them? How could this statue ever bring you good fortune and prosperity? Could it be that others wouldn't see the horrible spirit that lived inside the statue? Was I the only one picking up on its ratcheted energy? In my mind, the feeling of aversion grew and grew and every time I saw this Ganesha statue, I wondered about the person who had made it.

Then one day, I arrived at the store in a very agitated state. I had sat for the last few hours listening to a new friend I had made, feeling more and more invisible as time had passed and all she wanted to do was talk about herself. This kind of thing had happened before, but with every successive instance, the little child in me had screamed louder. This day, I had again felt my energy draining out of me and the little child in me becoming out of sorts. But it wasn't as simple a feeling as exhaustion. In my personal life, something else had been draining all my resources, so I was already in that space of having fewer strokes. It was all I could do to take one step after another, to not go hurtling into another anxiety attack.

Still, in my *Be Strong* frame of mind, I hadn't let that get into this friendship, this interaction. But now, this seemed to be forming into that same old pattern again. No matter how hard I tried, no matter how much I showed interest in others, no matter how hard I listened to them, there never seemed to come a time when they listened to me. A friend back home had told me to call out this person, to say in so many words that she didn't let me get a word in edgewise. But I just hadn't been able to do it. Some part of me also wished that she could see, all by herself, that I hadn't said much. Some part of me wished that she would be genuinely interested in me without my having to prompt her.

But this day, as I had sat listening, as I felt that shrinking feeling of wanting to both get away and to stay, as I felt my energy hacked to pieces as she talked about, what felt to me, little things and went *Poor me,* it seemed that this was to be the day when I really went under. I felt a terrible rage growing inside me even, as outwardly, I nodded and soothed her. Here again, there was one more proof that I wasn't seen, that everyone was just self-focused and self-absorbed in this transactional, cold, self-serving country. By the time we wrapped up and I rushed out of the coffee shop, the little one in me was screaming louder and louder and creating a terrifying uproar.

East West was nearby, and I thought of going in to sit near the indoor fountain. Water always soothed me. Water always helped. This time, as I sat near the little fountain, it felt as if all my wounds were climbing out of the walls, out into the open, where I couldn't control them. It was as if that ancient feeling that had followed me since a child, that feeling of being all alone in the world, of being unheard, invisible to everyone around me, it was as if that wound, usually ignored, had become full of pus and was turning rageful.

It was as if there was some part of me, some injured part that I couldn't control, that didn't understand why I kept listening dutifully, patiently to others when it was howling and crying inside. It would have no more of it. Revenge. Revenge. The little child in me screamed. It wanted to lash out, hurt people because no one listened to it, because no one felt the kind of hurt it felt.

What the hell was wrong with me? Why had I listened when I was feeling down myself? Why didn't I know my own limits, when I was running so close to my edge, almost tipping over? Why was I always clamping down on that now often-repeated feeling of my energy sinking right down, as if it had a stone tied to it? Why didn't I listen to the scrunching up of my own heart? Why did this feeling of remorse always come afterwards, after I had tipped into too much giving?

I sat near the fountain with my self-awareness see-sawing, with the little one screaming louder and louder, threatening to take me over. Something inside me thrashed around, feeling mangled. Again and again, that feeling of deep resentment flared up. I wanted to hurt someone, make them feel the way I was feeling. I almost felt like kicking someone, like an angry child. Thankfully, no one was sitting near me, and there were few people in the store.

Trying to calm myself down, I tried to listen to the water and look at the colors around me. That helped but only a little. Then, I tried to say to myself that it was my ego, just my ego that had taken such offence at not being seen. This didn't help at all. It just made everything worse. I felt like an animal that had been stepped on, in fact, worse than an animal, someone who had been hurt but couldn't cry out. The worst part of all this was that I thought that I had been doing the right thing. Giving first before wanting to be given back to. Wouldn't I be taken care of in return?

As the little child inside me howled, I did what I had now started doing once-in-a-while. I prayed. I prayed with whatever faith I had, whatever I could muster. *Help me God. Please help me.*

Slowly, gradually, I calmed down a little bit. I took a tiny step back from the cliff. Someone came out of one of the rooms at the back. I looked around. The little child stomped up and down inside me. I tried to anchor myself. I tried to breathe to calm it. It was then that I noticed the Ganesha statue staring back at me.

In my anxious panic, I had hardly looked at it even though it was right in front of me. But now, as I noticed it, at first hazily and then in definition, it looked nothing like the statue that I had always looked at. The expression on its face was wiped clean. It still had that stolid, ungraceful look that had irritated me. But there was none of the meanness in the eye, none of the spite on the face that I had seen time and again. It was inert wood that had nothing of that malevolent spirit that had alarmed me.

I had been working with my dreams on and off and learning about Jungian psychology for some years now.

225

The thought struck me, all at once, that after years of reading about the Jungian concepts of the Shadow and the Persona and about the unconscious aspects of our own selves, here, in this moment, I had seen my Shadow, seen that all the meanness and spitefulness in that statue had been poured in not by some craftsman who had made it, but projected into it by me.

The statue, which just looked expressionless and plain now, had been that part of myself I didn't consciously identify with, that I didn't consciously own. That mean, revengeful part had split off. I had looked at it as if it belonged to another.

In this moment of clarity, in this opening up of deep stores of resentment at feeling all alone in this new country but still feeling almost obligated to take care of others, I could see that all my niceness and patience had also created deep icicles of resentment that twisted my heart. Now, it was as if I was being shown that this part of me - this buried, unexpressed part - *this* was me too. I was bitter and spiteful now, even though I had never so much as used those words for myself.

It was as if I had been pretending that I could unendingly go on being some inexhaustible source of energy for others and that it wouldn't affect me. But it had. It was as if the best part of me had been contorted and twisted in so many ways. Maybe, this was what some of those animals in my dreams - the ragged looking ones, the ones who snapped at anyone who came close to them, the ones who were starving and feral - maybe this was what they meant. I hadn't fully seen them as a part of myself, even though I knew all the theory.

What had happened in my experience of the Ganesha

statue was a classic case of what depth psychologists call *projection*. I had projected this part of me that I had unconsciously created over the years, this mass of dark, cloudy material - this part that had no inclusion in my "nice" persona - on the statue. In a split-second moment of awareness and grace, I had withdrawn my projection and seen that what I was seeing in that statue was actually a part of me.

In that moment, stripped of my disconnection, the withdrawing of my projection felt crazy-making, as if the world had toppled over. Was nothing I saw true? Was everything just projection? Did I ever see things for how they were or because of who *I* was? Were all the things I was intuitively picking up untrue? But as time went by, I would see that wasn't the case. Everything wasn't projection. But there *were* things that were.

When Jungian depth psychologists talk about the Shadow, the part of us that lives in the unconscious, they tell us that it contains not just the negative but also positive qualities that might have gone underground. If our creativity, for example, wasn't affirmed or valued in early life, then that can also go underground. That can also become part of our Shadow, something that has been banished and that we don't identify as part of ourselves. In that case, we might project our creativity, seeing others as fabulously creative or talented (which they might be) but not seeing that we, ourselves, also have these qualities and possibilities inside. When we project the negative, the gunk in the Shadow, then, of course, our own unworked, unsaid, disowned stuff is seen as a characteristic in someone else.

So, our Shadow, Jungian psychology tells us, can contain both the gold in our soul - the best in us - as well as our problematic aspects. Our Shadow can contain desires and feelings that have been repressed, that don't comply with social norms, as well as positive and negative traits we don't consciously associate with. This is where Jungian psychology veers sharply away from Freudian thought. The unconscious is not just a rubbish heap, a pile of refuse, but also a place where you can find diamonds buried inside. But we have to sift through the refuse to get to the diamonds.

But that's not easy. The more we identify with our outer persona, the denser the Shadow becomes. This might not be a problem at first, depending on Shadow contents and also if the Shadow would just stay down forever. Then, it wouldn't really affect us. But Jungian depth psychologists tell us this is not what happens.

When things, both good and bad, are banished underground, they don't simply disappear. They are still there. They have a life of their own. The Shadow is more or less autonomous. It can act on its own, beyond our conscious will. If the contents of the Shadow are problematic, then this can be dangerous. Then, we live with the risk of our Shadow breaking off.

A story by Agatha Christie comes to my mind. In it, the murderer turns out to be a mild-mannered man who has been pushed and ridiculed by his employer for many long years. Then, one day, "something" comes over him, and he kills this person. This is the Shadow breaking, the part of this man that was buried deep inside him, that no one saw. It was, in fact, a part of him that he, himself, hadn't seen. It was cut off from his awareness.

This is why we need to integrate the Shadow. We have to come to terms with the opposites in us - the generosity and the greed, the strength and the weakness, the niceness and the resentment. Integration may be pulling out the good in the Shadow, such as a healthy quality such as "questioning authority" or our creative talents and starting to use these in daily life. If it is negative aspects that are buried, then we don't have to vent everything nasty inside us. That's not integration.

To me, integration means pulling out the qualities I might have disowned and thinking of specific, intentional ways to use them. If resentment had become a part of my Shadow, to me, it meant that I had to start being, in actionable ways, the opposite of merely nice. Sometimes, I had to be discerning. Sometimes, I had to let myself be "not nice" in situations that required being "not nice," such as when someone was blaming me when it wasn't my fault.

Internalizing the blame was taking nice way too far. It made me weak, both in other people's eyes as well as in my own. The little child in me got furious when it couldn't rely on me to "not be nice" when required, to stop smiling and instead flash out an angry warning, to patrol my boundaries and take charge of them.

As I became more aware of this dynamic, over the next few years, I withdrew some more bits and pieces of my projections. As I changed, some more things started to make sense and fall into place. An important way to know that we might be projecting, Jungian psychologists tell us, is if we have a very strong judgment of some quality in another person. Some of the people who really got on my nerves and whom I judged harshly as being full of it were people who self-promoted openly and loudly. They talked about themselves. They shared things they had made, even things that were, in my opinion, not that good. They tooted their own horn.

Why did this bother me so much? Why did I judge them so harshly? I think it was because my own voice was buried underneath a rubble. I almost took personal offence when I saw them sharing so openly. I also felt a lack, a gap in my artistic self. One of the only sources of recognition for my creative self was through reader comments and emails. But in day-to-day life, I often didn't share what I was doing creatively.

Part of this was healthy, protecting the little flame that could die out with ignorant criticism. But it also kept me from getting some more strokes of appreciation. But here were these overly loud people, openly declaring and sharing things they had created. No wonder they had gotten on my nerves. No wonder I had judged them so harshly. The peacock-like part of myself was completely buried. I judged it as harshly as I judged them.

Maybe, bringing out this part, expressing it in a way that felt authentic to me, would help. I wasn't trying to be like these people or copy them. At the root of it, what was triggering me was that I didn't share enough of myself, appropriately, with enough people who would recognize me. I was hiding. But as soon as I started to be more self-expressive, my judgment of these others went down. They didn't have the exact same charge as before. They were doing their thing, and I was doing mine.

I still do have some charge around this kind of person, which means I haven't completely changed my self-expression. But now, I know there is something inside me that causes me to judge so harshly, that takes them so very personally.

Another kind of person that I judged harshly, almost out of proportion, were the know-it-alls. Maybe, I had to stop being so self-censoring and pull my own know-it-all outside, to make it a little more normal. Once in a while, I think others *can* see this part of me that I can't see myself. As someone to whom accuracy is important, once in a while, I correct people when they say something inaccurate. Because this so bothers me in others and I also see glimpses of it in myself, the solution feels like both letting myself be more of a know-it-all in certain situations and also being conscious that I might be acting like that. Then, maybe, this becomes something more inside the range of choice, something I have more conscious control over.

But the most difficult thing to own about myself, I think, was and is my aggression. For years, I lived only as a flattened-out version of myself, the super-nice one and created a Shadow that is weighed down with anger and resentment. The interesting thing is, as I changed, it was the super-nice people who irritated me. It was almost like I couldn't see that they reflected parts of me.

Watching a YouTube channel on Food and Travel, I would loudly tell Rohit that this guy, with all his comments of "super-amazing" and "heavenly" each and every time, without fail, as he went around tasting street food all over India was super-annoying. He was just too much. But afterwards, I would think this was how I might have come across till a few years back, when I was going around complimenting everyone. Maybe, then, I didn't come across as accepting, which was what I was aiming for. Maybe, I just came across as fake.

It's in deconstructing "nice," this adjective I have so identified with - breaking down its good and bad, its healthy and unhealthy, its light and its dark - that I have moved some steps towards being a person who can access a broader range of behaviors, who is not locked into and limited by being polarized onto one side. If I have the capacity for being mean, for example, maybe I can use it for good to free myself from the pattern of being too generous to the wrong people. Then, the meanness won't add up over time into a big rubbish pile that is stuffed somewhere deep down and can explode. Then, it's just a part of something bigger.

It's okay to dip into the whole of myself.

These have been the little markers on my journey, these shifts in seeing myself more clearly and also seeing how others might see me. But before these little lights showed up, after my initial encounter with the Shadow, projected in that Ganesha statue, there also came a time when the light seemed to have disappeared. The old seemed to be dying. But there was nothing new to take its place, just a void. Things no longer made sense and life seemed fragmented.

All my old wounds re-appeared, gnashing their teeth, howling and screaming. It was then that I tumbled deep down into the dark night of the soul.

The Dark Knight of the Soul

By the time 2017 rolled around, my mind seemed to have come to a stand-still. I had been more creatively productive in the year gone by than I had been for decades, and now, it felt like I was empty. All I had really wanted to do for some time now was to get away from words, which now just seemed to be lopping off my mind instead of coming from a deeper place.

Actually, the only thing I had really wanted to do was to make art, to play with colors, to put my feet in some more fertile part of my psyche. I let myself do this a little bit. But the connection to my writing self still felt insecure and tiny, and I felt like I *should* make an even bigger effort. So, I willed myself to apply for a significant writing fellowship, something I wouldn't have even tried to get before, and got to work on that.

By now, I had already had that first encounter with my Shadow. Now, as I willed myself to write, it felt as if I was writing my way back to my wounds. It was more journaling rather than writing. I don't know why I wanted to write about my wounds. Maybe, it was because I wanted to be seen, even if it was just me doing the seeing. Maybe, I wanted to purge them, get rid of them. Or maybe, I just wanted to remember.

Whatever it was, in the process of writing, of remembering and of almost feeling my pain once again, I seemed to set into motion something. A part of me, numbed and bereft, abandoned and forgotten, uncared for and desolate, seemed to come up and show me its face.

Except for the few people close to me, no one saw this happening. This was my interior life. More and more, I had been realizing how little people saw about me. Of course, I often hid my true opinions and didn't reveal myself. I was also a quiet person, a listener. But also, as I had learned more about being an INFP, I had seen more than once that all those internet images showing the tip of the iceberg to describe INFPs were true. People not close to me didn't usually see *anything* that was under the water.

All they saw was the tip of the iceberg.

This was as true in this tumultuous time, when things seemed to be breaking down, as it was in my normal day-to-day life. But this break wasn't an outer break. It was more of a break in the way I saw things. Things that had felt meaningful before no longer felt meaningful. It felt like the life had been drained out of them. All of a sudden, it seemed like even if I, one day, got all the things I had ever dreamed of, say, I became a successful writer, I knew, for sure, that that wasn't enough. None of the things we are all supposed to want, that we look to for our happiness, seemed to make sense. They were not the answer.

It was as if the world was stripped of its illusions. It lay flat on the ground, a dead thing made of meat with nothing alive in it.

Was writing stripping away my illusions? Had it scratched too close to something that had better be left closed up? Had I poked my wounds unnecessarily?

Somewhere during this time of deep despondency, as someone holding onto a straw, I read some articles on empath-focused websites like *Lonerwolf* that talked about how these could be signs of "waking up." I felt some truth in that view but after that little intake of breath, it felt as if this me "waking up" was just me hurtling down, one step after another, into a deep, dark dungeon, getting more and more bruised.

By the time 2016 had ended, I had already gathered symbols that felt like a marking of some psychological crossing. Suddenly feeling attracted to the symbol of the dragon, a dragon-shaped incense holder had found a home in my altar. It was almost a year later, on a trip to visit family in Scotland, that a girl with a stall full of dragon-themed accessories would tell me that the dragon was considered the gatekeeper to a different level of consciousness, a different part of yourself. The image of the dragon was a formidable symbol, the beast you had to fight to get to the treasure within.

All through the previous year, 2016, I had felt as if the attraction to this symbol had been some portent of doom. For the first time in my life, I had felt pure hatred. It was something I had never experienced before, even in the worst of times, even when my soul had felt dismembered. But after the dragon had appeared, as I had journaled and dug deeper with my words, something else had come up. It had to do with an ancient, arrested wound.

In my life now, I was trying to set a boundary related to it. But it was being pushed against. Even when I tried to explain why that boundary was so important to me and how it was connected to my wound, it felt like I wasn't understood. Even when I tried to explain it, as best as I could, I felt like I wasn't heard.

That made me want to hold onto this decades-old wound like a mother does to a child, like you do to some precious part of yourself that no one understands but that you still want to keep, not for its terrible hurt but because it contains all those parts of you that have been rent from you, that no one else has seen. It's that part of you that remembers.

It's that part of you that cries for help, that doesn't hide quite so well as everyone else would like, that might remain underground for years but then it comes up when you are scarcely ready, staking its claim in your life, asking you for its voice.

The Lessons of Hatred

For months, I struggled with these overwhelming feelings. An infant part of me howled in pain. I felt an intense push and pull as I went between trying to people-please, unsure of whether it was even okay for me to have this boundary, and feeling deep anger at having to struggle like this again. During these long months, often rages took over my inner landscape. It seemed as if my Shadow was breaking. Afterwards, as I tried to tame that rage, I fell into apathy and depression.

What did those long, dark months of being shrouded in anger and swelling with hatred teach me?

I am hardly an expert on emotions and definitely not on hatred, but this is what I can say. Hatred, for me, came when it felt like no one understood the depths of my wound, the depths of my pain. I slipped down into an old feeling of being all alone in the world. It came because I was being asked to give of myself in a way that crossed the terrain of my wound. The thing that was being asked was not, in itself, huge. But it was a thing that crossed the boundaries of my pain, that struck it like you might strike some damaged creature with an iron stick.

Then, my wound howled and broke.

It was the little child inside, the one who liked to please, the one who found it very hard to say No and shore up its boundaries, that couldn't protect this vulnerable space. Because it couldn't hold the fort, because it didn't realize what it had let in through the gates, my wound got

236

contaminated. It festered. Hatred spun out of it.

It was during this tumultuous time, these months when I was feeling tossed here and there, out of control of my feelings, that Karla McLaren's work became my lifeline. I had read her book *The Language of Emotions* a few years back. Now, in a moment of grace, I remembered her work. She was a fellow HSP and she talked about emotions in a very nuanced way. Maybe, something in her work could help me.

Like other teachers who don't consider specific emotions "positive" or "negative," Karla McLaren also thought that each and every emotion serves a function. Sadness, for example, that thing that none of us wants to feel, is exactly the emotion we need to let go of losses. Like other emotions, sadness lives on a scale. The softest form of sadness could just be sighing, a physical movement in which we let go. So, after a day of hard work, we might instinctively sigh and physically let go of the day and its burdens. There's a sense of movement and change in this.

Then, there is the other end of the scale, those times when we feel saturated with sadness. Then, actually feeling this sadness and crying is what helps us let go, helps us move ahead. If we don't let ourselves feel this sadness in an effort to circumvent its pain and protect ourselves, we are also inadvertently holding on to whatever feeling our sadness would have helped us release.

When I had first come across her work, the way Karla McLaren talked about emotions had added another dimension to my understanding. I had learned earlier in life how important it was to feel my feelings. McLaren not only reemphasized some of these same concepts -

that even so-called "negative" emotions have a positive function - but she also added new information to the mix. Now, caught up in the currents of my cycling anger and my uncaring apathy, I again looked up her work. She had a YouTube channel. On her website, she also had an extensive Emotional Vocabulary list that described the different forms and degrees of different emotions.

She talked about many things that directly helped me. Apathy, she said, was anger in one of its less intense states. It was just one of the many forms anger can take. While apathy didn't sound helpful at all, especially to a layperson like me, psychologically, it played a very important role. Apathy helped us tolerate intolerable conditions.

Let's say we are in a situation that we find extremely disorienting and intolerable, but for some practical reason, we *have* to be a part of it. Then, in that case, apathy can help us withstand it. At least for the time being, we can still remain there physically. We can tolerate the situation to some degree because apathy provides a protective distance from it. So, even apathy, if it is specific to a situation and doesn't become something we *always* feel, plays a protective role just like other forms of anger.

Karla McLaren's Emotional Vocabulary list talked in detail about anger, this emotion I was so struggling with, and the different ways in which it showed up. I already knew some of these, but there were some I hadn't consciously thought about before. Words like resentment, of course, pointed to anger but even when someone was being sarcastic or acting cold towards you, that could be an indicator of underlying anger as well. In its most intense form, anger showed up as hatred and feeling vengeful and vicious.

When I read that, I thought about how I hadn't listened to my anger. I hadn't used it as fuel to build better boundaries. I had let it grow and grow till it had a life of its own. Now, it felt as if I had little control on this mass of hurt and aggression and resentment that was all bitterly fused together. It felt like my Shadow could take over me, as if my searing hatred had an alarming forward thrust that could be very destructive. It felt like it could break away, go rogue at any moment.

It was during this dark night of the soul that Karla McLaren's work became my guiding light to the other side.

When I looked on her website, a blog post she had written about hatred felt like a lifeline that could help me understand this terrifying, destructive, out-of-control anger that I was riding day in and day out. It explained something crucial about the nature of hatred.

Before, even in the most desperate times, I had never felt the need to exact revenge. Without having to learn it, I had always known that revenge did not work, that it would only take me down, that I was large enough to not retaliate. But now, in the throes of slashing rage, a feeling I didn't know I was capable of having had developed. It was a sense of wanting revenge, of trying to show people exactly how much pain they had put me through. It was a sense of feeling deeply angered at not being understood and feeling vicious about it.

What scared me the most was that this feeling had an energy all of its own, as if it was a stone boulder falling down a hill, not an ordinary feeling within my own hands, within my own control. Unconscious of it, I hadn't realized how much momentum it had gained. Again and again, revengeful thoughts played out in my mind. It was as if my normal persona, everything I thought I was, was stripped away, and I was just a mass of seething rage and anger.

It was McLaren's blog post on hatred that pulled me out of this ugly morass. She told me something very important about the nature of hatred. Hatred, she said, was a sticky feeling. While it has an element of disgust in it, the feeling of disgust itself only makes us want to recoil from someone or something unpleasant. But hatred is more than just disgust and revulsion. Hatred makes us attach to whatever we hate.

There's a forward-marching, aggressive movement to hatred, that onward thrust that was making me more and more scared. Instead of getting as far away as possible when someone truly disgusts us, with hatred, we become obsessively drawn to our targets. We not just *don't remove* ourselves from the situation or them from our lives, we intimately connect ourselves to them. It's as if some vein passes between them and us, and our intense feelings are focused on the object of our hatred.

This was certainly true for me. My hatred seemed to be focused on one particular person. Intellectually, I knew what I was feeling was out of all proportion. But my wound was paining so much and my feelings had grown so violent that rationality had no part to play in it. It was all about raw, seething emotion.

In the end, it was becoming aware of this obsessive nature of hatred that saved me. It was a little gap, a little pause in the tornado of feeling. This understanding became a life raft, a tiny piece of knowledge at a time when I was sinking down fast. It did not make the hatred go away all at once. Over months of raging and trying to purge and control it, there was an intense negotiation every moment between me and my out-of-control feelings.

It was only this leftover awareness and some tools I had learned earlier in life that saved me. Bit by bit, inch by inch, every day, I swam a little further in the chasm, not knowing whether I was going to sink or swim. But somehow, with help, I came out on the other side of the shore. After I was done with hatred, apathy and depression overtook me completely. But they were still more welcome adversaries than that terrible deluge of rage and hatred.

Even now, I know I have pockets of resentment in my heart. Sometimes, I fear the chasm might open again if I don't heal the unhealed parts of myself. My hatred, after all, was anger not listened to, anger disowned, anger intensified. My hatred, after all, had hurt and sadness mixed up in it. Hatred, after all, was trying to get my attention, when I hadn't listened to less threatening emissaries.

It was asking me to repair my boundaries, to stand up for myself and for my own experiences. So, I now know that one way or another, I must tear away all those blanket agreements I have made to keep quiet, to not say what I am thinking, to play dead even though I am very much alive. Anger is the sentry on my boundaries, and hatred means I have ignored the sentry and let my sacred self be breached.

This battle with hatred told me, for the first time in my

life, something about *some* kinds of hatred. While McLaren also talked about bigger problems like racism and homophobia when she talked about hatred, problems I didn't know enough about, as one single person feeling the emotion of hatred, I could see how hatred might sprout in the heart of someone who is disenfranchised. Of course, not all hatred works like this. Racism, for example, is often about making people, who are themselves disenfranchised, the "other."

But I think *some* hatred happens when something has been torn away, and only you have felt its absence for a very long time. This hatred comes from a deep hurt that goes unacknowledged, a hurt that you feel all alone in the world with, that makes you feel as if a gulf separates you and the rest of humanity. In these cases, hatred can tell us that someone has fought a hard, long battle, a battle they still might be fighting and that maybe, just maybe, we should see things from their perspective.

Like many people, I used to think that I was beyond hatred. I am a relatively loving person. I am a quite forgiving person. But with the experience with my hatred, I see I have to do a better job of honoring my own self. If I had been firm and sure of my boundaries and not given them up in the first place, I would never have felt hatred. I would not have gone through those venomous months. I would not have felt as if I was psychologically teetering on the edge, gazing at an abyss, almost ready to destroy all the wonderful things in my life because I got so attached to my hurt and anger.

In truth, I gave my power away. The message in anger is *always* to protect the precious self within and to stand up for it. But I kept on discounting the voice of anger till it grew and grew and collected charge and feeling. I did not

242

consider myself important enough, sacred enough to listen to my own feelings and what they were telling me.

That's the risk so many of us have, if we are sensitive and have developed a way of being where we give indiscriminately. Sometimes, we are giving good things from a healthy place. But sometimes, we are just giving away pieces of our soul. I don't think empaths are somehow different from other people in this basic sense. We all have the capacity for hatred and love, for strength and weakness, for courage and cowardice.

For empaths, with our common struggle with boundaries, it's important to see that we are not unlimited beings. Only the divine is unlimited. We are human beings and like everyone else, we have both light and darkness, good and bad inside. We also have our own needs, needs that can fall by the wayside when we take on the task of caretaking another person.

Living in a different country and having to build a new structure has shown me that my energy *is* limited. I have to create a sustainable system where I am getting energy as well as giving energy. It's important to see when someone is encroaching on my energy or goodwill.

Otherwise, like a car run out of gas, I stall. I can't go on any longer. I also have to learn about my boundaries and know that the interior of my life is mine alone. It's not something for other people to charge into, to know everything about, to get into. It's my sacred space. If giving and healing are part of my purpose, then I have to also heal me and learn to give in a way that works for not just the other, but for me as well. That's not selfish. That's self-protective.

Maybe, being confronted with the Dragon of my wound was worthwhile. Maybe, it was as the Dragon girl in Scotland said later on. That symbol had risen just before I felt enclosed in my wound, just as I dropped into its raw, fleshy parts, just as I felt as if any movement would set it off, make it scream louder and louder for revenge. The fight had felt exactly like I was fighting some giant creature or my inner demon. It was a confrontation that could have gone this way or that. If I had fallen, the Dragon would have been the portent of doom just as how I had first thought about it. But maybe, it was also something more.

Later on, when I read more works by depth psychologists, I came across a related, but different idea for the meaning of the symbol of the Dragon. In *Soulcraft*, that book I had left without completing it, Bill Plotkin talked about how the call, *"the opening of a destiny,"* is signaled across the mythologies of many different cultures by the appearance of a herald - a frog, a serpent, a dragon or even some dark and mysterious person. These dark but bewitching creatures are mythology's way of embodying the mystery as well as the power of the call to adventure.

Of course, as I found, there are no guarantees on an adventure, whether it's outward or inward. Things can go either ways. But reading this felt hopeful, as if our dragons are not just portents of destruction but challengers on a path that we've chosen. It was amazing how in the couple of years before my dark knight had come riding on its horse, *all* the symbols that Plotkin mentioned had become attractive to me. The serpent had been there, of course. I had also become more interested in animals. I read about them and drew and painted them more and more. I had painted a frog, a coyote and then, towards the end of my struggle with hatred, a mountain lion.

It was one of my favorites. I had drawn its outline in pencil, looking at and copying just its outline from an illustrated book on Shamanic animals. But then, inside, I had filled it with my own colors, shades of red in the body set against a black and teal background. I had somehow managed to give the mountain lion my own expression. It looked fierce and angry, as if it could tear you to pieces, as if I could tear you to pieces.

This mountain lion has become my symbol for the necessary anger I am learning to hold and channel. It's a symbol for honoring my self-protective instincts. In a way, it's like a symbol for *Kaali* or *Durga*, in their hands, the power to destroy and renew. Maybe, my anger can destroy the brambles of my adapted, docile self. Maybe, I can then give in a way that's an authentic expression of me and not mixed in with people pleasing and placating other people's momentary emotions.

Today, the mountain lion lives inside a black frame on one of my living room walls. At first, I thought whether it was okay to put it there, in this more public space of the house. But isn't it here, in these public spaces that I need to channel and assert my anger? Isn't it here that my anger must learn to live, must learn to ferociously walk my boundaries?

So, here, the mountain lion stays now, solitary and alone, unafraid of striking out on its own. It is my guidepost, the symbol for a way of being I hope, one day, to become, someone unafraid to live on a mountain, someone unafraid to walk all alone, even if no one around understands them. The battle with my hatred, seeing how it points the way to some ravaged, lost part of me, has brought this symbol to me. Now, when I feel weak and unsure, I know that I am this too, this fierce, solitary part that has walked its own path before and that can again gather the strength to go it alone again.

Chapter 6

Coming Back Home

Again and again, over the last six years, I have thought a lot about self-compassion and how being in this new country was so much tougher for me because I didn't know how to hold and comfort myself. I didn't give myself enough space to make mistakes, to be imperfect and to move slowly.

In the beginning, I even doubted my own perceptions. I discounted the validity of all the subtle nuances my sensitivity brought me. I looked at myself just like everyone else looked at me. I found myself wanting. But learning about the SPS trait from Dr. Aron's *The Highly Sensitive Person* and then exploring it for myself opened up my sensitivity for me.

What if I didn't see myself through other people's eyes? What if I understood that although we are basically the same, I was also different from other people in a fundamental way? Wasn't it violence to keep on trying to make myself into something I just wasn't? Wasn't it true that many of my problems with my sensitivity were because of how much I was always pushing against it, trying to flatten it out? What if bit by bit, piece by piece, I could redraw the picture of my sensitivity?

In the last six years, experiences, both big and small, have showed me that I often do notice things that other people don't seem to register. Of course, when I am overstimulated, I am not this perceptive. Then, I am just overwhelmed. But on a day-to-day level, my sensitivity brings me nuances and shades of things. Because these are little tendrils, little threads of feelings and sensations, in the beginning, it's hard to even articulate them. They are also invisible to people who don't notice such things, so it's sometimes hard to stand up for them. But that doesn't mean that they are unreal or invalid.

For the first time in my life, during these last few years, I have experienced little shoots of self-compassion growing inside me as I have looked back. A decade ago, in my corporate job in Delhi, there were times when I treated myself so much like a machine that I wouldn't even eat till late afternoon or evening. That would be my first meal of the day. Those were the years when I found even giving myself these simple biological strokes hard. So, I know what it means to struggle with self-compassion.

All these years later, now, when I leave the house, more often than not, I carry a bottle of water. Now, I think about myself. I consider my needs. I am no longer trying to cut myself down to fit inside a box. That's what change looks like to me, that's what self-compassion looks like.

My journey to self-compassion has included looking at *why* taking care of myself has sometimes felt like such hard work. I think for some of us, self-care is hard because it feels like an obligation. It's another thing we have to do for ourselves. In her lovely book, *Wellspring of Compassion*, Sonia Connolly talks about how self-care can even sound like abandonment if we were emotionally or physically neglected as children but still longed for someone to take care of us. Imagine that, imagine how hard it can be if taking care of ourselves feels like abandonment.

I definitely resonate with this. There have been times in my life when *not* taking care of myself has almost felt like a protest. No. I wouldn't take care of myself. Wasn't I lovable enough for someone else to take care of me?

But the task of growing up, and I am still growing up in my late 30s, is to realize that I, myself, need to give myself many of the things I have looked for from others. Maybe, the reason I have rescued so much is because I feel such sympathy for anyone who is in trouble. Maybe, it means that the little child inside me is not looking at people and situations as they are, but as how that little child feels inside or how it imagines *they* feel inside. When I rescue others, sometimes, I am also attempting to rescue myself in some weird, contorted way. I am projecting my needy, vulnerable self onto others. It's this self that needs my compassion.

In the past few years, there are two things I have learned that have helped me in this journey. They are two things I am still learning to be, both at the same time. The first is to go deep into my feelings and really feel them. *Don't feel your feelings* is an injunction I have lived with for most of my life. *Be Strong.* Or rather, *Appear Strong, Act Strong Even When You Don't Feel Anything Like That. In fact, Go against Your feelings. Just Don't feel your feelings.*

This is a tricky injunction to undo. Sometimes, I do need to go against my feelings. Once in a while, I do have to be stoic about things. But *always* discounting my feelings is not healthy. It means discounting all the information my feelings bring me. It means not giving importance to my discomfort, to my sense of things being off, to my intuition, to my curiosities, to my loves. So, in the past few years, I have turned towards my feelings, imperfectly and clumsily at times, but turned nevertheless and given them the importance they deserve.

The second thing is something that looks like the opposite of feeling my feelings. It's becoming more pragmatic and putting a stopper on all the places from where my energy leaks. It's about constructing more boundaries, both physical and emotional. It's about getting to the roots of my unhealthy patterns, so they don't masquerade as empathy. So, part of my journey has been about unlearning unhealthy emotional habits.

Uprooting Emotional Patterns

During the time when I was taking photography courses in the first few years after the move, for a class assignment, I went to the San Jose Museum of Art to view a traveling exhibition I had to write a report on. That day had started normally. I had walked through the exhibit, making notes, looking at the little blurbs on the sides of the photographs and the paintings. I had wondered once again why museums made art so inaccessible.

Why were there only these snippets of technical specifications, such as what paper and ink had been used? Apart from artists and photographers, why would this even matter to anyone else? Why was there no story, no context for these artworks?

As I had walked through the main hall, I had been slightly bored that day, even as someone who so loves art. I had made notes, felt a little awkward about staring at something for too long, and thought about how nothing was appealing to me emotionally. As it is, I was up in my head. Now, this was also an empty intellectual exercise. I had ambled along like this, half-interested, till I had finally meandered to the other side of the hall. There was a door here, and the exhibit seemed to spill over into several other rooms at the back. I had stepped in.

As soon as I walked through that door, it was as if the energy had shifted. I was already feeling it. I was already starting to get affected. As I walked around, reading the descriptions, it turned out that these rooms were filled with works by artistes who had suffered from AIDS. If art is about moving someone, there was definitely art here. There was one canvas with black scrawled-out paint lines. It looked dazedly confused and endlessly jumbled up. Another work was by an HIV-positive photographer whose partner and several friends had passed away as part of the AIDS epidemic.

As I had walked through this area, I had tried to *not feel*, tried to focus and just read and make notes. But the more I had looked, the longer I remained in that room, the more and more overwhelmed I had gotten, even though I tried to be "normal." This was not an empty intellectual exercise. This was not looking at things from a distance.

This was like walking headfirst into someone's pain, touching their raw despair and confusion hurled on pieces of paper. This was looking at suffering which had congealed and solidified, that felt as dank as tar. It felt as if I was inside the pieces of someone's soul, inside someone's life as they sat emotionally naked, flogged down on their knees, not knowing why these terrible things were happening to them, not knowing how to deal with them.

This was the record of the suffering of a community.

By the time I had made my way through these rooms, pretending this wasn't affecting me, I had a terrible, pounding headache. It felt like I had "caught" some of the depression of these amazing photographers and painters, some of their utter hopelessness. The world was tightening around me just as I imagined it might have tightened around them.

By the time I had reached home, all I had wanted was to stop feeling like this, stop feeling so overwhelmed. All I had wanted was to get away, to hide myself under a blanket, to escape somehow. All clogged up with these feelings, I had thought of how sensitivity *was* a weakness, this uncontrollable feeling of being so taken over by someone else's emotions.

This happened during the time when I had already come across the word "empath" and started becoming a little aware of what it might mean. I had thought then that maybe, this was why, consciously or unconsciously, so many people didn't like visiting museums. Art could be so many different things. Sometimes, it was soul-touchingly beautiful. But sometimes, it was also like this, this feeling of being set ablaze, this feeling of being scorched right through. Maybe, those people who didn't like museums were on to something. They had an impulse, a quite natural one, to move away from pain.

So why had I kept on *making myself* go through the exhibit? I could have seen some part of it, written my report and let it go at that. Why had I kept on exposing myself and getting more and more overwhelmed? Part of it was that I was still trying to pretend that I didn't *feel* as affected as I did, that I was "normal," that intense experiences like this didn't impact me. It was flogging myself into appearing like everyone else. I was also so used to willing myself forward, discounting my feelings, even when they got more and more turbulent. It was as if

I was again treating myself inhumanely, like I used to do when I willed myself to work without eating anything for hours on end.

All this was true, but there was also one other thing.

I think I have a tendency to keep fiddling with, to keep going into those places of my being that have been contaminated, that have pus oozing out, that are the receptacles of my greatest pain. It's a rebellion at not being seen, at not being witnessed, at being told that I feel too much, at being told that these feelings don't matter. I don't know what to do with whatever pain I have inside, and it almost feels like honoring this pain, honoring my experiences to hold on to it.

Of course, I hadn't thought about this in so many words and so clearly that day, but that was really part of it. This is one of the reasons why when I see extreme pain, I keep on walking with it. I feel sympathy, not empathy, sympathy because I see someone else who is walking alone in their pain.

But in reality, this dysfunctional way of honoring others' pain as well as my own hasn't ever worked. These kinds of intense experiences always leave me overwhelmed. I think there is a healthy part to avoiding *some* pain. Going through this exhibition was like watching an open wound and having that intense pain jump out of it and into my own wound. Even if I didn't have my wound, it would have still affected me. But because I do have a wound, it left me doubled up with pain.

That day, afterwards, I had thought that walking away from this exhibition as well as these kinds of situations was one emotional boundary I could possibly set.

Realizing when my own pain was triggered and taking care of it instead of obstinately charging through was one way to have compassion for myself.

Did that mean that I should *always* walk away? No, that wasn't it. It was not that I wouldn't ever go to another exhibition like this. These were important, valuable experiences. But it was wise to see whether I was emotionally filled up or half-empty *before* I approached any experience that might be emotionally exhausting. I did believe that creating this kind of art was useful, both for those artistes who had created it as well as for anyone who could watch it. For those artistes, it was catharsis, moving some of their pain out, expunging it, burning it. For other people, it was a bridge into an experience, an entry point. But was taking on this writhing pain and feeling it helpful?

That's where many of us get stuck as empaths. There have been countless times when I have felt so overwhelmed by others' feelings that I have been on the floor with them, crying out in pain. Then, all I have wanted to do is to get away from everyone, to hide myself under a blanket, to get away from the world. That's not helpful to anyone. It obviously doesn't help me. But it also doesn't help anyone else. It creates nothing except feeling disintegrated and felled down.

That day, I thought, maybe, it's wise to see the limitations of my energy. Maybe, it's wise to learn discernment and understand what actually helps and what doesn't. Maybe, it's even crucial to see that I can't be of any use if I am excessively open all the time or always abandoning the little child inside who needs to be helped first.

This was just one way to put a stopper on energy leaks.

This was just one healthy boundary to set. Just as I had learned that I wasn't a lightning rod for other people's feelings, I could choose to tune in to my own self and energy level first. Only then could I not be overwhelmed and washed ashore, only then could my attunement to feelings serve me well.

This is just one emotional boundary I have learned to practice in the last few years. Another boundary I am still learning about has to do with understanding the different faces of my resistance. As a creative person, I have often come across one particular kind of resistance, the unhealthy kind, the one that makes me procrastinate, the one that is my fear talking. But there's also another kind of resistance, one that is both healthy and life-affirming, and that's something to pay attention to.

Sonia Connolly talks about this kind of resistance in her book *Wellsprings of Compassion*. In it, she talks of an experience she had with a client in her practice that underlined how resistance can sometimes be healthy. As someone who combined different therapeutic approaches like Massage Therapy, Reiki, Craniosacral Therapy and Trauma Work to help others heal from trauma, Sonia Connolly was again working with someone who was learning to inhabit their body.

But at the beginning of this specific bodywork session, her client admitted that he had been feeling extremely resistant to coming and seeing her. When she asked him why, he said that he was extremely exhausted. He just didn't want to pay any more attention to his pain. Already, it took up such a large chunk of his life. This day, he was fatigued just by the thought of all the healing work he still needed. He was so tired of feeling his pain.

In the book, Sonia Connolly talks about how after this conversation, she changed the focus of the session to a relaxation massage so she could support her client instead of trying to dig deeper. In this case, her client's resistance was a genuine expression of his exhaustion. He was already taking the action needed to work through his pain. But it was hard work. He was tired of it, tired of feeling his pain, not sure when it would finally end. He was dispirited and not up to dealing with his pain that day. His resistance was a genuine call to take things slow, to let his trauma be for a while so he could rest and take a break, so he could come back to the process with his energy renewed.

What would have happened if he hadn't expressed these resistant feelings? What would have happened if he had judged himself as weak and thought his resistance was self-sabotage? What would have happened if he had tried to bulldoze his way through?

If he had gone through the more demanding session, it's very likely he would have felt completely overwhelmed by the end of it. He would have thought that he just couldn't take the process any more. He might have completely backed off from this healing work entirely. Instead of understanding he needed a break from what felt like a never-ending struggle, he would have fallen fast into the murky depths of helplessness.

When I read this, I thought about how I had often done the opposite in cases like these. I had often tried to bulldoze my way through hard things. This pattern came from a combination of different beliefs, but one of them was a loud, internal voice that repeated how my sensitivity was a weakness, that derided it, that told me to move against it.

What these past six years have given me is a little inroad into self-compassion. They have taught me to ask: *When I don't judge others for their different needs, why do I then judge myself?* They have showed me that I do notice subtle differences and that all these details keep bothering me till I can place them in a context.

These are two sides of the same coin - noticing gradations and then getting overwhelmed. I can't have one without the other. When I can acknowledge my needs and take care of them, I function well. But when I get into the game of comparing myself with others whose needs are different and internalizing the voice that questions whether I *should even get overwhelmed in the first place when others don't,* it's then that sensitivity becomes a cross to bear. It's then that I am at war with myself.

But if I can be this different self, then I have lessened my burden almost by half. If I can stop comparing myself to others and see that we have different ways of being, each as valid as the other, then that's one way of honoring myself. This is something I am still practicing and still learning to do. But now, from my new vantage point, I have given up at least some of other people's filters.

I have learned, for example, that caution and fear are different things. It's my fear that I have to get rid of, not the slow, considered style that is part of my very being. Like every style, this deliberate thinking and then acting has its pros and cons just as acting first and thinking later has its pros and cons. But now, I can finally see the pros and cons of *both* styles. They are just different approaches, not better or worse in themselves.

Now, I can see how my attunement to details and my curiosity give me a more complete picture if I can just stay with these scratchy, irritating subtleties instead of prematurely drawing conclusions. Now, I can see that my intense feelings are raw materials I can shape into many different things. Now, I can see that if I listen to their deeper messages, I come closer to myself.

Now, I can see that authenticity is not about idolizing the past. It's about rooting myself in the present. In this great melting pot of the world, my Indianized Green Curry with fresh *kadipatta* and *dhania* powder and Rohit's Indian tacos with chicken *keema* and *garam masala* are not compromises with traditions, but notes in new songs. When I do go deeper into my own culture and take two hours to cook a dish the same way my mother makes it, it gives me more appreciation for all cooks everywhere. Whether we are making *Pakode-wali kadi,* breaking chocolate to add to our *mole* sauce, or making pasta from scratch, we are all attempting to weave together our worlds.

In all of these worlds, behind the different tastes and sounds and colors, there are similar myths and monsters, demons and deities, tricksters and heroic figures. Whether we are familiar with Sophia or Pele, Saraswati or Aphrodite, we are all being called by the currents of deeper energies. Now, I know that I need to look inside to commune with these energies. Now, I can sense how they can be my guiding force.

Now, I am no longer as impressed by outer forms. Just because someone appears more confident does not mean that they know what they are talking about. Some of my "maybes," some of my not declaring black and white, is exactly because I notice nuances. There's a maybe that comes from not believing in yourself, something I am giving up by and by, but there's also a maybe that comes from seeing subtleties. Owning that "maybe," owning the different shades of gray I see means I now own my perceptions instead of just going along with the more surely-articulated opinions of others.

Some of the laying down of my "nice" is exactly this. It's owning that I see things a little differently or notice different things.

Over the last few years, I have been able to reframe at least some of my ideas of sensitivity.

In part, it finally happened because finally, I also started doing something I have struggled with for most of my life. I started to give myself, however slowly, gradually and imperfectly, positive strokes. This was something I didn't even have the capacity for earlier in my life. But miraculously, in the tumult of constructing a new life, new shoots appeared. They grew and grew, till I could finally start doing something I had struggled with so terribly, for so long.

Finally, I could start becoming my own good mother.

Giving Yourself Positive Strokes

Giving yourself positive strokes is an idea that comes from *Transactional Analysis*, a system of psychotherapy that I first came across during my Delhi days. Specifically, the idea of Strokes comes from the work of Claude Steiner, a psychotherapist who created the concept of the *Stroke Economy* in the 1960's. So, what exactly is this Stroke Economy, and why is this a helpful concept?

Just as we are all part of the monetary economy, the

marketplace, in the same way, psychologically, we are all part of a kind of marketplace as well. But we are in this market not to earn money, but to earn psychological currency like acceptance and appreciation, to get what Claude Steiner called *strokes*, which we can think of as imaginary units of recognition.

We all want to be acknowledged, paid attention to, appreciated, and valued. That's what most of us are trying to do in our interactions with people. We are trying to get strokes, whether it's a simple stroke like being said Hi to when we walk into the office or more profound strokes such as wanting love and appreciation in our families. All of us are looking for these different kinds of strokes, these different forms of recognition, and many of the things we do each and every day of our lives are simply bids to get these strokes.

But aren't these emotional strokes, like praise or a hug, aren't these all free, unlike physical goods or services that require money? Why aren't we then all filled up and satiated? Why do some of us feel like we have to go to such extreme lengths to get these strokes, such as being overly nice to people or working way too hard?

Steiner tells us that this is because of the way the Stroke Economy works. In a way, the Stroke Economy is very much like an economy based on money. Let's say money is in short supply and hard to get. Then, people will work very hard just to earn enough to get their basic needs met. In such as situation, we could, in fact, control all these people by controlling their access to money. If we had the capital, the resources, we could get them to work very, very hard for very, very little.

The psychological *Stroke Economy* works in the same way.

Even though strokes like love, appreciation or acknowledgement are supposedly free, many times, our parents or caretakers have many restrictive rules about how to give or receive strokes. This sometimes makes these strokes, these little packets of recognition, very hard to get. These limiting rules might have been part of our parents' own conditioning. They might never have consciously considered them or realized they were passing on these behavioral rules about giving and receiving to us.

But, whether it happens consciously or unconsciously, these restrictive rules mean that these strokes, these little bundles of love and acceptance, are often in short supply for us as children. Many of us have to work extra hard to earn them, to get them, to keep them.

Once these unsaid "rules" are passed on to us, they also become our own internalized rules. They become part of our conditioned, scripted self that learned its lessons well as a child. As an adult, these rules are part of our automatic behavior. Unless we think about them and consciously change them, we can keep on doing the same things we always did, keep on doing the same things that, in fact, our parents did.

So, what are these five restrictive rules?

Don't give strokes you would like to give. Don't ask for strokes that you would like to get. Don't accept strokes you would like to accept. Don't reject strokes you don't want. Don't give yourself strokes.

Let's say we unconsciously learned this unspoken rule: *Don't give strokes you would like to give.* In this case, we will hold ourselves back even when we could give a positive stroke. We might hold ourselves from praising someone, for example.

If we have the second rule operating somewhere deep inside us, *Don't ask for strokes you would like to get*, then we won't ask directly for what we want. We keep on waiting because we don't have the internal permission to directly ask for what we need. Sometimes, this is where I fail miserably. Rohit is a very thoughtful person, but like many wives, I expect him to guess what I want. But the reality of life is that sometimes, he gets so busy and tired that he doesn't have a lot of energy left over.

Then, if I can remember this rule and what trouble I have with asking directly, I can then remind myself to directly ask him for strokes, such as doing something like going to see a show together. Often, he will readily agree. But because I haven't gutted this part of my conditioning completely, sometimes I just wait and wait and feel more and more like I am not getting what I need. But I am the best authority on what I need at any given moment.

Changing the scripted, automatic self is about doing what my conditioning tells me *not* to do. *Don't ask for strokes you want*. But why not? At least with the people we are close to, asking can mean getting. It can mean filling ourselves up.

Just like this negative rule, most of us have also either ourselves been or seen people who operate from *Don't accept strokes you would like to accept*. If we have this internalized rule, we deflect compliments. We don't easily take in what we genuinely like or need. There is a prohibition inside us that tells us to not take the good stuff in.

Then, there is the fourth rule: *Don't reject strokes you don't want*. This destructive rule makes it hard for us to say no to what doesn't work for us and to uphold our boundaries. One example of this is someone standing physically too close to you when you are not comfortable with it but you don't say anything to that person.

The last destructive rule is something I have struggled with all my life. In the past few years, I have managed to shift some of it. As someone learning to fill myself up, it has been and still is a crucial rule to break: *Don't give strokes to yourself.* Till just a few years ago, I was always a little puzzled by this rule. How do you actually give strokes to yourself? How do you give yourself acceptance, appreciation and love?

It was in Delhi that I had first learned about the Stroke Economy and started working with it. It was another period of my life, another inner journey. That time, I had, in fact, even been part of a group where we freely gave each other positive strokes. In those circles of women, we would go one by one, giving each other words of praise. When someone's turn would come, first one person, then another, would clearly tell them what they appreciated about them. Someone might praise them for their gentle energy. Someone else might say how much they admired the way they carried themselves. We would go one by one, till every person had received positive strokes.

More often than not, these were what are called *unconditional positive strokes*, strokes for *being*, rather than *doing*. These are the kind of strokes we are most hungry for, recognition that people see us as who we are, that they appreciate our intrinsic being, who we are in our very essence. We more deeply want to be told that people notice our shining qualities and not just what we do well, such as what a great worker we are. We want to be told that we are good, kind, brave, thoughtful, resilient or strong.

Of course, conditional positive strokes like being told we are a great team player also have value. But really, it's the unconditional positive strokes that we most long for. We want to be appreciated for those inherent qualities in us that make us, us.

This is exactly what we gave each other in those circles. As we went around the circle, each and every woman would have tears in her eyes as the others counted and acknowledged all the wonderful things about her. It was an amazing thing to see how people came alive when they were seen. It was almost as if we were suffused by our very essence when we saw our deepest self being mirrored back. It was as if a light that had been dimmed shone bright. After all such meetings, I went away feeling like myself, instead of feeling hazy and vague, instead of feeling unseen and invisible.

But during this time, while I had gotten better at giving strokes and practicing saying No to some strokes I didn't want, I always struggled with giving positive strokes to myself. Sometimes, even when I tried to recall the five rules to remind myself, I would tellingly forget *Don't Give Yourself Strokes*. It was as if I couldn't even conceive what that meant.

How could you give yourself what you needed? How was this even possible? What if you needed love? Wasn't love what other people are supposed to give you? What if you wanted acceptance? Wasn't acceptance what other people are supposed to give you? How could you give these things to yourself?

Because I didn't even begin to understand this, because I was so needy for others to give me what I wanted, again and again, I would feel empty. If someone didn't praise or acknowledge me, if someone didn't say something nice to me, then that was how it was. I would walk around unfilled. I would live on unfilled.

Although I had struggled on and off with this rule before and had gotten a little better at it, it was only after moving to the States that I really grappled with it. Of course, it wasn't that I hadn't ever given myself positive strokes before. There had been times when I had done things like affirmations to give myself the positive words I so longed to hear from others. I had successfully given myself parts of what I needed, parts of what I liked. But this was the first time that I really wrestled deeply with this rule. This was the first time that I thought that maybe, if I weren't so stroke-starved, I would find it easier to set boundaries.

Maybe, if I weren't so stroke-starved, I would not neglect the red flags that showed up early on with many people. Maybe, then I would make swifter progress, feel more at home in this new country. Maybe, then my home would be inside me and not outside, a place of refuge that I carried everywhere with me. It was during this time that I started doing art, first with simple coloring books and then on my own and started working with my dreams and my intuition. These were all ways to fall back on myself and give myself the energy and guidance I so needed.

At first, this process of giving myself what I needed was a huge effort, as if I had to construct something I didn't have, the caretaker inside me. It was a frustrating process of two steps forward and one step back. Even today, it remains an effort for me. But like anything else you keep persisting at, this once mysterious process of giving myself what I needed, on my own, by myself, opened up a little space inside me.

Just attempting added bits and pieces to my sense of self, to my ability to nurture myself. Making sure I gave myself basic biological strokes, like drinking water or having breakfast, made a dent in the *Don't Exist* injunction I have carried inside forever. *Don't Exist. Don't be Yourself. Don't Feel your feelings.* Practicing existing, practicing being myself, and practicing feeling my feelings are ways in which I have become more self-loving. Loving myself means considering my unique needs, whether it's more time or less stimulation. Loving myself means seeing that it's okay to be a little different from the norm. Loving myself means gutting out my negative beliefs about sensitivity. It's about not flogging myself to fit into the square box.

It's still a process, and I lose the connection many times. But then I pick it up again. I count how far I have travelled, from five years ago, from ten years ago. Now, I am more of my alternative self than I have been for decades. Now, I let myself follow my curiosities, whether it's picking up books on herbs and flowers or learning more about the symbolic world. Tuning in to my intuition has shown me first-hand how much wisdom my body has, how much it knows before my mind knows. This journey into body-based intuition has led me in another interesting direction.

It has led me towards a deeper respect for my own body. Although I am still very early in my journey towards taking care of myself physically, one way in which I have fostered this connection in the last few years is by learning more about my menstrual cycle. Like my other curiosities, this felt very weird in the beginning. In fact, it often felt taboo. Or maybe, considering how we treat women's bodies, the feeling wasn't so weird after all.

But the more I have learned about the ebbs and flows of my energy during different times of my cycle, the more I understand both my body as well as my cyclic way of being. Now, I can see how my energy changes throughout the month in a very predictable way. It is inextricably linked to what's happening in my physical body. This is a step deeper into my own journey with the feminine. It reaffirms how going in a circle is as valid as going in a straight, linear line. Every month, in the pre-ovulation phase, for example, I often get clarity about problems I am dealing with. It's as if my reasoning is clearer during this time. This is also the time when I want to be out and about more. My energy is growing, just as the moon waxes and becomes fuller over the month.

Ovulation is my full moon. It is when I have the most energy. It is when I most want to go out, when I most want to do concrete, actionable things. After this comes pre-menstruation. During this time, the filament crackles. The line between this world and that becomes blurred for me. Now, the symbolic moon is waning. It's getting darker. My energy feels different. This is a period when my intuition seems to be gathering new things by the minute. Pictures emerge, giving hints. My energy is shifting, and now some part of me just wants to purge things.

When I write during this time, ideas spill out. They connect one by one into a long chain. This is also a good time to spot grammatical errors in my writing. It's as if the part of my brain that notices details gets switched on. It's an Editor that organically notices distinctions. I feel both highly intuitive and as if I want to release and let go. I feel like discarding things. So, it's a good time to declutter. But I also have to be a little careful that I don't discard too much in my zeal to unburden.

Working with these deep rhythms of my body instead of against them has given me a new perspective on how there are different ways to accomplish the same things.

I see how predictably my energy morphs once again as I inch towards my periods. Instead of a heightened ability to tune in to details, now I get irritated if I have to pay attention to puny, little things like grammatical errors. I don't want to be bothered about organizing paragraphs. I am open, receptive, vulnerable. This is winter-time, a time of slowing down, a time of letting go. All my unnamed, unspoken feelings rise with full force, as if they are a monster lashing in the sea. But now I know that this is a time of reckoning. It's truth time. Like other women, I get cranky, irritable, and sometimes fall in a pit of despair during my periods.

But unlike before, now, I know that the seemingly sudden appearance of all this angst is because there was undealt-with angst in the first place. I feel stretched and porous, less able to keep it all in. The difference is, now, instead of believing tales about how femininity is erratic and unpredictable, now I know that femininity is cyclical, not haphazard. It ebbs and flows. It waxes and wanes, almost to a schedule.

It creates. It destroys. It grows full. It sheds its skin. It undulates. It makes things in a kind of process that's less like joining pieces together and more like letting something emerge. Like water, it carves out a shape slowly, gradually, persistently. This is not one plus one logic. This is riding the waves of a current.

Falling deeper into this rhythm of my body has also served me in other practical ways. I have used some of this understanding of my energy while writing a part of this book. Even if all I could find was a stream of words, knowing my ebbs and flows, I was sure there would also come a time soon when I would want to organize. I have learned that it's okay to do what comes naturally. It's okay to flow and be receptive sometimes. It's also okay to *only* feel like organizing at other times instead of doing inspired writing. Just understanding that I have easier access to certain aspects of my writing at different times of the month is a powerful tool in my arsenal.

Of course, I haven't written like this all the time. But being attuned to changes in my energy helps me understand where I am and when I can go for a ride with that energy. It makes writing that much smoother. Just like my experience with dreams, I only had to scratch through the misshapen, hardly-spoken judgments about women's bodies lodged deep within me to find another energy current.

This process of connecting with my physical body has also led me to another insight.

Working with energy really is about *working with energy*. It's not wishing that the energy was different. It's not trying to ride flat water. It's about getting your board out, your boat out at a time when you can most easily get into the water. It's timing yourself so you ride the currents that are already there. It's working with nature, not against it. It's working with the energy that's *already* present. I think this is what working with energy really means. It's not some non-understandable process. The fact that empaths are so tuned in to energy simply means that we use our heightened sensitivity to pay attention to subtle changes in energy and then use them in any practical way we can figure out.

This tuning into the deeper current of my femininity has felt like the deepening of the circle, the deepening of the spiral. Now, I think that part of the reason so many creative people find it so hard to work in a straight line is because creativity is a circular process. But when we try to practice it, try to write or paint or make music, we try to work in the way we *think* is normal. But no, what comes through us is normal. It's not understanding this that sometimes makes creativity feel so monstrous. But it's just energy. It's just energy that is shifting and changing.

We are not meant to control it. We are meant to work with it.

As I have learned to work with and not against my true nature, this is exactly what I have attempted to do. In the last few years, I have re-written at least a portion of the story I was told about my sensitivity. Synchronicities have often showed up in my path. Sometimes, a dream will come, and then soon afterwards, I will find exactly the explanation I need for it.

In one recent dream fragment, a beautifully-dressed woman takes me through a chain of one beautiful, unused bathroom after another. They are all pristine and luxurious, fitted with bathtubs and jacuzzies. Soon afterwards, I open a book on menstruation to the exact page that talks about how premenstrual women often instinctively take long baths and showers. It's just before my periods. I have been full of shaking energy that feels almost destructive. So, I take the book's suggestion and take some long baths. Afterwards, I physically feel better.

Giving myself permission to be myself, to follow my interests, my feelings, my inner nudges has helped me give myself some of the positive strokes I need. It's in

270

being myself and validating my own needs, my own feelings and my own seeings that I can gather what gives me energy, whether it's encouraging, positive symbols or good, kind words.

I am still beginning. I am still learning. I still have many moments of being half-full and even less than half-full. But now, I know that I do have a capacity to give myself what I need. I can look inwards and strengthen the young, clueless mother inside me. She is still learning. She is still making mistakes. But finally, she is there.

What was once empty is now full.

Saying No to Strokes You Don't Want

As I finally complete this book, it's the end of 2018. Around a month ago, I was in India after many years. On the lane outside my parents' house, *raat ki raani,* the Queen of the Night, as night-blooming jasmine is called in Hindi, was in full bloom. It's ensnaring, enchanting perfume was a high note, a memory clip. In Delhi, I spent a delicious night finding and reading Hindi names for Indian flowers, trees, and perfumes online.

Periwinkle was *sadabahar,* literally translated as "always spring." Narcissus or daffodil was *nargis. Nag Champa* incense, it turned out, combined the fragrances of sandalwood and *Champa,* a kind of Indian plumeria that looks very much like those white *pua melia* with yellow centers that Hawaiian *leis* or flower necklaces are often made of.

At the end of the trip, I brought back what has become my favorite gift from India - essential oils and incense -

tiny glass bottles of *Kesar Chandan, a* saffron and sandalwood mix, *Nag Champa*, Lotus, and Vetiver or *Khus*. It was like buying a long-lasting sweet that I could enjoy bit by bit and really relish.

But along with these sweet-smelling memories, there also came a stench. During the trip, I had told many people about this book. Some were positive and happy for me. Some didn't care that much. But then, one person said something very dismissive. I had only told them that I was almost finishing my first book. I hadn't even told them what the book was about. But their discount seemed to center on the fact that I was wasting my time doing something so pointless as writing a book. A little while afterwards, they also made another remark about "*sensitive*" people, entirely disconnected with the book, but entirely connected with me.

I was low on energy that day, so I didn't reply in the self-affirming words I had used throughout this trip. That day, I just kept quiet. I don't know what it was about this particular remark that so did me in. A few other people had been slightly discounting as well, but maybe, some of the sting of this remark had to also do with the utter dismissal of my "sensitivity."

When I came back to the States, I felt utterly exhausted, completely overthrown by these casual words. *Nothing. Nothing. What I was trying to do was nothing. What I am was nothing.* I had worked very hard over a decade to exorcise just these words, but here they were again. *Nothing. Nothing.* I was so close to finishing the book. I had put in so much of myself in it. But now, all of a sudden, I felt a strange disinterest in it. *Who cared? I didn't.*

This was shame talking. It's something I have felt acutely

both as an empath and just as a person, at different times, for different reasons. Some of it was warranted, and some of it completely unwarranted. This time it told me once more that my very being was faulty.

As if this wasn't enough, I even felt ashamed at having let this person's remark get to me. Hadn't I learned anything at all in all these years? Hadn't I made any progress? Why was I back inside this archaic feeling? I had done so well through most of this trip. I had held up many different boundaries with many different people.

Even out and about in what felt like boundary-injured Delhi, I had said No more than I had ever before. I had said No when people had stood too close to me at a posh South Delhi mall and had told them to step back. I had even yelled at the cab driver who was trying to take a shortcut through a deserted lane late one night just to save some time. *Don't you know you are taking back two ladies at night in a place like Delhi? Don't you know that you should take the main road with its busy traffic and not some unlit lane?* Although the cab driver had protested, he *had* taken the main road. By the time our silent cab had reached my parents' home, he had even apologized. Overall, throughout the trip, I had been less "nice" and more self-protective than I had ever been before.

But now, maybe because I was exhausted, maybe because I had travelled so much and also because I still have more boundary work to do, this person's passing comment had pierced into some old, shaky place inside me. That place didn't know what would happen to this book. This place felt a lot of fear about exposing its vulnerable underbelly. This place was not entirely sure what it was doing or exactly what was driving it.

But one way or another, over the course of a few weeks after coming back, I wrestled out of this place of not good enough. But after shame and fear came what's become my companion emotion for the last few years. Anger.

As I had dismantled the *"nice"*, after I first dealt with the ensuing guilt, that terrible guilt that is the bane of all nice people, that a lot of women know so intimately, there had come anger. The less nice I was, the more and more anger showed up. It was there for different reasons.

It came when I encountered swathes of blank space, grounds of unlived life. Some of it also masked the real vulnerability I felt as I changed myself. Some of it was anger at other people. If only they behaved, I wouldn't have to say No in the first place. If only they behaved, I wouldn't have to doubt whether I was doing the right thing. If only they behaved, I wouldn't have to feel so guilty for being less than a nice person.

This time, when the surge of anger came after coming back from India, it was actually a mask for grief, for sadness. I felt exhausted by the emotional work this book has taken. I felt clenched in the heart at being misunderstood once again. I felt deep resentment once again. Why was this never-ending, this feeling of not being good enough? It was like peeling the layers of an onion. But as soon as I had peeled one layer, there was still another one, still more work to be done. It was exhausting.

At first, I didn't know what to do with this new, uncontrollable rage. At first, I didn't realize that I needed to get to the sadness hiding inside it. But then, I cried. I realized I hadn't used any tools for catharsis for a very long time. So, I did some art. I also thought about all I had learned about anger in the last few years. There had been times when I had handled anger well and when I had handled it badly. So, what exactly had I learned about anger?

I understood now that neither repressing nor venting anger were good things. Whenever I had channeled my anger effectively, I had first expressed and released my overflowing anger to lessen its charge, either through art or journaling or by beating pillows. Sometimes, one of these ways worked. Sometimes, another. After releasing some of this explosive energy, I had then used my anger to change *behaviorally*.

I had looked at what was bothering me, and then I had taken a concrete action that enforced a boundary. To do this, I hadn't asked for anyone's permission. I hadn't tried to change anyone's thinking. I hadn't talked reactively. Instead, I had thought about what was making me angry and decided what I wanted to do next. Then, I had simply done that.

Some of this learning had come from looking at previous experiences where I hadn't handled anger quite so well.

There had been a time in one of my corporate jobs in Delhi when I had expressed anger quite ineffectively. It was a small interaction but I had thought about it over the years, as my perspective had shifted. It had gone like this. I had been at this job for years and years. I was very quiet, the "good" employee. I was also completely invisible. Looking back, I think I was the classic pushover who was always doing more, always getting left back. But after many long years at this workplace, that day, I had reached a breaking point.

Someone else had recently been promoted instead of me. Now, at last, I was really angry. A few days later, my anger came out in an entirely different interaction when, I, for once, challenged a colleague about something I thought was wrong in an angry tone. There were two other colleagues of ours sitting nearby who had overheard our conversation. One of them burst out laughing at my mini angry outburst.

I was mortified. *He had burst out laughing.*

The colleague that I had spoken angrily to was someone I was friendly with. Although he was younger than me, afterwards, he had sagely counseled me. He had told me something like, *Just as when you get married, you have to adjust to different people in your new family, in the same way, in a team, you have to adjust to different people.* He wanted me to adjust and *"be mature"* about what he had been talking about.

I remember feeling ashamed at this time. I remember feeling confused. I had expressed my feelings. I had gotten angry and out of control publicly, probably for the first time ever in that office, and someone had laughed at me. They had not taken me seriously. They had found me insignificant. What was the use of anger? What was the point? Why did I feel so helpless?

Now, when I look back, I can hardly remember all the details of this incident. But I do know that even though my real anger was displaced and came out in the wrong way, the point that I was questioning during this discussion was valid. Now, I also know that my friendly colleague's remark was sexist even though I had been confused about it then. *"Adjusting"* is the kind of thing Indian women are often advised to do.

Now, I also know that men's expression of anger is viewed differently than women's expressions. Experiences like this and insights from books like Dr. Harriet Lerner's wonderful book *The Dance of Anger* have shown me that. Women's anger is more likely to be discounted and downplayed. Women are often called irrational and overly emotional for the same emotion that is seen as normal in men. So, there was a real bias at play here.

But as Dr. Lerner points out in *The Dance of Anger*, I had also behaved like many other women who don't even get to the real issue that's at hand for them. Although I was aware that I was angry at being passed over for the promotion, I didn't clearly articulate how embarrassed I felt about the reception of my anger in this other interaction. So, I wasn't sure what to do with my real anger. I was scared of getting out of control again. I used my experience in this one interaction as an excuse to not go and ask my manager clearly about the promotion. That would have been a real step towards change.

If I had done that, I could have found out any number of things. Maybe, I was qualified for the next position. Maybe, I wasn't. Maybe, they were being fair. Maybe, they were not. But feeling ridiculed for expressing what I felt in this small instance, I thought that I might be discounted once again. I also felt that I wouldn't be able to express myself calmly. What if I got angry again? What if, worse, I started crying? What was the use then? See how easy it was to dismiss someone who got out of control even though I knew the underlying point I was making with my colleague was a valid one.

So, at that time, I just repressed my anger. I didn't even approach my manager. I didn't get any real-world feedback about what might have happened or what I could have done differently in the future to improve my chances. Even if I had decided that I was being treated unfairly after such a discussion, that would still have been information. It would have made it clearer sooner that I needed to act on my behalf, one way or another.

It was quite a while later on that I used my anger to take action and move to a different position in a new company with a much higher salary. But I stayed stuck for a long time because I got scared of even feeling my anger. I got stuck because I didn't know what to do with it except feel it storm inside, get scared of it, and then repress it.

But as many experts on feelings tell us, anger is about clarifying what we want. Repressing means we are shoving the message of our anger aside. Venting also doesn't work unless we just do it to blow off some steam with a safe person in a safe place. But venting, in itself, doesn't change anything.

There's a third option to help direct our anger to shift things. It's first taking charge of it and expressing it cathartically - through physical movement, journaling or some other means - and then really thinking about what's behind our anger. Once we've decided our position on what's really at stake, then it's about taking a concrete next step and sticking to that next step even in the face of opposition. This is how anger can create positive change in our lives.

Harriet Lerner tells us that sometimes, it's just because of this discomfort we feel about the inevitable change that's around the corner if we get clear about what we want that causes us to unconsciously stay confused and stuck. For me, getting clear about my anger would have shown me the need for taking some uncomfortable action, such as confronting my manager or finding another position, so I just marinated in the anger and stayed paralysed.

This is just one way in which we stay stuck. Another is when we are angry about something but try to get someone else to change their mind instead of taking action. Let's say there is a religious tradition that you want to change. It's something that you grew up with. It's something that your mother finds really important and valuable. But now, as an adult, you have a different perspective. You do it every year, out of obligation or nostalgia, but there's a big part of you that feels inauthentic doing this. It just doesn't sit right with you.

So, after years and years of going along, you decide that you want to do things differently. You decide to talk to your mother and explain your position before you make the change. You don't want to upset her. You want her to understand. You want her to get your point. You want it to be peaceful.

But when you bring it up, it goes even worse than expected. Your mother feels like you are betraying and criticizing her by letting go of this important tradition. You give her your reasoning. You try to provide logical arguments. You try to get her to see things from your perspective. But she doesn't. Instead, she gives you counter-arguments about her position and how important it is that you follow this tradition. Now, you are at a deadlock.

You feel angry at her for not listening to you, for not agreeing with you. You feel angry at her for not respecting your boundaries. You feel angry with her for emotionally blackmailing you. So, now, what do you do?

Are you going to go ahead and do what you want? Maybe, you will do what you want behind your mother's back but then feel even more resentful and irritated. After all, you have a right to do what you want openly. Or could it be that as a "nice" person, you think you have to win her over *before* you can do what you want? Maybe, you get more and more angry about how you have such little freedom to live your own life. Your mother just doesn't get it. There's no way to convince her. You start thinking that anger is useless.

In this trap of thinking that you have to get someone else to change their mind before you can do something for yourself, you forget that you do have the power to do what you want. That's the problem with being *"too nice."* It prevents us from listening to the message in our anger. It prevents us from thinking about the actual boundary that has been invaded. The real issue here is not the specific tradition, but the fact that your mother and you are two separate people. You have a right to decide what you are comfortable doing, and the boundary that needs to be set is about defending that right.

Yes, there might be hurt feelings if you don't get agreement and change the tradition yourself. Yes, there might be discomfort and tension. But you have drawn your line in the sand, acted on your conviction that you have the right to make choices for your own life. Instead of verbal back and forths, you have taken a real action and started to change the dynamic with your mother.

As a recovering *"nice"* person, I know this isn't easy to do. It's a process. But I have understood one thing in the past couple of years. Earlier, I used to read articles about how nice people try to control other people. I didn't understand those at all. *Me? Controlling people? Of course, I wasn't controlling anyone. They, in fact, were controlling and getting into my space.* But control, in our case, if we're being overly nice, isn't about controlling someone by dominating them, it's about trying to pre-emptively control their reaction to us.

So, we shape-shift because we are hyper-aware of how the other person might react. We censor our true feelings. We trip over ourselves trying to ensure we don't have to deal with any "bad" feelings towards us. Staying with this discomfort of not being able to control others' reactions that saying No brings has been part of my journey back home to myself.

My feelings are telling me something. If I don't listen to them, they will only become stronger and stronger and much more likely to overwhelm me. If it makes me angry that some people take me for granted, then it's up to me to do something about it. If they don't understand or acknowledge my anger, then I don't need their permission to change my own behavior. I have many options. I can stop being so available. I can choose to give only what I have decided I can give unconditionally and stop giving in ways that are too costly for me. In the end, the only real power I have is over me.

At an earlier point in my life, I would have also thought things like: *Am I going to be petty and count what I am getting before I give something? No. I am bigger than that. That's not how I operate.* I would have been open and giving just because I was so used to the idea of the value of being open and giving, no matter what, no matter how resentful it made me. But now, at this point, I know it's not about keeping score or giving tit for tat. It's about a fair exchange of energy.

281

It's about discernment. It's seeing that my anger is telling me about my needs and often also about the reality of my relationship with another person. If I am the one always giving, then what kind of a relationship is that? It's not really a friendship or a relationship then, is it?

Another belief that I have undone the hard way and that I think many empaths struggle with is: *If I am good to the other person, the other person will also, in return, be good to me.* As empaths or HSPs, we do often see the good in others. So, when the outer world matches this belief, all is good in our world. This happens sometimes. But then, at other times, it doesn't happen. The truth is there are all kinds of people in the world. There are those people who will match niceness or kindness, but that's mostly because of who they are.

There are also those people who believe in competing and getting the upper hand. These people will only perceive us as a weak fool if we over-give. Their focus is on how much they can get. We might think we are being loving, but, well, they don't think so. This is also mostly about them, about how they see the world. But imagine where we would be if we just keep giving to this latter kind of a person.

This has been a hard belief for me to let go of because it challenges a fundamental way in which I see the world. I desperately want the world to be just. But the world is not always fair. The scales of justice don't always balance out. That's painful to feel. But it's possible that what I am here to learn is not just how to give, but also learn who to give to.

I think many of us, as empaths, stick quite obstinately to this belief in a fair, just, idealistic universe because someone has directly or indirectly, made fun of this tendency in the past. They thought we were naive or stupid when we were trying to be open and giving. Being made fun of something fundamental about us hurts. So, we tend to dig our heels in. The world *should* be fairer. It *should* be more just. So, we stick stubbornly to being open and almost choose to trust people indiscriminately. I know that I have been like this.

But now, after falling down many times and then getting up again, I realize that my energy is limited. It's about creating a sustainable system that can nurture both me and others. I also realize that caught up in the draining loop of hooking into the wrong people, I discounted all those people who *did* give to me in the past. I wasn't present enough for them. I took more than I gave. For them, I wasn't a giver, but a taker. I was the needy one. That's not fair, and so I have begun the task of thinking and consciously choosing how I exchange energy.

Like everyone who struggles with boundary problems, I do think sometimes about how amazing it would be if I never came across problematic people in the first place. After all, I don't have issues when I am by myself or when I am with anyone who has even relatively good boundaries themselves. But that's not how it works.

Everything might work great in my life, but it's unstable if I have beliefs and habits that allow even one person who shouldn't have too much access inside my life. Constructing good boundaries is especially important for dealing with these encroachers. I can't prevent them from coming, but I *can* create a barrier between them and me.

Letting bad behavior slide in the name of loving someone is something I have done less and less of as these last six years have gone by. When I don't say No to strokes I don't want, I am not being loving and compassionate. I am just creating a story in my head and making excuses for bad behavior. I am inadvertently positively reinforcing what I need to discourage. In the past few years, I have gotten a lot better at this and learned to figure out what ways of saying No work for me.

Whether it's by limiting time with someone, consciously filling up my own well before meeting someone challenging or saying direct Nos, I have laid down a concrete framework that I can now build from. I have made imperfect, messy progress, but I think that is what real progress looks like.

In the end, the only one I can control is myself. The only person I have real power over is myself. It's not possible to change people. It's not likely that I can rationalize or talk a bully out of pushing me if they want to push me again and again. For some reason, that makes them feel good. It's not possible to get someone I think is a narcissist to realize they are treating me badly. In the end, they won't change if they don't want to.

The only person I can change is myself. That's where the point of power is. That's enough. That's more than enough.

Part of my growth has been about realizing that controlling and manipulative people are just paper tigers. It is I who gave my power away when I wanted to please them. On their own, they had no power. They only had the power I let them have. In fact, anyone who needs to put someone else down to make themselves feel better has very little internal power, very little internal control. When I laid down my "nice" and stopped enabling them, when I was not afraid of being called "selfish" because I didn't do what they wanted, when I realized that I didn't need their validation, it was then that I came into my power. It was then that I stopped laying down the soft, vulnerable parts of myself out for any random person to come and sink their teeth into.

I have gotten much better at protecting myself over the last few years. I also know there's more work ahead. I know that some of the arrows that people like these can hurl get us so deeply because they hit us on our sore, unhealed spots. I still have many of those. I have often felt unheard, unseen. Like other HSPs and empaths, I have heard many derogatory comments about my "sensitivity" over the years. I have felt as if I was "less than," as if I wasn't quite upto the task of dealing with this world. I have felt overwhelmed, isolated, withdrawn. I have turned against my very self.

At this point in my life though, the question I have come to ask is this: How come so much I heard about being sensitive was so negative? Although I did hear some good things (otherwise I wouldn't be here), how come so much I heard put down something so essential about me and made me a stranger to myself for years?

Why is it that we devalue a quality of being, a way of seeing that can call enough "enough," and not run around for bigger, larger, more? Why is it that we devalue the capacity to feel for other people? Why is it that so many of us feel that we have to numb out as sensitive people in order to survive? Is it really only because we can't bear feeling so much? Or is it because we don't find a direction for our intense feelings? Could it be that we invalidate ourselves even before we can start our real work? Could it be that we take in other people's judgments about ourselves and not even get to know who we are in the first place?

Being *more* of myself, not less, has helped me find my way back home.

My ability to notice details can serve me well. It can help me see the world in full-color and notice all the shades of gray that are in-between black and white. My intense, overwhelming feelings don't have to be self-destructive. I can create channels in which they can flow. They are the raw materials for my art and the raw materials out of which I can create my very self. Instead of being scared of them, I can get to know them. Instead of locking them up, instead of locking myself up, I can see the directions in which they are pointing.

In the last six years, I have created some of the love and belonging that I was always looking for outside within myself. My home is within me, in my dreams, inside my very capacity to give more to myself. Now, I know things about me that I didn't know before. Now, I know that being authentic is more important to me than mere harmony. When you are authentic, you say things in your own voice. You own where you have been as well as where you are hoping to go.

When you are authentic, you don't have to be perfect or flawless to say what you really believe. When you are authentic, you won't always keep outer peace and harmonize with everyone else. But when you are authentic, you will tune in to the lost pieces of your own self and harmonize with yourself.

Now, I know I don't have to choose between two ill-fitting ways. Now, I know I can create a new option. I know that connecting with India does not mean doing rituals by rote. It means creating my own links back to my own memories. Now, I worship both Lakshmi on Diwali and Saraswati on Basant Panchami. My prayers are those I have never learned. They are the ones I have always carried inside me. It's not that I don't have doubts. I do. All the time. But now I allow myself those doubts. I know they are part of faith, part of being a person, part of feeling pain and hurt.

Now, I know that I belong first to myself, and only then, to everyone else. Now, I know my creativity a little more intimately. Now, I know that when we do something creative, the energy that is flowing has a movement all of its own. When I first started writing this book, I wanted it to be a sort of self-help book about Highly Sensitive People that connected different psychological theories in a very intellectual way. There is solid research backing the SPS trait, and I wanted to write a book that wouldn't be questioned at all. But at some point, the book that was coming through me shifted its gait a little to the right.

This book shape-shifted into a book about Empaths without my controlling it. When it changed its form, I resisted it hard. I fought it. "Empath" was a nebulous, still-being-formed word. I was wary of using it, although I was identifying with it more and more. I knew it was a label, and it might turn out to be a flawed label in the end.

But I also knew it was a helpful word. It spoke of my peculiar struggles. It spoke about the potential inside me and pointed to the nature of my challenges. It spoke about why setting boundaries felt so hard for me at times. It spoke about how important my intuition and my felt sense seemed to be in my journey as well as how much I needed to give them more voice in my life.

So, after wrestling and trying to contain it for a while, I let what was coming through show me the way. Instead of remaining my biggest block and tripping over myself, I gave up my rigid ideas, and I followed the moving energy of what felt true.

In completing this book, I have now thrown open a door to my true self. I have cut through some of the fear that has caused me to lock anything that looks different about me in the basement. Trying to look "normal" has been one of my biggest defenses. It was my attempt to keep myself safe, to merge into the background. It's also what kept me from really seeing myself. But now, through writing this book, I see that different is not abnormal. It's just different. Whether you are gay or straight, Hindu or Christian, left-handed or right-handed, whether you have a gift that helps you analyze or synthesize, whether you are quiet or you like to talk, a difference is just a difference.

With owning what's different inside me, what's unique, and what comes naturally, I am crossing over to my own side. I am throwing my hat over the fence and letting myself be seen as I am. Like everyone, I have a lot of fear around this. I know everyone has biases, and any word, any label you apply to yourself, that you self-identify with, can bring up many reactions. But it's this fear that I am now unwrapping from around myself.

It's this old, archaic, deep-seated fear that anyone who removes any mask feels. I feel it now at the base of my spine. But to really be myself, there is no other alternative. I have to feel and shake with my fear. I have to see that I can only walk my path when I am true to myself.

I have spent enough time creating a deep divide inside myself. I have spent enough time being the opposite of who I really am. I know it wasn't all my fault. I know I misunderstood myself, and looked at myself through other people's eyes. But now, at this point, it *is* all my responsibility to call back all those parts of myself that are still frozen, that have hidden in shame, that live in an orphaned state. It *is* my responsibility to feed them, hold them and sing to them. Only then will my real self crystallize, only then will its underlying shape become clear. Only then can I be the whole of myself.

Only then can you be the whole of yourself.

It really is what is inside you, that very sensitivity that you have been told so many false stories about, that is your biggest hope. It's what will see patterns and show you things you've missed. It's what will help you sense your way through the dark of the night. It's what will alert you when you are taking the wrong turn. It's what will throw open new, exciting doors to you, whether it's the door to your dreamworld or another deep current that's already a part of you.

Maybe, you've always been good with animals. Maybe, your passion is working with them. Maybe, you will grow up to become one of those researchers who are now telling us new things about the true nature of trees. Did you know that redwoods in ancient forests join their roots together and help feed stumps of trees that might die out otherwise? They are a family of trees.

If you, with your great sensitivity can say those things that are still unsaid, if you can see those things that are still being born, then we need you. You are part of our family of trees, and just like those old redwoods that keep old stumps alive, maybe, you too will help keep some of us alive, some of us who might have died out because of those old stories, because of those old poisons that might have gotten into us, that told us that we were "*too sensitive*," that really meant we were not enough.

But you, my beloved, are enough. Not just enough, but more than enough, and I hope that you will find that all that crackling sensitivity that you didn't know what to do with will find a place in the container of your life and form deep, smooth bowls that can hold the water that everyone is looking for so blindly, that everyone is so thirsty for.

If you enjoyed this book, please consider leaving a review. Reviews help other readers know that you found a book helpful or insightful. They are the seeds that help spread a writer's work.

Subscribe to the Author's Newsletter at https://www.walkingthroughtransitions.com/ for insights, tips and tricks about meeting life as an emotional empath and sensitive creative.

You can also contact Ritu on Twitter @ritukaushal2.

Acknowledgments

Thank you first to my husband Rohit for all your love and support during the process of writing this book. This book wouldn't have been possible without you. Writing a book, especially a first book, is a hard, lonely process. You encouraged me through all my meltdowns and all my phases of self-doubt. Thank you for always being the patient, kind one, the one who kept on believing in me when I didn't believe in myself. Thank you also for your many helpful inputs and suggestions that have helped make this book better. There were many times when I felt stuck and the next step I needed to take was an organizational step. You were the one who pointed that step out and who helped me move ahead when I felt overwhelmed.

Thank you to Bruce Cuthbertson. You were part of the beginning of this book and one of the first people who looked at its outline. Thank you for your valuable suggestions that have helped give shape to this book. Thank you also for believing in me more than once. You took precious time out for this book when you had so much going on in your life. I really appreciate it and as you know, I deeply admire and look upto your talent.

Thank you to Ramesh Menon who was my first writing teacher. Those few months in your Delhi workshop helped me remember my true self and helped kickstart my artistic journey. Thank you for believing in me and supporting me.

Finally, this book wouldn't have been possible without a circle of women.

First comes Lauren Sapala. Thank you for helping me birth this book during its more than 2-year gestation period. Your valuable insights and encouragement helped this book find shape and form. Your suggestions about how to approach my writing helped me find and express my voice. Your many insights, such as how a book is a little plant that has its own soul and takes its own time to grow, have helped me immensely in my journey. Thank you for all the nourishment you have given me and this book.

Thank you to Amanda Linehan, fellow INFP and HSP, for your generosity. Your valuable suggestions have helped make this book better. A first-time writer always wonders when their work is connecting and by giving your time to this book, you have helped add another layer to it.

Thank you to my sister Priyanka for your insights and direction that have helped make this a better book. Thank you also for all your words of encouragement over the years and for believing in me.

Thank you finally to Mandira, my guide and teacher. It's simple. I wouldn't be here without you. You know how much of a difference you've made in my life and I hope through this book, I will make a little bit of difference in this world as well.

Finally, this book is dedicated to all the women who have helped me find my voice.

It's also for all the women in my lineage who didn't have a voice. Now, you do.

References

Aron, Elaine N. The Highly Sensitive Person: How to Thrive When the World Overwhelms You. Citadel, 2013.

Meyer, Erin. The Culture Map: Decoding How People Think, Lead, and Get Things Done Across Cultures. Public Affairs, 2016.

Gogarty, Jim. The Mandala Coloring Book: Inspire Creativity, Reduce Stress, and Bring Balance with 100 Mandala Coloring Pages. Adams Media, 2013.

Fincher, Susanne F. The Mini Mandala Coloring Book. Shambhala, 2014.

Taylor, Jeremy. Where People Fly and Water Runs Uphill: Using Dreams to Tap the Wisdom of the Unconscious. Grand Central Publishing, Reprint Edition, 1993.

Fromm, Erich. The Forgotten Language. Rinehart, 1951.

Mellick, Jill. The Natural Artistry of Dreams: Creative Ways to Bring the Wisdom of Dreams to Waking Life. Conari Pri, 1996.

Rosetree, Rose. Become the Most Important Person in the Room: Your 30-Day Plan for Empath Empowerment. Women's Intuition Worldwide, 2009.

Judith, Anodea. Eastern Body, Western Mind: Psychology and the Chakra System As a Path to the Self. Celestial Arts, Revised Edition, 2011.

Plotkin, Bill. Soulcraft: Crossing into the Mysteries of Nature and Psyche. New World Library, 2010.

Connolly, Sonia. Wellspring of Compassion: Self-Care for Sensitive People Healing from Trauma. Sundown Healing Arts, 2011.

Lerner, Harriet. The Dance of Anger: A Woman's Guide to Changing the Patterns of Intimate Relationships. William Morrow Paperbacks, Reprint Edition, 2014.

De Becker, Gavin. The Gift of Fear: Survival Signals That Protect Us from Violence. Gavin De Becker, 2010.

Other Resources

Halpern, Steven. Deep Alpha: Brainwave Synchronization for Meditation and Healing. Inner Peace Music.

Segal, Inna. The Secret Language of Color Cards. Atria Books/Beyond Words, 2011.

McLaren, Karla: www.karlamclaren.com

Fehmi, Dr. Les. www.openfocus.com.

Bartlett, Scout: www.ifidknownthen.com

Made in the USA
Monee, IL
09 August 2021

75309030R00177